THE LAST POEMS OF
D.H. LAWRENCE

For Russell

The Last Poems of
D.H. Lawrence
Shaping a Late Style

BETHAN JONES
University of Hull, UK

Routledge
Taylor & Francis Group

LONDON AND NEW YORK

First published 2010 by Ashgate Publishing

2 Park Square, Milton Park, Abingdon, Oxfordshire OX14 4RN
711 Third Avenue, New York, NY 10017

Routledge is an imprint of the Taylor & Francis Group, an informa business

First issued in paperback 2018

British Library Cataloguing in Publication Data
Jones, Bethan, 1971–
   The last poems of D.H. Lawrence : shaping a late style.
   1. Lawrence, D. H. (David Herbert), 1885–1930 – Poetic works.
   I. Title
   821.9'12–dc22

Library of Congress Cataloging-in-Publication Data
Jones, Bethan, 1971–
   The last poems of D.H. Lawrence : shaping a late style / Bethan Jones.
      p. cm.
   Includes bibliographical references and index.
   ISBN 978-0-7546-6700-1 (hardback : alk. paper) — ISBN 978-0-7546-9926-2
   (e-book) 1. Lawrence, D. H. (David Herbert), 1885–1930—
   Criticism and interpretation. I. Title.
   PR6023.A93Z6355 2010
   823'.912—dc22

                                                                    2009030827

ISBN 13: 978-0-7546-6700-1 (hbk)
ISBN 13: 978-1-138-37633-5 (pbk)

Contents

Foreword

The aim of this book is to reveal the sheer breadth and profundity of D.H. Lawrence's late poems, also considering their status as late or last works. I have taken as my starting-point the two poetry notebooks filled by Lawrence in 1929 and posthumously published: notebooks encompassing some of his great acknowledged masterpieces such as 'Bavarian Gentians' and 'The Ship of Death'. I am equally concerned, however, with the unacknowledged masterpieces and even with poems that are less stylistically accomplished but engage fascinatingly with key preoccupations of Lawrence's last years. Since the publication of Edward Said's book *On Late Style* in 2003, there has been a wave of interest in artistic 'lateness' or 'lastness' – with all that these terms imply and entail – across the arts. Current issues and debates within this field serve as useful catalysts for a discussion of the works composed by Lawrence between 1927 and 1930, with particular focus on the late poetry.

'Lateness' and 'lastness' are slippery terms, while the 'shaping' of any poem (or poetry collection) is a complex process that tends to elude definition. A poem created within a sequence exists in relation to the other surrounding poems rather than in a vacuum; arguably, then, it is best considered in its place. The development of poems might also be explained through recourse to the word 'reshaping', given that they evolve through draft stages and often undergo an intricate process of correction, revision and even rewriting. In Lawrence's case, the complexity is heightened by the fact that he was working with and between two notebooks in 1929, deriving material from the earlier manuscript for interpolation into the later, so that drafts of the same poem frequently occur in both. The notebooks were not in any sense finalized and Lawrence's intentions for them remain unclear. These poems thus retain the tantalizing provisionality so often associated with – or imposed by – lateness.

This study adopts a contextual approach, in which the last poetry notebooks are discussed not only in relation to their earlier draft stages but in conjunction with the works written by Lawrence during the last three years of his life. Individual chapters indicate connections between the late poems and *Lady Chatterley's Lover*, *Sketches of Etruscan Places*, *Apocalypse*, *The Escaped Cock*, selected articles from this period and his last review. More broadly still, Lawrence's late works are discussed here as products of a lifelong process of intertextual assimilation, though the books read or re-read by him during his last three years are prioritized. Works on mythology, cosmology, primitivism, mysticism, astronomy and astrology are brought into play, illustrating the way in which ideas or images are borrowed and transformed through incorporation into the late verse. The resulting poems emerge as astonishingly rich and diverse.

A crucial question raised in this book is whether Lawrence's late writing can be justifiably perceived as a glorious summation of his literary career, rounding off a life, or whether such imposed closure would falsify and underestimate the works themselves. Perhaps it would be more appropriate to discuss lateness in terms of ragged ends, thwarted endeavour and a fierce determination to continue and create against the odds. In his last years, Lawrence sometimes referred to the 'fresh start' that would propel his life and work in new directions, and this is borne out by his experimentation even after *Last Poems* with another kind of poetry.

I am extremely grateful to a number of people who have made the writing of this book possible. Above all, I would like to thank Katherine and Gareth Elwyn Jones for their unfailing support over the years, for their utter dedication to my academic pursuits and (in recent months) their expertise in assisting with the final stages of this project. I am also deeply indebted to John Worthen, who has given me invaluable help and advice since the initial conception of this study. Christopher Pollnitz has been particularly generous in providing me with essential material and sharing crucial insights particularly regarding the textual evolution of the late poems.

I am grateful to George Bryers, David Ellis, Mark Inman, Jane Kingsley-Smith, Dennis Low, Andrew McBirnie, Michael Pringsheim, Keith Sagar and Julia Scott for their assistance with various aspects of the book. I would also like to thank Ginette Katz-Roy and Stephen Rowley as organizers of the annual D.H. Lawrence conferences at Nanterre, Paris, for creating such an invaluable environment in which scholars can meet and exchange ideas. The International D.H. Lawrence Conferences held in recent years at Nottingham, Eastwood, Cambridge, Santa Fe, Naples, Florence and Kyoto have been equally inspiring; I am very grateful to all my 'Lawrentian' friends and associates who have participated in these events, both intellectually and socially. My academic and secretarial colleagues in the English Department at the University of Hull have been highly supportive of my research, and I would particularly like to thank Valerie Sanders and James Booth: the two Heads of Department since my arrival in 2002.

My research has been enhanced by access to the manuscript notebooks of *Last Poems* held at the Harry Ransom Humanities Research Center, University of Texas at Austin, and to further xeroxes held at the Department of Manuscripts and Special Collections, University of Nottingham. I would like to thank the staff at the Brynmor Jones Library, University of Hull, for their assistance over the past six years. The Estate of Frieda Lawrence Ravagli has generously granted me permission to quote from copyright material fundamental to the book. It has been a great pleasure to work on this project with Ashgate Press; I would like to thank Ann Donahue and the rest of the team for their efficient yet humane approach to the publishing procedure.

My brother Matthew, a fluent Italian speaker, was invaluable during an extensive tour of the Etruscan tombs at Tarquinia. I also have a number of friends who have given their constant encouragement and followed the progress of this project with great interest. Finally, I would like to thank my partner Clive and his children, Holly and Jake, for their support and forbearance during the composition of the book.

Bethan Jones
University of Hull

Abbreviations

A   *Apocalypse and the Writings on Revelation*, ed. Mara Kalnins (Cambridge: Cambridge University Press, 1980).

2A   *Apocalypse and the Writings on Revelation*, ed. Mara Kalnins (London: Penguin, 1995).

AU   James M. Pryse, *The Apocalypse Unsealed* (New York: J.M. Pryse, 1910).

BBF   D.H. Lawrence, *Birds, Beasts and Flowers* (London: Cresset Press, 1930).

BR   John Oman, *Book of Revelation* (Cambridge: Cambridge University Press, 1923).

CC   George Dennis, *Cities and Cemeteries of Etruria*, vol. 1 (London: J.M. Dent, 1907).

CP   *The Complete Poems of D.H. Lawrence*, ed. Vivian de Sola Pinto and Warren Roberts (London: Penguin, 1993).

DA   Frederick Carter, *The Dragon of the Alchemists* (London: Elkin Mathews, 1926).

DH   Keith Sagar, *A D.H. Lawrence Handbook* (Manchester: Manchester University Press, 1982).

DP   Christopher Pollnitz, *D.H. Lawrence and the Pensée* (Paris: Carrefour Alyscamps Press, n.d. [1996]).

EGP   John Burnet, *Early Greek Philosophy* (London and Edinburgh: Black, 1892).

3EGP John Burnet, *Early Greek Philosophy* (London: Black, 1920).

EL   Christopher Pollnitz, 'Cough-Prints and Other Intimacies: Considerations in Editing Lawrence's Later Verse', in *Editing D.H. Lawrence*, ed. Charles L. Ross and Dennis Jackson (Ann Arbor: University of Michigan Press, 1995).

F   'Fire', in T.A. Smailes, 'D. H. Lawrence: Seven Hitherto Unpublished
           Poems', *The D.H. Lawrence Review,* 3 (Spring 1970), pp. 42–6.

FS   Gilbert Murray, *Five Stages of Greek Religion* (Oxford: Oxford University
           Press, 1925).

IR   *Introductions and Reviews*, ed. Neil Reeve and John Worthen (Cambridge:
           Cambridge University Press, 2005).

L i   *The Letters of D.H. Lawrence*, vol. I (1901–13), ed. James T. Boulton
           (Cambridge: Cambridge University Press, 1979).

L ii   *Letters* II (1913–16), ed. George J. Zytaruk and James T. Boulton
           (1981).

L iii   *Letters* III (1916–21), ed. James T. Boulton and Andrew Robertson
           (1984).

L iv   *Letters* IV (1921–24), ed. James T. Boulton, Elizabeth Mansfield and
           Warren Roberts (1987).

L v   *Letters* V (1924–27), ed. James T. Boulton and Lindeth Vasey (1989).

L vi   *Letters* VI (1927–28), ed. James T. Boulton and Margaret H. Boulton
           with Gerald M. Lacy (1991).

L vii   *Letters* VII (1928–30), ed. Keith Sagar and James T. Boulton (1993).

LCL   *Lady Chatterley's Lover*, ed. Michael Squires (Cambridge: Cambridge
           University Press, 1993).

2LCL   *Lady Chatterley's Lover*, ed. Michael Squires (London: Penguin, 1994).

LEA   *Late Essays and Articles*, ed. James T. Boulton (Cambridge: Cambridge
           University Press, 2004).

LP   Lawrence Lipking, *The Life of the Poet: Beginning and Ending Poetic
           Careers* (Chicago: University of Chicago Press, 1981).

N   Notebook (Roberts E192) held at the Harry Ransom Humanities Research
           Center, The University of Texas at Austin, containing poems published
           in *Pansies*, *Nettles* and (posthumously) as 'More Pansies' by Richard
           Aldington in 1932.

OLS   Edward Said, *On Late Style* (London: Bloomsbury, 2006).

SEP   *Sketches of Etruscan Places and Other Italian Essays*, ed. Simonetta de Filippis (Cambridge: Cambridge University Press, 1992).

SP   *D.H. Lawrence: Selected Poems*, ed. Mara Kalnins (London: Dent, 1992).

SS   Holly Laird, *Self and Sequence: the Poetry of D.H. Lawrence* (Charlottesville: The University Press of Virginia, 1988).

VG   *The Virgin and the Gipsy and Other Stories*, ed. Michael Herbert, Bethan Jones and Lindeth Vasey (Cambridge: Cambridge University Press, 2005).

WL   *Women in Love*, ed. David Farmer, Lindeth Vasey and John Worthen (Cambridge: Cambridge University Press, 1987).

Chapter 1
Lawrence and Late Style

Shaping a Poet's Life: How to Make an End

> How dull it is to pause, to make an end,
> To rust unburnished, not to shine in use!
> As though to breathe were life. Life piled on life
> Were all too little, and of one to me
> Little remains; but every hour is saved
> From that eternal silence, something more,
> A bringer of new things[1]

This quotation from Tennyson's poem 'Ulysses' indicates some of the problems and paradoxes entailed in the consideration of late or last works. These lines express the awareness of impending demise, a reaction against its accompanying debility and a sense that the precious hours remaining ought to be life-affirmingly vivid: lived to the full. Lawrence's two last poetry notebooks[2] obviously occupy a position at the tail end of his life, and it is impossible to read such collections without attributing to them a particular significance, even if that significance is primarily biographical and imposes on the poems a retrospective awareness of the poet's impending death. Adhering to a biographical model, editors and scholars are keen to chart a neat trajectory that incorporates a sense of closure, while labels such as 'late' and 'last' are attached to the pre-death utterances.

However, Michael Wood rightly observes that 'It's worth pausing over the delicately shifting meanings of the word *late*, ranging from missed appointments through the cycles of nature to vanished life'.[3] Equally, the attribution of 'lastness' comes with its own complexities and ambiguities. 'Last' usually denotes the final

---

[1] Alfred Lord Tennyson, 'Ulysses', *The Poems of Tennyson*, ed. Christopher Ricks (London: Longmans, 1969), p. 563. This poem was written on 20 October 1833 and published in 1842.

[2] The first is Richard Aldington's MSB or 'More Pansies', designated as the '"Nettles" notebook' in Christopher Pollnitz's impending Cambridge University Press edition of *Complete Poems*. The second is Aldington's MSA or 'Last Poems'. I will refer to the notebooks together as *Last Poems* (following Aldington's edition of 1932), and to them separately as the 'Nettles' notebook and 'Last Poems'. Both are listed as E192 in Warren Roberts and Paul Poplawski, *A Bibliography of D.H. Lawrence*, third edn (Cambridge: Cambridge University Press, 2001).

[3] Edward Said, *On Late Style* (London: Bloomsbury, 2006), p. xi. Hereafter *OLS*.

item in a sequence, so how many works by a specific author can be given this label? Should every author's pre-death achievements be evaluated according to one last work or according to a last work in each genre: a last novel, a last poetry collection, and so on? The issue of multiple versions also becomes a complicating factor here. In the case of Lawrence's last novel, *Lady Chatterley's Lover*, there are three separate versions of which one is – without doubt – chronologically the last (though not necessarily the best). Within the late poetry notebooks, however, where a number of lines have been corrected or scored out and replaced, it is sometimes impossible to ascertain at what point these revisions were made, and whether the revisions to one poem post-dated the actual composition of subsequent poems. The case is illustrated by reference to 'Bavarian Gentians', which appears in two consecutive versions within the 'Last Poems' notebook (having previously been drafted several times in the 'Nettles' notebook[4]), and it is impossible to ascertain which version contains the author's final revisions. Defining the boundaries of a late or last *phase* is also deeply problematic as it entails the placing of a caesura within the apparently continuous evolution of a writer's life. The attempt to isolate definite stylistic or semantic traits that may be associated with lateness tends to raise more questions than it answers, harbouring its own contentious issues and problems of definition.

Lawrence, of course, died young (though after a lifetime of illness), raising a further question regarding the point at which it is possible to designate lateness or lastness. Is it possible or appropriate to attribute lateness to the plays written by Shakespeare before he died at the age of 52, or to the works composed by Mozart before his death at 35? In such cases we might identify (in Wood's terms) a 'sudden lateness, as distinct from maturity' (*OLS* xiii) in which the 'late' style comes paradoxically early, coinciding with the middle (or even early) phases of artists who lived to old age. There are also paradoxical instances of works that apparently possess many of the traits associated with late style (discussed in more detail below), yet which occur too early in the chronology of a life to count as late. Rossini's *Guillaume Tell* (1829), written two years after the death of the composer's mother but long before his own death in 1868, was perceived at the time of composition as the height of sublimity – a perfect fusion of Italian and French styles – both challenging and innovative. Thomas Mann's *Death in Venice* was published in 1911, when Mann was 36, and is thus a relatively early work; it is therefore 'all the more paradoxical for its autumnal and even at times elegiac qualities' (*OLS* 149). It seems that late works can come early, just as early works can be made late by the relentless chronology that hastens an untimely end.

It is also necessary at this point to introduce the question of foreknowledge, which differentiates accidental lateness from lateness that has been confidently predicted. Euripides and Sophocles lived to almost 80 and 90 respectively, and must have at least been aware of the possibility that the works they were producing

---

[4]   For a discussion of the evolution of this poem through its draft stages see Chapter 6, pp. 131–4..

at such a time might be their last. Yet if foreknowledge of this kind can exist – leading to self-consciousness regarding one's own impending death – then surely it is possible for a younger writer in the final stages of a fatal illness to produce works that are analogously 'late'? According to this interpretation, illness simply precipitates the ageing process, so that a life might be seen to preserve its trajectory across a shorter span. It is sometimes possible to make a distinction between late works that have been created as such, in the full expectation of death, and 'accidental' late works, penned prior to a sudden loss of life which could not have been foreseen. The extent to which Lawrence predicted his own lateness and prepared for it will be considered below, in relation to the works he was producing towards the end of his life.

The most interesting and directly relevant discussions of the thorny issues outlined above are to be found in Edward Said's *On Late Style* and *The Life of the Poet: Beginning and Ending Poetic Careers* by Lawrence Lipking. Said's book (his last, left incomplete) is a genuinely enlightening interdisciplinary study of lateness among writers, composers, performers and visual artists. Lipking (focusing specifically on poets) considers lateness merely as one significant stage within the writer's span, yet – though writing in 1981 – he interestingly anticipates many of the current debates on late style. He proceeds from the assumption that a poet's claim will have been to forge an identity, to have 'shaped his life into art':[5] a claim which is either borne out or disproved not by the claim itself but by the works *them*selves. Unlike Yeats, who suggested a dichotomy in which an artist could either achieve perfection in his life or his art, Lipking argues that life is shaped through becoming art, and that the life of a poet is therefore best investigated through reference to his poems. Focusing, then, on 'the shape of his life *as a poet*' (*LP* viii), Lipking acknowledges the existence of numerous stages, constantly shifting direction, but identifies three 'testing moments' that are of crucial importance:

> Three points, in particular, will focus the investigation: the moment of initiation or breakthrough; the moment of summing up; and the moment of passage, when the legacy or soul of the poet's work is transmitted to the next generation. (*LP* ix)

Analogously, Said identifies 'three great problematics, three great human episodes common to all cultures and traditions' (*OLS* 4), although his categories do not reflect the onward dissemination of influence; they focus instead on the stages within an artist's life. 'Passage', in his sense of it, is a progression beyond 'the moment of birth and origin' (*OLS* 4), which is 'always subject to revision' (*OLS* 4):

---

[5] Lawrence Lipking, *The Life of the Poet: Beginning and Ending Poetic Careers* (Chicago: University of Chicago Press, 1981), p. x. Hereafter *LP*.

> Beginnings ... necessarily involve an intention that either is fulfilled, totally or
> in part, or is viewed as totally failed, in successive time. And so the second great
> problematic is about the continuity that occurs after birth, the exfoliation from
> a beginning: in the time from birth to youth, reproductive generation, maturity.
> (*OLS* 4–5)

The third problematic, with which Said is principally concerned, is 'the last or
late period of life, the decay of the body, the onset of ill health or other factors
that even in a younger person bring on the possibility of an untimely end' (*OLS*
6). Said's notion of an 'untimely end' might already be set against Lipking's
deliberate 'moment of summing-up', indicating the kind of discrepancies within
two approaches.

In the case of Virgil, it is possible (though not sufficient) to divide his career
as a writer neatly according to a tripartite model. He might be seen as progressing
from the 'early' style of the *Eclogues* through the middle period of the *Georgics*
to the late flowering of the large-scale, epic *Aeniad*. Said would attribute to this
progression the idea of timeliness, in which events or works of art occur at the
appropriate moment in history, or within the trajectory of a life:

> For it bears saying explicitly that both in art and in our general ideas about the
> passage of human life there is assumed to be a general abiding *timeliness*, by
> which I mean that what is appropriate to early life is not appropriate for later
> stages, and vice versa. (*OLS* 5)

Employing the term 'Harmonium'[6] to categorize the summing up of a poet's life
and career, Lipking focuses on those who achieve a timely end. He applies this
term in particular to the case of ageing poets, who possess (in T.S. Eliot's words)
'the gifts reserved for age / To set a crown upon your lifetime's effort.'[7] Ageing
(and by implication dying) poets feel, according to Lipking, the need to 'put their
affairs in order' in the creation of a final book. He goes on to say that 'Last works,

---

[6]   'Harmonium' literally means a keyboard wind instrument or reed organ. Lipking
comments: 'Like Peter Quince's clavier or the blue guitar, a harmonium furnishes the poet
with a rare distinctive instrument on which to play his tunes ... But "harmonium" also
suggests deeper strains, the harmony in which a poet hopes the pieces of his book will join
... Though blind and clumsy, not ready as yet to make the parts of his world into a single
book, he struggles toward a more cohesive whole—his own *Harmonium*' (*LP* 71).

[7]   T.S. Eliot, 'Four Quartets', in *T.S. Eliot: Collected Poems, 1909–1962* (London:
Faber, 1963), p. 218. Lipking's use of this quotation (*LP* 67) does not take account of the
fact that Eliot is here writing with withering irony, as is evident in the words that follow
in 'Little Gidding'. The 'gifts' referred to are 'the cold friction of expiring sense'; 'the
conscious impotence of rage / At human folly' and 'the rending pain of re-enactment / Of
all that you have done, and been'.

like last words, have a special aura of authenticity' (*LP* 67), and quotes John of
Gaunt's lines in Shakespeare's *King Richard II* as illustration:

> O, but they say the tongues of dying men
> Inforce attention like deep harmony.
> Where words are scarce they are seldom spent in vain,
> For they breathe truth that breathe their words in pain.[8]

According to Lipking, the last literary efforts of a dying poet will, through sheer
urgency, be free of ornament and deception, as their author is faced with 'a vast
silence into which every word reverberates' (*LP* 68). The mythologized visionary/
dying poet is, in this account, prompted to transcendental utterance by necessity:
necessity imposed upon him by the passage of time, and by the sense of duty
urging him to produce a totalizing final vision. This definition of lastness points
to the glorious summation of a life of artistic endeavour that would accord with
the way in which Lawrence's *Last Poems* have often been perceived: as a kind
of pre-death summation on the brink of visionary insight, sliding over into death
because there is no other possible progression.[9] Vision of this nature entails its own
destruction: it rips the parasol protecting us from the wider cosmos into shreds (to
adopt the terms of Lawrence's essay 'Chaos in Poetry'), and leaves us shivering
in the midst of chaos.[10]

The last phase of an artist's life has frequently been identified as the phase in
which the writing acquires a visionary profundity hitherto unknown. Said alludes
to the 'accepted notion of age and wisdom in some last works that reflect a special
maturity, a new spirit of reconciliation and serenity often expressed in terms of a
miraculous transfiguration of common reality' (*OLS* 6), while another formulation
suggests that the process of ageing might bear witness to a 'ripening ... often
blossoming before its season under the foreshadow of death ... the reaching of a
new level of expression'.[11] According to this late-style model, last works either
achieve a renewed (seemingly youthful) artistic power or the 'unearthly serenity'
that Said identifies with Sophocles and Shakespeare's plays *Oedipus at Colonus*,
The Tempest and *The Winter's Tale*, which have 'settled their quarrel with time'
(*OLS* xiii). Stylistically, timely and serene last works are often perceived as
childlike, archaic, dreamlike or abstract: they testify to the 'triumph of artistic

---

[8]   William Shakespeare, *King Richard II*, II. i. 5–8, quoted in *LP* 67–8.

[9]   See, for example, Keith Sagar, *The Art of D.H. Lawrence* (Cambridge: Cambridge
University Press, 1966), p. 245 and Helen Sword, 'Lawrence's Poetry', in *The Cambridge
Companion to D.H. Lawrence*, ed. Anne Fernihough (Cambridge: Cambridge University
Press, 2001), p. 133.

[10]   *Introductions and Reviews*, ed. Neil Reeve and John Worthen (Cambridge:
Cambridge University Press, 2005), p. 111. Hereafter *IR*.

[11]   Hermann Broch, 'Introduction', in *On the Iliad*, Rachel Bespaloff, trans. Mary
McCarthy (New York: Pantheon, 1947), p. 10 (quoted in *OLS* 136–7).

achievement over final degeneration', asserting the supremacy of art over life (*OLS* 149).

Yet this is not the kind of late style with which Said is primarily concerned. Using a slightly modified version of the Eliot phrase also cited by Lipking (again unironically), he establishes a dichotomy in which the transcendental model is set against one of resistance and conflict:

> Each of us can readily supply evidence of how it is that late works crown a lifetime of aesthetic endeavor. Rembrandt and Matisse, Bach and Wagner. But what of artistic lateness not as harmony and resolution but as intransigence, difficulty, and unresolved contradiction? What if age and ill health don't produce the serenity of 'ripeness is all'? (*OLS* 7)

Wood asserts that 'every artist who is late in Said's sense of the word will be unreconciled' (*OLS* xv), and indicates the crucial influence of Theodor Adorno[12] on Said's thoughts regarding lateness: it is the 'notion of tension, of highlighting and dramatizing ... irreconcilabilities'[13] that remains Adorno's legacy and underpins the writing in *On Late Style*. This 'tension' is described as 'nonharmonious' (contradicting Lipking's harmonium) and 'nonserene' (opposing the transcendental, elevated model; *OLS* 7). Unlike Said, who does not dismiss other kinds of lateness beside his own, Adorno solely acknowledges lateness that presents a 'bristling, difficult, and unyielding—perhaps even inhuman—challenge' (*OLS* 12). Late-style maturity, he argues, 'does not resemble the kind one finds in fruit'; such works are 'not round, but furrowed, even ravaged. Devoid of sweetness, bitter and spiny, they do not surrender themselves to mere delectation'.[14] Beethoven's late works – referred to as unreconciled, uncoopted, unsynthesized, wayward, eccentric, alienated, obscure, stubborn and forbidding (*OLS* 10–17) – testify to an antithetical model of resistant, hostile, enraged lateness. If the works are difficult they could be perceived as deservedly so: liberties taken during a late phase are justifiable and might reach a new level of innovation and accomplishment precisely through being alien and obtuse.

The notion of the artist as hero-figure who must 'Rage, rage against the dying of the light'[15] can result in the assumption that s/he will somehow produce from

---

[12]   Theodor Wiesengrund Adorno (1903–69) was a German philosopher who also wrote on psychology, musicology and sociology.

[13]   *The Edward Said Reader*, ed. Moustafa Bayoumi and Andrew Rubin (New York: Vintage, 2000), p. 437 (quoted in *OLS* xv).

[14]   Theodor W. Adorno, *Essays on Music*, ed. Richard Leppert, with new translations by Susan H. Gillespie (Berkeley, Los Angeles and London: University of California Press, 2002), p. 564 (quoted in *OLS* 12).

[15]   Dylan Thomas, 'Do not go gentle into that good night', *The Poems*, ed. Daniel Jones (London: J.M. Dent, 1971), pp. 207–8. This poem was written in response to the death of the poet's father.

within unsurpassed works against the odds. Yet it is equally appropriate in some cases to see this final struggle as futile: part of a trajectory in which an early period of apprenticeship and a middle period of consolidation are followed by a late period of decline. Relentless chronology can be a powerful and unremitting force, taking its toll, and the artist is sometimes aware of fighting a losing battle against debility and fading strength. Writers are not restricted to the same degree as visual artists by the physical effort entailed in the creative act. Yet their work may – literally or figuratively – bear the stamp of their increasing lack of physical functionality. In his article 'Cough-Prints and Other Intimacies: Considerations in Editing Lawrence's Later Verse', Christopher Pollnitz alludes to the spots of blood evident on the *Last Poems* notebooks, providing evidence of the way Lawrence coughed onto the page when writing these poems.[16] This poignant reminder of the correlation between physical deterioration and artistic endeavour compromises any model of lateness predicated upon an abstract sense of elevated, controlled, creativity.

Radicalizing the Past

> Strangely enough, Euripides' very last tragedies—*The Bacchae* and *Iphigenia at Aulis*—are works that self-consciously return in subject matter to some scarcely remembered beginning point. (*OLS* 137–8)

The concept of 'return' is crucial to an understanding of Lawrence's late style, and will be discussed extensively in subsequent chapters. In the sense employed by Said above, Lawrence's late works frequently engage with early influences, settings and preoccupations, apparently subscribing to the model of lateness that suggests an endpoint which connects with its origins and rounds off a life. Lipking refers to the way in which 'each [poet] makes a whole and satisfying poetic world by redeeming the first sources of his inspiration. "In my beginning is my end." ' (*LP* 15) – and it is possible, at first glance, to identify this process within late Lawrence. The essay 'Hymns in a Man's Life', written in 1928, demonstrates links with the past, provoked as it was by an event reminiscent of an Eastwood family gathering. Banal Nonconformist hymns, plays by Shakespeare and poetry by Keats, Wordsworth and Goethe are cited as instances of texts that were assimilated early but resurfaced throughout Lawrence's life.[17] The verse of the 'Last Poems' notebook in particular does illustrate analogously significant links with youthful influences: with the

---

[16] Christopher Pollnitz, 'Cough-Prints and Other Intimacies: Considerations in Editing Lawrence's Later Verse', in *Editing D.H. Lawrence*, ed. Charles L. Ross and Dennis Jackson (Ann Arbor: University of Michigan Press, 1995), p. 155. Hereafter *EL*.

[17] 'Hymns in a Man's Life', in *Late Essays and Articles*, ed. James T. Boulton (Cambridge: Cambridge University Press, 2004), p. 130. Hereafter *LEA*.

poetry of Keats, Shelley, Swinburne, Tennyson and Whitman, which had filtered into Lawrence's consciousness early like the hymns of his childhood.

'[Autobiographical Fragment]' (*LEA* 50–68), written in October 1927,[18] returns to Eastwood for its vision, amalgamating youthful experience with intermediary events and accumulated knowledge (particularly of the Etruscan civilization) to articulate a visionary conception of the future. *Apocalypse* and *Lady Chatterley's Lover* revert to youthful preoccupations: one is quite literally a 'last testament' that begins with recollections of childhood experiences of religion; the other is a fictional portrayal of the relation between the sexes, played out against a Nottinghamshire backdrop. Adorno identifies in Richard Strauss's late work an 'extraordinary capacity for surprisingly and involuntarily recalling a lost childhood world' (*OLS* 28). Said (interpreting Adorno) alludes to the regressive tendency through which Strauss 'escaped the rigours and the horrors of his time', so that 'his music was a throwback to an earlier age, as well as an index of how much his own had faded and decomposed' (*OLS* 28). One attribute of late style implied here is its nostalgic recapturing of a lost, past world in the process of vilifying the impoverished present. Such a vilification of the present is, without a doubt, one of Lawrence's concerns in the late fiction, non-fiction and poetry. Yet his appropriation of youthful experience is never straightforwardly nostalgic; rather, the late works testify to an intransigent and essentially radical revisioning of the past.

For instance, while *Lady Chatterley's Lover* returns to the region in which Lawrence grew up for its setting (indicating an affinity with the early novels *The White Peacock*, *Sons and Lovers*, *The Rainbow* and *Women in Love* rather than the intervening novels of the 1920s) it is perhaps the most striking instance of a book in which the author pushes ahead of his time. This last novel provided the ultimate challenge to contemporaneous readers due to its sexual frankness and breaking of class taboos. Lawrence's late paintings proved equally controversial: as a consequence of the British authorities' prudish reaction to his representation of the naked human form, his exhibition at the Warren Street Gallery, London, was raided by police on 5 July 1929. Thirteen of the paintings – those in which pubic hair was showing – were confiscated, impounded and finally returned to Lawrence on condition that they would not be exhibited in Britain again. His last travel book, *Sketches of Etruscan Places*, aims to 'correct' previous misconceptions regarding the customs, religious practices and relationships of a past culture, creating a compelling and imaginatively inspired, wilful, idealistic and sometimes wrong-headed alternative. *Apocalypse* offers a radical rewriting of the Bible in which the last book of the New Testament (Revelation) is reworked through reference to cosmology, astronomy, paganism and pre-Socratic philosophy. The late story *The Escaped Cock* is more controversial still[19] in its re-conceptualizing of the biblical

---

[18]   For alternative titles allocated to this fragment by previous editors see *LEA* 49.

[19]   For the reception of this story see *The Virgin and the Gipsy and Other Stories*, ed. Michael Herbert, Bethan Jones and Lindeth Vasey (Cambridge: Cambridge University Press, 2005), pp. xlviii–l. Hereafter *VG*.

resurrection story as a tale in which the re-born Christ renounces his mission, retreats into solitude to recover, experiences sexual awakening amid the trappings of pagan iconography, then sails away, leaving the woman he has impregnated behind.

Other late stories adopt a newly satirical and wonderfully comic style, evident both within completed tales and those left as fragments, such as 'The Man Who Was Through with the World' and 'The Women Who Wanted to Disappear' (*VG* 237–40 and 251–5). The late essays, articles and reviews are forthright, often astringently satirical, rhetorically charged, sometimes combative and often dismissive (examples will be discussed in Chapter 8). Said 'sees "amusement" as a form of resistance' (*OLS* xiv), while Lawrence suggests that the purpose of satire is partly didactic or rhetorical: 'Satire exists for the very purpose of killing the social being, of showing him what an inferior he is, and, with all his parade of social honesty, how subtly and corruptly debased'.[20] Yet the 'amusement' in these works can also be exuberant, or simply playful.[21]

Of course the flouting of convention is not a unique attribute of Lawrence's *late* style: *The Rainbow* provides just one much earlier instance of radical writing that provoked controversy and led to censorship. Yet it is my contention that in the last works in every genre, Lawrence was facing conflict and contradiction head-on, perhaps revealing a strengthening of imaginative power and conviction rather than any sense of decline. This growing power might also, paradoxically, be a consequence of increasing physical debility: there is a sense of urgency and defiance, also reflected in Lawrence's recurrent denial that he had tuberculosis.[22] Said and Adorno emphasize that late works are hard-won out of a struggle with life; that they are often riven with the tension arising from the series of irreconcilable dualisms inherent in the act of impeded or accelerated creativity.

While lateness might provoke focus, clarification and condensed utterance, it might also possess a roughness occasioned by the need to hasten to a finish. These paradoxical attributes appear to co-exist in the poetry written by Lawrence after the publication of his *Collected Poems* in 1928; poetry including *Pansies, Nettles* and the two late notebooks discovered posthumously and published by Richard Aldington under the title *Last Poems*.

---

[20]   D.H. Lawrence, 'John Galsworthy', in *Study of Thomas Hardy and Other Essays*, ed. Bruce Steele (Cambridge: Cambridge University Press, 1985), p. 213.

[21]   For a fuller discussion of Lawrence's comedic craft in his prose works of this period see Bethan Jones, 'Disappearing Tricks: Comedy and Gender in D.H. Lawrence's Late Short Fiction', in *New D.H. Lawrence*, ed. Howard J. Booth (Manchester: Manchester University Press, 2009).

[22]   See, for example, David Ellis, *D.H. Lawrence: Dying Game 1922–30* (Cambridge: Cambridge University Press, 1998), pp. 376–7 and 473–4.

Collected Poems – **and a Fresh Start**

Lipking identifies the epic as the most appropriate and common genre adopted by poets in the past to express their visionary last words. In modern times, he argues, the Collected Poems edition has taken the place of the epic, because such an edition enables the poet to engender his 'longest poem' which is 'the ensemble of all his poems together ... "an assemblage of all the powers" a poet can muster' (*LP* 70). Lipking cites Yeats and Cavafy (the latter also foregrounded by Said in his seventh chapter, 'Glimpses of Late Style') as examples of modern poets who 'seem to regard the ultimate fruit of all their work as a poetic autobiography in the shape of a single book'. He continues: 'To make such a book is to redeem individual poems from their solitude and the poet's life from time' (*LP* 70). This contextualizing is, arguably, an extension of the approach already adopted by Lawrence in relation to the collections *Look! We Have Come Through!* (1917) and *Pansies* (1929): he had referred to the former as 'an essential story, or history, or confession'[23] and asks the reader of the latter volume to fill in the biographical and circumstantial background so the poetry can be better understood.[24] Both these approaches prioritize the book as an entity rather than the individual, by implication fragmentary, poems that form merely a part of the whole. Lawrence did in fact create his own *Collected Poems* edition two years before he died, yet he still cannot be easily fitted into the category of a pre-death visionary neatly summarizing his own poetic career, in Lipking's sense of it. Lawrence's case is complicated, of course, by the fact that he was not only a poet: he was not even primarily a poet. Even as far as the poetry writing is concerned, however, it is evident that his late work undermines a model that categorizes *Collected Poems* as a summary or conclusion.

Lawrence collected his poems between 1927–28, having refused to respond to a suggestion that he might do so eight years earlier.[25] A model based on timeliness would emphasize the fact that in 1919 he was still mid-career: that the time was not propitious for the creation of a volume that would constitute a

---

[23] *The Complete Poems of D.H. Lawrence*, ed. Vivian de Sola Pinto and Warren Roberts (London: Penguin, 1993), p. 191. Hereafter *CP*.

[24] *D.H. Lawrence: Selected Poems*, ed. Mara Kalnins (London: Dent, 1992), p. 281. Hereafter *SP*.

[25] The idea that Lawrence should collect his poems came from Martin Secker in 1919: see Lawrence's letter of 6 August in *Letters* III (1916–21), ed. James T. Boulton and Andrew Robertson (Cambridge: Cambridge University Press, 1984), p. 379 (hereafter the *Letters* volumes will be cited as *L* i, *L* ii and so on). The subsequent suggestion also came from Secker in September 1927 (see *L* vi 167–8). The idea of dividing the work into two distinct halves labelled 'Rhyming' and 'Unrhyming' poems came in November 1927 (*L* iv 206 and n. 1), at which time Secker also stated that he was sending Lawrence volumes of his published poetry. By 14 November 1927 Lawrence was at work (*L* vi 213) and by 11 January 1928 he had organized both volumes and was typing: at this stage he was using the new titles 'Lyrical Verse' and 'Free-Verse' (*L* vi 264).

summing up of his life and poetic career. By 1925, however, he was obviously beginning to think about shaping his life: it was at this time that he started to produce autobiographical essays.[26] By 1928 Lawrence's health was failing and he knew that death was a possibility (though not an imminent certainty, yet), so it may be considered in retrospect to have been a good time to choose for collecting the volumes of poetry that were to sum up his poetic oeuvre. An alternative interpretation, however, foregrounds pragmatism rather than romance. By 1928 Lawrence was not particularly productive as a writer, and had published only one book (*Mornings in Mexico*) in the previous year. The offer to publish two weighty volumes of poetry which would involve an effort of revision and selection rather than of original composition must have been an attractive prospect. By this time, too, Lawrence would probably have considered that he had sufficient material to include in such a project. In 1919 a *Collected Poems* edition would have been much less accomplished as well as less substantial, for the *Birds, Beasts and Flowers* book, published in 1923 (and containing much of Lawrence's most successful free-verse poetry), had not then been written. An edition of the poems published in 1928 would also come at a time when Lawrence was plagued by the censorship issue: unlike *Lady Chatterley's Lover* it would be a relatively 'safe' edition that would avoid allegations of obscenity and notoriety. It seems, then, that Lawrence was driven as much by practical and commercial motives to create his *Collected Poems* edition when he did as he was by a sense of vocation and poetic destiny.

It is arguable that the resurgence in Lawrence's poetry writing in his last years (subsequent to *Collected Poems*) also testifies to a process of consolidation and compensation through which he abandoned larger-scale works due to failing health and focused on short pieces more compatible with his physical state. This argument runs counter to the transcendental model; it acknowledges late-period decline and posits lateness as dictated by practical necessity. Rather than building up to a Virgilian epic as the climax of a life's work, a writer might have to scale down in order to render his output manageable. Yet in Lawrence's case, the notion of 'scaling down' is to an extent belied by the sheer number of poems composed during the period 1928–30, and by the fact that he wrote a full-scale book – *Apocalypse* – subsequent to the composition of the poems.

Rather than functioning as a summary or endpoint, Lawrence's work on *Collected Poems* seems to have spurred him on, provoking the wave of creativity that resulted in the post-1928 poetry. Lipking emphasizes the way in which exposure to earlier writing can have a regenerative impact on future work:

> A poet who wishes to grow must learn to read his own early work, to explore its secret life and hidden meanings. Even apprentice work often contains some gist of everything to come—if the right eye sees it. The only singing-school, as Yeats

---

[26]   See John Worthen, *D.H. Lawrence: The Early Years 1885–1912* (Cambridge: Cambridge University Press, 1991), pp. 500–503.

would have it, studies monuments of its own magnificence; poetry itself is the
source of poetry, poems beget poems. (*LP* 15)

When creating *Collected Poems* Lawrence was re-reading, revising and re-
categorizing his earlier poems, notably assigning poems to the 'Rhyming' and
'Unrhyming' categories, according to the volumes in which they had appeared
(rather than their actual poetic form). The idea that poems beget poems indicates
continuity rather than a caesural severance: a sense that *Collected Poems* merely
remains one poetic landmark in an evolving oeuvre. This continuity is further
indicated by Lawrence's ongoing attempt to embody spontaneous expression
through the use of direct and unfettered utterance. Ever since the composition of
his first two poems, 'To Guelder Roses' and 'To Campions' (of which he wrote
'Any young lady might have written them', *SP* 280), Lawrence's aim had been
to liberate his poetic demon, with all its outspoken, uncompromising radicalism.
From early on, then, Lawrence had anticipated the intransigence that Said and
Adorno attribute specifically to late style, while in the 1919 essay 'Poetry of the
Present', he had set forth his views on modern poetry (the liberating free-verse
of Whitman in preference to the gem-like lyrics of Shelley and Keats, *SP* 267),
which would be supplemented (rather than contradicted) by the late essay 'Chaos
in Poetry' (April/May 1928).

   Stylistic continuity might also be inferred from the fact that Lawrence had
used free-verse closely modelled on that of Whitman throughout his poetic career.
Nonetheless, the 1928–30 poems are characterized by formal diversification and
experiment, suggesting that this period was 'a bringer of new things'. Lawrence's
own attitude to his progression beyond *Collected Poems* is, in fact, one that
emphasizes a clean break rather than continuous development:

> I'll sort of feel I've got everything behind me, when they are done, – and the
> novel [*Lady Chatterley's Lover*]. Then what next? Some sort of a new start?
> (*L* vi 271)

Lipking recognizes that the sort of planning inherent in the shaping of a life or
career 'can inhibit the fresh starts in unexpected directions, the ever-quickening
sense of discovery, that many writers live for' (*LP* 79). Appropriately he cites the
specific example of Walt Whitman's *Leaves of Grass* (1855), which he categorizes
as 'a poem of beginnings' (*LP* 114), remaining uninhibited. This conception of a
new start – or a series of new starts – seems a more profitable way of considering
late poems than to force them into a coherent pattern illuminated clearly by
retrospect. Another (rather fanciful) way in which such constant renewal might be
envisaged is through reference to Heraclitean metamorphosis:

> Confronted by a Heraclitean nature where flux and transformation rule the
> rhythms of life, swept along by a Heraclitean self, the poet submits to the stream,
> trusting that something imperishable will survive. (*LP* 95)

The Heraclitean river of the self is clearly a bringer of newness: a source of constant replenishment. The above quotation is useful in revealing the arbitrary yet invigorating nature of the creative process: the poet 'submits', 'trusting' rather than knowing that some vestige of poetic immortality will be left behind. Interestingly, Lawrence defines the literary products of such creativity in an antithetical sense, celebrating their perishability; associating poetry of the present with the blossoming and dying of plants or the erection and decay of wooden Etruscan towns.

The originality of the 1928–30 poems is largely attributable to Lawrence's approach to flux and impermanence, as expressed in 'Foreword to *Pansies*' (April 1929):

> So I should wish these *Pansies* to be taken as thoughts rather than anything else; casual thoughts that are true while they are true and irrelevant when the mood and circumstance changes. I should like them to be as fleeting as pansies, which wilt so soon, and are so fascinating with their varied faces, while they last. And flowers, to my thinking, are not merely pretty-pretty. They have in their fragrance an earthiness of the humus and the corruptive earth from which they spring. And pansies, in their streaked faces, have a look of many things besides hearts-ease. (*SP* 290)

The disregard for fixed, stable form implied above resulted in Lawrence adopting a fragmentary, aphoristic method for the first time in 1928: one which could, therefore, be seen as a defining trait of his late poetic style (though it is used in only some of the poems). Fragmentation is often identified with lateness, and has been attributed to the writing of Adorno, 'whose distrust and hatred of the totality caused him to work entirely in fragments, aphorisms, essays, and digressions' (*OLS* 86–7). According to Said, Beethoven's late work possesses an 'episodic character'; an 'apparent disregard for its own continuity' (*OLS* 10); a 'new sense of private striving' and an 'instability that is quite different from earlier works' (*OLS* 135). These labels would be appropriate in describing the newly aphoristic snatches of poetry that Lawrence began after *Collected Poems* in *Pansies*. His use of aphoristic verse was a conscious attempt to encompass conflicting snippets of poetic insight, so that the juxtaposition would result in 'one eternal moment easily contradicting the next eternal moment' (*SP* 291).

Pansies was the first book by Lawrence written entirely in France, and his aphoristic method was directly modelled on

> those slightly didactic opinions and slices of wisdom which are laid horizontally across the pages of Pascal's *Pensées* or La Bruyère's *Caractères*... Let every *pensée* trot on its own little paws, not be laid like a cutlet trimmed with a *patte de mouche*. (*SP* 286)

In addition to Pascal and La Bruyère, Lawrence was reading La Rochfoucauld's *Les Maximes* in June 1927, while the pre-Socratic fragments collected in John Burnet's *Early Greek Philosophy* (discussed in chapters 5 and 9) may also have furnished a formal precedent for *Pansies* and some of the poetry within the 'Nettles' notebook (a notebook actually headed 'Pensées'). Pollnitz emphasizes Lawrence's fascination with the literary culture of seventeenth-century Paris during this period, and his determination 'to make his own thing of it'.[27] Pollnitz suggests that Pascal appealed to Lawrence partly as an 'apostle of angst and self-loathing' (*DP* 7), and that Lawrence's aphoristic verse functions as a 'gunpowder plot against all high culture', subverting bourgeois and literary convention (*DP* 6). Bridging the gap between working-class satire and the 'aristocratic moralist's elegant dismemberment of vulgar prejudice' (*DP* 17), these 'pensées' – categorized by their author as 'real doggerel', employing a 'loose little poem form' (*L* vii 64) – achieve an original fusion of apparently antithetical literary modes.

Paradoxically, too, the poems strive for newness through stylistic anachronism: their origin lies in French neoclassical tradition yet they are 'almost postmodern in [their] casualness' (*DP* 5). They exemplify instability through fragmentation and self-contradiction more than anything written by Lawrence previously in this genre. Unlike his previous collections, too, many of these late poems are stringently iconoclastic. The social critique that fuels the ire of the poems reaches an apotheosis in *Nettles* (published on 13 March 1930, just after Lawrence's death): this is his most obviously combative, spiky and embittered collection, in which the poems reflect a violent and often bludgeoning response to society's authority figures. Fuelled by the confiscation of Lawrence's paintings, these poems were retaliatory and aggrieved. The 'Last Poems' verses (as well as some poetry within the 'Nettles' notebook) – often mythopoeic, mystic or deeply philosophical in tone – are not as obviously iconoclastic as *Nettles* or even *Pansies*, but are arguably just as radical in their refusal to settle. They are constantly shifting; only fleetingly serene. They confront the painful process of dying and remain true to the struggle it entails: 'it is hard to die, it is difficult to go through / the door, even when it opens' (*CP* 721). The originality also lies in their challenge to preconceived notions of death, god and the 'afterwards',[28] also evident in *Apocalypse* and *The Escaped Cock*.

Lawrence's poetic late style drew on previous stylistic models that provided him with an essential flexibility, enabling him to compose stringent political satires, philosophical fragments and profound lyrical or mythopoeic verse about death. Late style is sometimes associated with closed systems and imposed limits: Said refers, for instance, to the 'logical circuit that allows no escape and very little

---

[27]   Christopher Pollnitz, *D.H. Lawrence and the Pensée* (Paris: Carrefour Alyscamps Press, n.d. [1996]), p. 5. Hereafter *DP*.

[28]   See David Ellis, 'Death and the After-life', in *Death and the Author: How D.H. Lawrence Died and Was Remembered* (Oxford: Oxford University Press, 2008), pp. 63–73.

elevation' (*OLS* 63) through which Mozart exerts compositional control over his late opera *Cosi Fan Tutti*. Lawrence would have seen this circularity and imposed closure as tantamount to the 'serpent of eternity with its tail in its own mouth' (*SP* 269), against which his poetry was in revolt. It is also necessary to recognize that late work often eludes such control through being hurried and provisional; sometimes even unfinished.

Late Works in Progress

Said's book *On Late Style* itself testifies to the provisionality of lateness, and to the resistance to closure identifiable also in Lawrence's late phase. It might appear an apposite, timely composition, crystallizing an evolving interest in lateness within a final work – a last testament – yet the book is less timely than it initially appears. Given that Said's death was occasioned by disease rather than old age, his last, unfinished book might be perceived as late in its aborted creativity:

> Said wanted to continue with the self's making, and if we divide a life into early, middle, and late periods, he was still in the middle when he died at the age of sixty-seven in September 2003, twelve years after the first diagnosis of leukemia. Still a little too early, I think he would have said, for real lateness. (*OLS* xviii)

Interestingly, Wood goes on to suggest that there is something appropriate about the book's incomplete status, considering its subject matter and the way in which it might otherwise have imposed closure on a life:

> And yet I find I can't believe that he wanted to finish this book. Or rather, he wanted to finish it but was waiting for a time that would perhaps never have come. There would have been a time for this book about untimeliness, but this time was always: not quite yet. Completing the work would have been too much like writing the end of a life, closing the long chapter about the making of the self that opened with Said's book *Beginnings* or, even earlier, with his book on Conrad—and the whole point about beginnings, as distinct from origins, is that they are chosen. (*OLS* xvi–xvii)

The book's composition had been deferred – 'next week I'll concentrate on completing *Late Style*, which will be finished in December' (*OLS* vii) – and as Said's life did not extend to that proposed date of completion it remains tantalizingly incomplete. Unfinished works are never treated quite like those that are complete: Schubert's *Unfinished Symphony* is a celebrated anomaly, novel in its provisional status. A current fascination with the unfinished has elevated Turner's late paintings to a lofty height: these works are now thought, by many, to be of greater interest than the preceding ones through anticipating Impressionism in the effect of light they create.[29] Cézanne's late paintings were fascinatingly provisional in that, attempting to regain an initial freshness, the artist recurrently wiped his canvas clean, leaving only an outline, so that the painting could be approached anew the next day (although it is also notable that he had experimented with this technique much earlier in life).[30]

Significantly, the literary works on which Lawrence was engaged between 1929–30 were mostly left unfinished: they are thus examples of work in progress, drafts rather than completed literary artefacts. It is the provisional, unfinished status of the late poetry notebooks that cuts against any approach suggesting that the 'new start' or wave of creativity beginning after *Collected Poems* with *Pansies* culminated, appropriately, in *Last Poems* (profoundly reflective, religious and sublime): the end.

It is important to emphasize the distinction between works that Lawrence had completed and prepared for publication – works clearly intended for a public – and the books/poems that were abandoned before they reached this stage of development. *Pansies* clearly had the status of an ordered book, a completed volume, as did its offshoot *Nettles,* although the latter was not published until shortly after Lawrence's death. Before moving to the Ad Astra Sanatorium in Vence (France), where he died, Lawrence was described as sitting propped up in bed at the Villa Beau Soleil, correcting galley proofs of the *Nettles* volume.[31] These poems were very obviously intended for the public domain: they must be in the hands of the public, for they must have someone to sting. The case is rather different both with *Apocalypse* and *Last Poems*. I will look briefly at *Apocalypse* (the later work) first.

It is easy to assume that *Apocalypse* is a finished volume, as it gives such a powerful impression of an ending: its final affirmation that 'the vast marvel is to be alive…'[32] seems suitably conclusive and – according to the dying-poet myth – appropriately poignant in its life-affirmation in the light of Lawrence's death shortly afterwards. In fact Lawrence did not actually finish *Apocalypse* but felt he had to lay it aside. In a letter to Frederick Carter circa 5 February 1930, he wrote: 'Have not finished my longer essay on Revelation – and am abandoning it' (*L* vii 640). The text of this book exists in different versions, some of which are included as lengthy

---

[29]   This point was made by Sam Smiles in a paper entitled 'Unfinished Business: the Construction of Late Turner', at the conference *Rethinking Late Style*, held at King's College, London (16–17 November 2007).

[30]   Richard Shiff, 'Late and Later', paper presented at the conference *Rethinking Late Style*.

[31]   The following description is given by Earl and Achsah Brewster: 'When [the door] was opened it disclosed Lawrence propped up in bed, galley sheets piled thick around him, correcting proofs of his "Nettles"', in *D.H. Lawrence: Reminiscences and Correspondence* (London: Secker, 1934), p. 309.

[32]   *Apocalypse and the Writings on Revelation*, ed. Mara Kalnins (Cambridge: Cambridge University Press, 1980), p. 149. Hereafter *A*.

fragments in the Appendices to Mara Kalnins's Cambridge and Penguin editions of *Apocalypse*. She also incorporates a draft fragment entitled 'Apocalypsis II'. This fragment, written into a different notebook from the other apocalyptic texts, extends to only a few pages, ending enigmatically with the assertion 'Before men had cultivated the Mind, they were not fools' (*A* 200). Significantly, the conception of God in this fragment is radically different from that (or rather those) found in *Apocalypse* and *Last Poems* (discussed at length in later chapters of this study). Was the fragment a new start, a continuation or a second part of the *Apocalypse* book that would take the argument in new directions? Alternatively, it could be a rewriting of parts of the longer book, broadening the previous discussion of Pythagorean number symbolism and its cosmological ramifications.

Apocalypse was clearly intended to inhabit the public domain, right from its initial conception as an introduction to Frederick Carter's book on the symbolism of Revelation.[33] Yet it was left incomplete, and its status as work in progress is highlighted by Carter himself, who emphasized Lawrence's reticence when it came to exposing the contents of the book to his companion and collaborator. Relaying his discussions with Lawrence on the apocalyptic theme which 'came up again and again whilst we talked',[34] Carter emphasizes Lawrence's reluctance to comment on his actual writing:

> But he said little of what he was doing, stopping his writing and putting aside the exercise book in which he did his work without remark, as one arrived. In fact, he usually was secretive about his work in progress, whatever it might be.[35]

Lawrence's reticence may be attributable to his reluctance to expose material to Carter, for reasons which may be conjectured. Carter no longer held the fascination for him that he once did: Lawrence thought of him in 1929 as someone who has gone 'a little more dead' (*L* vii 570). This loss of respect may have meant that Lawrence valued his opinion less, and believed that a discussion of his text with Carter would have been unprofitable. Another possibility is that Lawrence, having broken free of Carter's original intentions for the joint book in order to write a volume of his own, may have wished to play down the fact in his collaborator's presence. He may not have wished Carter to realize the size and significance of his new endeavour, or to become familiar with the new ideas that in fact signified a break with the person who had impelled him initially into a lasting fascination with

---

[33]   This manuscript was revised and published in 1926 as *The Dragon of the Alchemists* (see Chapter 7, p. 143–6).

[34]   Frederick Carter, *D.H. Lawrence and the Body Mystical* (London: Denis Archer, 1932), p. 61.

[35]   Ibid.

apocalyptic/cosmological writings. In short, Lawrence may not have considered Carter an appropriate audience at this time.[36]

Nevertheless, the distinction between more private 'work in progress' and material collected and prepared for publication is a significant one, and one that reflects interestingly on *Last Poems*. Lawrence, writing copious numbers of poems into two notebooks (see Chapter 2, pp. 24 ff.) after May 1929, scarcely refers in the correspondence of this period to the fact that he was composing verse. Apart from very occasional exceptions, such as the poem 'The Triumph of the Machine', which was revised and sent to Faber before appearing, in October 1930 as No. 28 of the *Ariel* series,[37] there is virtually no evidence of Lawrence reading these late poems aloud or discussing them even with Frieda. The only evidence of such a design is recorded by Achsah Brewster:

> One afternoon we were with him and Frieda at Villa Beau Soleil, he began selecting some of his 'Nettles' for a small volume. There were to be others called 'Dead Nettles,' because they were to have no sting in them. He turned the pages of his notebook, adding that he had been writing some verses about death and would read them; then, shaking his head wistfully, he closed the book, saying: 'I can't read them now.'[38]

The 'Dead Nettles', poems without a sting, are distinct from the *Nettles* in remaining intimate rather than overtly public, not geared towards an audience. The same applies to the 'verses about death', and Lawrence's inability to read them invites obvious interpretations about his sensitivity and vulnerability in the face of death. They could be seen as a way of dealing in private with an untimeliness that cannot be publicly acknowledged. It is also likely, though, that the Brewsters' retrospective account is coloured by this inevitable contextualizing: the adverb 'wistfully' seems entirely appropriate in the circumstances, yet we must recall that it has been subjectively and posthumously applied. Lawrence's reluctance to read the poems may in part have reflected the same feeling about his subject-matter and audience as his refusal to engage with Carter over *Apocalypse*. Perhaps his reticence is provoked by a sense that the poems are as yet incomplete – they are merely works in progress – and not yet ready to assume a public identity. It is possible that he never wanted, or expected, the 'Dead Nettles' or 'verse about death' to enter the marketplace, although the many localized revisions and the way in which he selected material from the earlier notebook for incorporation in the later one (discussed in Chapter 2) indicates that this is unlikely. Lawrence

---

[36]   It seems that Lawrence did read some of *Apocalypse* to Frieda later on, as she writes: 'In those days he wrote his *Apocalypse*; he read it to me, and how strong his voice still was, and I said: "But this is splendid" ', Frieda Lawrence, *Not I, But the Wind...* (London: Heinemann, 1935), p. 270.

[37]   See Roberts and Poplawski, p. 195.

[38]   Brewster, pp. 308–309.

had clearly shaped and reshaped many of these poems subsequent to their initial drafting, perhaps working towards final versions that could be gathered into a book.

The two last poetry notebooks are undeniably incomplete. In this sense the poem versions are drafts rather than fair copies, work in progress rather than a finished volume. Provisional writing of this kind is often made posthumously collaborative, as exemplified by Franz Xaver Süssmayr's completion of Mozart's *Requiem*.[39] Lawrence did not provide a title for *Last Poems*: this was retrospectively added by Richard Aldington, just as Ernst Roth (chief editor at *Boosey & Hawkes*) used the title *Four Last Songs* (in German *Vier Letzte Lieder*) for an important final work by Richard Strauss. Aldington categorized Lawrence's *Last Poems* and made certain claims regarding the status of the two notebooks: claims for simultaneous composition that have now been contradicted by detailed study of these manuscripts (this issue will be considered at length in my next chapter). He chose to place 'More Pansies' (now the 'Nettles' notebook) before 'Last Poems' in his edition, and made a number of editorial decisions regarding ordering. These decisions, these impositions (though necessary, perhaps), find a parallel in the creative evolution of *Four Last Songs*. Strauss composed this work between April and September 1948 when he was 84 – barely a year before he died – and it is often seen as an aestheticization of his life. The earliest movement to be composed was *Im Abendrot* ('In the Sunset', based on a poem by Joseph von Eichendorff), followed by *Frühling* ('Spring'), *Beim Schlafengehen* ('Going to Sleep') and *September* (poems by Hermann Hesse). Strauss died without making clear his intentions for these movements: he did not specify an order and it is possible that he did not even conceive of a single work that would bring together these settings. It was Roth who decided on a logical order for the movements when first published in 1950 – namely, *Frühling, September, Beim Schlafengehen*, and *Im Abendrot* – thus altering the sequence of the first performance.[40] Roth's new order has subsequently been adopted for most performances and recordings. *Four Last Songs*, then, has been posthumously reshaped with no available recourse to authorial intention, its provisionality affording considerable license.

Editors of Said's book might 'do [their] saddened best to imagine what Said might have written if he had written more' (*OLS* xviii), but this is clearly an impossible task and the subjective ordering of material is subject to editorial discretion. In order to create the book now known as *On Late Style*, Wood has drawn together different sets of material from sources as diverse as the Lord Northcliffe lectures given by Said at Columbia University, the *London Review of Books*, lectures given to a group of doctors and individual essays. His seventh chapter is an assemblage of four different elements including reviews, essays and articles on Beethoven,

---

[39]   See, for example, H.C. Robbins Landon, *1791: Mozart's Last Year* (London: Thames and Hudson, 1988), pp. 78–82.

[40]   John Deathridge, 'Late Style as Fiction: the Case of Strauss's "Four Last Songs" ', paper presented at the conference *Rethinking Late Style*.

Euripides, Cavafy and Britten. Wood has cut and spliced this diverse material (admirably, in my opinion), making the decision not to include bridging passages or a commentary. After the introductory section the words are Said's, but the book is profoundly collaborative: the editor has shaped the writer's literary end.

Lipking also highlights the reader's participation in creating the fiction of poetic careers. Ends are made perhaps not by the poets themselves but retrospectively by readers, critics and biographers who impose a fictional order – a wholeness or harmony – on the poet who (once dead) can be thoroughly placed in the context of his life. This is emphasized in the case of Keats, who (according to Lipking) 'did not finish his career', and left the alleged great epic that was to 'advance the grand march of human intellect' unwritten (*LP* 180). Lipking summarizes the way in which attempts have been made to impose upon Keats's life an appropriate order and alternative 'shape':

> Each succeeding generation, each new biography, has labored to shape his
> life and his career as a poet into a satisfying whole. It seems almost a moral
> obligation. If Keats himself was robbed of the chance to end what he had begun,
> all the more reason for the rest of us to give him back his destiny and repair his
> loss of time. The perfect Keats lives in us. (*LP* 180)

It seems that such a retrospective shaping by readers or biographers is (to adopt Ursula Brangwen's phrase) 'an obstinacy, a theory, a perversity':[41] a conscious attempt to impose an order by becoming the divinity that shapes the poet's ends.

It is also the case that scholars are drawn to artists who conform to their own predetermined notions of late (or earlier) style; they are often unafraid to reshape both life and art to fit their mould. Adorno, a 'European intellectual who refused to compromise with the culture industry as he saw it' (*OLS* 92), and whose own prose style 'violates various norms' (*OLS* 14), adopts an uncompromising model of lateness that searches for contradiction and rebellion in his chosen artists. He can pull this off (as Said puts it) only through a careful selection of writers such as Berg, Beethoven, Husserl and Hegel (*OLS* 92), and Said accounts for the prominence of Beethoven in Adorno's discussions of late style as follows:

> I think it is right therefore to see Adorno's extremely intense lifelong fixation on
> third-period Beethoven as the carefully maintained choice of a critical model,
> a construction made for the benefit of his own actuality as a philosopher and
> cultural critic in an enforced exile from the society that made him possible in the
> first place. (*OLS* 21–2)

Adorno's late-style model of exile and resistance occupies the opposite pole to that of serene harmony, but both approaches are subject to the 'hopeless confusion that

---

[41]   D.H. Lawrence, *Women in Love*, ed. David Farmer, Lindeth Vasey and John Worthen (Cambridge: Cambridge University Press, 1987), p. 481. Hereafter *WL*.

arises when we attempt to contain the inscrutable pressures of self guiding artistic destiny within the neat, historical summation of collective chronology'.[42]

While Lipking's premise is to assert the necessity for poets to make an end, he stands back momentarily to bring into play the following perspective:

> But why should they need to end? The business of a poet, after all, is to make poems, not to shape a career. Would not his best last words be something unfinished—the new poem he was writing, like a soldier in the field, when death interrupted him? (*LP* 74)

Ultimately, the notion of an interrupted process of active creativity seems appropriate in defining a poet's career, one that is inevitably extended beyond the moment of death by transmitted influence and posthumous collaboration. In this way, artistic careers can be left with their ragged ends intact.

It is wrong, I feel, to think of *Last Poems* as an end, a conclusion, a summing up of the process begun in early life or even after *Collected Poems*, particularly as Lawrence's last book celebrates vivid life in the 'phenomenal world'. He was used to periods of near-fatal illness followed by recovery, and even as late as 14 February 1930, he did not anticipate imminent death: 'I'm not in any sudden danger – but in slow danger' (*L* vii 646). In letters to Earl Brewster, Aldous Huxley and Enid Hilton in early September 1929 Lawrence refers to the 'masculine change of life', and discusses the way in which 'the animal man is in a state of change' between 42 and 49, demanding 'different food and different rhythms', and needing 'a new diet and a new man': a new lease of life.[43] The poem 'Shadows' is as much about the changes within life as the transition between life and death. Lawrence is a poet of phases or waves of life and creativity, always imagining and predicting 'new blossoms of me' that will be engendered when he is sent forth 'on a new morning, a new man' (*CP* 727).

Like many other late texts such as *Apocalypse*, '[Autobiographical Fragment]' and his very last (and unfinished) review (of Eric Gill's *Art Nonsense and Other Essays*) the two last poetry notebooks reveal a lack of closure that must be accepted as an attribute of their interrupted composition. These unfinished, fascinatingly provisional last poems will be the subject of this study. In his book *Reading Late Lawrence*, Neil Reeve expresses the conviction that 'while much of D.H. Lawrence's later fiction ... has received relatively little critical attention, it contains some of the freshest and most stimulating writing he ever produced'.[44]

---

[42]   *The Glenn Gould Reader*, ed. Tim Page (New York: Knopf, 1984), p. 86 (quoted in *OLS* 26).

[43]   Lawrence's ideas regarding the masculine change of life were inspired by a doctor who visited him in Rottach in early September: 'One [of two doctors] is a new, very modern one, who was a *Pfarrer* – a priest – and has a *Klinik* in München and does wonders, chiefly with diet and breathing' (*L* vii 466).

[44]   Neil H. Reeve, *Reading Late Lawrence* (Basingstoke: Palgrave, 2003), p. vii.

He focuses on a different range of late works to substantiate his claim, but I hope to lend weight to this argument and to show that the same degree of freshness and originality is evident in the late poems. It is necessary, however, to point to a final irony here, in observing that the poems posthumously given the title 'Last Poems' do not in fact seem to be the last poems Lawrence wrote. Through 1929 and early in 1930, he turns out to have been exploring a new style of poetry which we can observe in the fragments created as prefaces to the Cresset Press (1930) edition of *Birds, Beasts and Flowers*, as well as in a short piece entitled 'Fire'. These fragments, reaching beyond alleged lastness, will be the subject of the final chapter of this book.

Chapter 2
The 'Nettles' and 'Last Poems' Notebooks

In 1932 Richard Aldington published an edition of two manuscript notebooks filled with poetry by Lawrence and discovered posthumously. The contents of the two notebooks were published in the same volume under the title *Last Poems*, but Aldington categorized them separately as 'More Pansies' and 'Last Poems'. Given that the former contains a number of poem drafts also incorporated in the published volume *Nettles*, Christopher Pollnitz has decided to rename it the 'Nettles' notebook in his impending *Complete Poems* edition: a practice which has been adopted throughout this book. The 'Nettles' notebook (completely filled), which Aldington described as a 'catch-all' text, is diverse in style and genre, ranging from poems under the heading 'Pensées', which continue the style of the previous *Pansies* volume (see Chapter 1, pp. 13, 14), to serious and contemplative death poems, including early drafts of 'Bavarian Gentians' and 'The Ship of Death'. The 'Last Poems' notebook (containing less poetry and not entirely filled), seems more unified, incorporating several mythological poems, philosophical and religious verse and later drafts of the death poems. Aldington chose to place 'Last Poems' before 'More Pansies' in his posthumous edition, acknowledging in the introduction that Lawrence had left no indication of his intentions for this material (*CP* 592).

When considering the nature and significance of Lawrence's last poetry notebooks, it is essential to engage with the process of composition and revision that determined the nature of the poems. It would be impossible to discuss the late poetry without acknowledging the critical debate surrounding the way in which the manuscripts may be considered to interrelate. It was originally assumed by Aldington that the two texts were composed simultaneously, and that the 'Nettles' notebook served as a jotting-book from which certain poems were taken and transcribed into the other book: an interpretation which suggests that Lawrence was selecting his best work for inclusion in 'Last Poems'. However, Aldington also asserts that the two books remain distinct in content and preoccupation: they 'represent two different books, one a continuation of *Pansies*, the other a new series leading up to the death poems, for which Lawrence had not found a general title' (*CP* 592). This implies selection according to type rather than quality, but does not throw into question the simultaneity of the two books' composition.

This notion of simultaneous composition was challenged by Keith Sagar, then later by Christopher Pollnitz in 'Cough-Prints and Other Intimacies: Considerations in Editing Lawrence's Later Verse':

> Keith Sagar has proved erroneous Aldington's assumption that the *Nettles* and
> *Last Poems* notebooks were used contemporaneously, the one serving as 'a first
> jotting-book' from which Lawrence redrafted certain poems into the other. Sagar
> shows the two notebooks were used sequentially: when the *Nettles* notebook
> was filled, Lawrence went on to the *Last Poems* notebook, which he left unfilled,
> and unfinished, at his death. (*EL* 154)[1]

It is likely that Lawrence began writing poems into the 'Nettles' notebook during
or after December 1928; he probably started to compose the 'Last Poems' verse
in October 1929 and broke off in mid-November (*EL* 167). If the two notebooks
were consecutively rather than simultaneously created, it becomes impossible to
argue for a clear-cut division according to type, style or subject-matter, in which
Lawrence split his poetry into a collection continuing *Pansies* (the 'Nettles'
notebook) and a collection that is serious, profound and contemplative ('Last
Poems'). Pollnitz challenges the approach that places a division between the two
notebooks by arguing instead that a stylistic break ought to come before the last
nine poems of the 'Nettles' notebook. He refers to this break as an interestingly
abrupt shift from epigrammatic 'pansy'-like verse to the mythopoeic or religious
death poetry. He asserts that:

> The transition, from the scurrilous squibs of summer to the elevated autumnal
> mood of the nine poems that conclude the *Nettles* notebook, is as sudden as
> any to be found in the notebooks. For Sagar, the move from Lichtenthal and
> Lawrence's ill-health in Rottach are sufficient to account for this change. (*EL*
> 165)

Pollnitz replaces a division separating one notebook from the other with a division
that sections off the last nine poems in the 'Nettles' notebook from the preceding
verse, and gives a circumstantial explanation for the 'transition'. This placing of a
caesura seems appropriate in the context of late style categorization, as it provides
the means of designating a literary and biographical hiatus: the beginning of a last
phase.

Nevertheless, it seems to me that any attempt to indicate a caesural break
between poems should be balanced by an acknowledgement of connection and
continuity. Pollnitz's new division is placed between the untitled poem beginning
'Dearly-beloved Mr Squire' and 'Let there be Light!'. A consideration of the
differences in tone and style between the ending of the former and the beginning
of the latter is sufficient to explain why critical analysis has identified a distinct
break at this point. The untitled poem (hitherto referred to as '[Mr Squire]') has as
its final verse the following lines:

---

[1]   See Keith Sagar, 'The Genesis of "Bavarian Gentians" ', in *The D.H. Lawrence Review*,
8.1 (Spring 1975), pp. 47–53. Pollnitz here italicizes 'Last Poems' which I always designate
using quotation marks, so as to differentiate unfinished manuscript from published text.

So now we beg you, Mr Squire,
do now, once and forever, retire
and leave the critical piggy-wiggies. (*CP* 681)

This colloquial, ironic style, employing tight rhythms and end-rhymes in order
to embody and reveal the absurdity of the person targeted, is characteristic of the
satiric doggerel throughout the 'Nettles' notebook. In stark contrast, the following
poem – 'Let there be Light!' – begins:

If ever there was a beginning
there was no god in it
there was no Verb
no Voice
no Word. (*CP* 681)

Immediately this poem seems to locate itself in a different context and tradition:
one of profound philosophical reflection and contemplation. It is engaging with
religious beliefs, both using and undermining the biblical story of the Creation
by asserting a contrary faith in the 'incomprehensible plasm of life, of creation'
(*CP* 681) that struggles to come into being. It is also written in free-verse, without
recourse to the rhythms or rhymes of '[Mr Squire]'. This poem seems at first
glance to be entirely unlike the previous satiric piece, while it is a clear precursor
to the poem that follows it – 'God is Born' – which again deals with the mystery
and wonder of Creation, and with the constantly regenerative (unbiblical) births of
the 'plasm of life', now referred to as 'God'.

However, the break between '[Mr Squire]' and 'Let there be Light!' is by no
means as sudden as it initially appears. The latter is not solely an intensely serious,
'religious' poem; rather, it is characterized by the Lawrentian wit evident in his
habitual satirizing of human nature and society. It contains the lines:

There was nothing to say:
Let there be light!
All that story of Mr God switching on day
is just conceit.

Just man's conceit!
—Who made the sun?
—My child, I cannot tell a lie.
I made it!

George Washington's Grandpapa! (*CP* 681)[2]

---

[2]   In an apocryphal story of the childhood of George Washington (1732–99), these
were the words of the future first President of the USA when his father accused him of

The poem is, in fact, not about 'God' as such, but about the 'Mr God' who springs from man's need to have things explained. The poem focuses on the deficiencies of *human* perception, and the inadequacy of the words through which perception is made palpable. The use of words ('Let there be light!') to express the primal moment of creation becomes absurd when it is seen to occasion a ludicrously mundane, literalized and anachronistic picture of 'Mr God switching on day'. The biblical 'Word' is deflated through becoming merely a synonym for 'Verb', while 'Mr God' is a figure bearing a marked resemblance to the 'Mr Squire' who leads 'the gawky choir / of critical cherubs that chirrup and pipe / in the weekly press their self-satisfied swipe' (*CP* 680). While the poem 'Let there be Light!' employs satire in order to deflate and mock religious conceit, '[Mr Squire]' employs religious language and metaphor in order to satirize the character described initially (and bitingly) as 'Dearly-beloved' – the hyphen revealing that the conjoined words have assumed an identity as an orthodox cliché. The term 'self-satisfied' epitomizes the preoccupation of the two poems, applicable as it is to the fanaticism both of undiscerning critics and fundamentalist Christians.

Perhaps the most striking link between the two poems, however, is their shared contempt for superficial utterance: when considered in the light of this concern, the progression from the first poem to the second becomes more comprehensible. In the untitled poem beginning 'I heard a little chicken chirp' (hereafter '[Thomas Earp]'), appearing only one poem earlier than '[Mr Squire]' in the 'Nettles' notebook, Lawrence has already mocked the 'chicken' who can 'neither paint nor write' but whose 'chirp' is employed in order to 'set other people right':

> All people that can write or paint
> do tremble under my complaint.
> For I am a chicken, and I can chirp;
> and my name is Thomas, Thomas Earp. (*CP* 680)[3]

This depiction of the foul, fowl-like critics is continued with some variation in '[Mr Squire]', in which the 'critical cherubs that chirrup and pipe' express themselves as follows:

> So long will they lift their impertinent voices
> and chirrup their almost indecent noises
> almost as empty as belching or hiccup
> in grand chorale to your monthly kick-up. (*CP* 681)

---

chopping down a prized cherry tree.

   [3]   On 24 August, Lawrence received from Charles Lahr a negative review by Thomas W. Earp (1892–1958) entitled 'Mr. Lawrence on Painting', from the *New Statesman* of 17 August 1929. On the same day, Lawrence returned to Lahr this retaliatory 'squib' or 'Earp cackle' with a request that Lahr 'circulate it' (*L* vii 447).

Language is shown to have become indecent and obscene through its empty use in modern society, particularly among those who have been vested with authority.

This explains the insistence on non-utterance ('there was no Verb') in the following poem – 'Let there be Light!' – in describing the creative mysteries. Similarly, in the next poem – 'God is Born' – the ultimate, most miraculous moment of creation is accompanied not by the 'wild crying of every electron' (*CP* 682) but by a suspension of breath and being:

> When the little eggy amoeba emerged out of foam and nowhere
> then all the electrons held their breath (*CP* 682)

The holding back of breath seems an outward manifestation of the experience of wonder, which is the only appropriate response to the mysterious, multiple 'birth[s] of God' (*CP* 683). In 'The White Horse' (the poem that follows 'God is Born'), it is through being 'so silent' that horse and youth are able to become mutual inhabitants of 'another world' (*CP* 683).

It is arguable, then, that the poems '[Thomas Earp]' and '[Mr Squire]' are not merely satirical 'squibs' entirely distinct from the nine profound, 'religious', meditative poems that follow. Rather, they function as catalysts, provoking a conceptual recoil from debased utterance to the opposite extreme: suspended utterance, or even non-utterance ('silence'). A stupid misuse of words leads to the rejection of the Word as insufficient in responding to the wonder and mystery of creation: something presented as unutterable. What sustains and is corrective and necessary is therefore wit, intelligence and play: the kind of writing that describes a 'little, eggy amoeba' rather than (for instance) a primitive life form.

A further argument against the placing of any absolute caesural break in the 'Nettles' notebook between the satiric and mythopoeic verse lies in the observation that the 'mythopoeic' poetry is not confined merely to the last nine poems in the book. The most striking example of an earlier poem that would fit readily into a category of mythopoeic, philosophical, religious, lyrical or visionary poetry is 'Gladness of Death', which ends:

> I shall blossom like a dark pansy, and be delighted
> there among the dark sun-rays of death.
> I can feel myself unfolding in the dark sunshine of death
> to something flowery and fulfilled, and with a strange sweet perfume. (*CP* 677)

This (unrhymed) meditation upon death may be located in several contexts and explored in relation to any (or all) of them. It may be said to spring from the previous sparky, satirical verse which, through a consideration of debased human contacts/utterance, has provoked the insight: 'Men prevent one another from being men' (*CP* 677). When placed in a satirical context, the botanical imagery may be considered instrumental in provoking the following anti-human poem 'Humanity needs Pruning' (discussed further in Chapter 4, p. 79).

Yet the stanzas are clearly lyrical rather than satirical, and bear closer resemblance to poems such as 'Glory of Darkness' (later redrafted as 'Bavarian Gentians'), 'Flowers and Men' and even 'Shadows', which appears in 'Last Poems'. In fact, the similarities with 'Shadows' are most striking, as both poems are concerned with the progression from a broken state of dissolution (in which a man is prevented from being a man) to a curious blossoming, associated with death but envisaged as a kind of revitalization:

> and still, among it all, snatches of lovely oblivion, and snatches of renewal
> odd, wintry flowers upon the withered stem, yet new, strange flowers
> such as my life has not brought forth before, new blossoms of me— (*CP* 727)

The correlation of imagery between the two preceding quotations from 'Gladness of Death' and 'Shadows' is sufficient to suggest that an attempt to arrange these poems according to aesthetic impression would result in 'Gladness of Death' being placed either towards the end of 'Last Poems', or at least with the nine 'mythopoeic' poems concluding the 'Nettles' notebook: certainly not earlier on, which is where it actually appears.

Although 'Gladness of Death' is the most striking example of a poem that defies the analytical categorization dividing satire from mythopoeia, there are many others, even near the beginning of the 'Nettles' notebook. Poems such as 'Andraitx.— Pomegranate flowers' and 'The Heart of Man' are lyrical and philosophical respectively, while many poems concerning the gods, fallen angels and astrological/astronomical changes are interspersed with the stinging, nettle-like satires. It appears, then, that the attempt to categorize and label last poems incurs the same kinds of problems as the attempt to define the boundaries of a late phase or style.

Verse-books, Groups and Sequences

An alternative strategy to that which identifies a single caesural break might emphasize multiple divisions. In his essay 'Some Issues for Study of Integrated Collections', Earl Miner defines the principal traits of 'sequential continuousness' as 'beginnings and endings (in addition to *the* beginning and ending) that are separated-joined by continuances'.[4] The elision 'separated-joined' creates a useful problem term to describe the links between poem sequences within a collection. In her book on Lawrence's poetry – *Self and Sequence* – Holly Laird adheres to a sense of order achieved through sequential continuousness, resulting in definable groups or clusters of poems. She is concerned with exploring the nature of a

---

[4]   Earl Miner, 'Some Issues for Study of Integrated Collections' in *Poems in Their Place: The Intertextuality and Order of Poetic Collections,* ed. Neil Fraistat, (Chapel Hill and London: University of North Carolina Press, 1986), p. 40.

'verse-book' (a book of poems) as a collection, proceeding methodologically from a conviction made explicit by William S. Anderson: 'A normal book of poetry should have some order, some kind of arrangement that can be appreciated by readers as an enhancement of the separate poems'.[5] Neil Fraistat similarly argues that it is necessary to allow poems to remain in place, and that failure to do so results in significant losses:

> Because reading is a process of patterning, to read an individual poem in isolation or outside of its original volume is not only to lose the large retroactive sweep of the book as a whole—with its attendant dynamics and significance—but also to risk losing the meanings within the poem itself that are foregrounded or activated by the context of the book.[6]

Fraistat employs the term 'contextual poetics' to describe a critical approach that 'would study a wide range of forms, including paired poems, sonnet and other types of sequences, poetic works published in parts ... individual collections—as well as clusters of poems within them, and the shape of a poet's canon'.[7]

Laird's emphasis on the 'book' or 'volume' as an entity is partly a response to her sense that 'The printed book seemed to [Lawrence] a vital form, both vulnerable to its readers and capable of changing them.'[8] She discusses verse-clusters and groupings, examining the diverse ways in which poems are 'linked' together stylistically, thematically or through the modulation of recurrent images and symbols, as well as the ways in which poem clusters generate and relate to other clusters. While considering these sequential patternings, she also attends to some incongruities and oddities within groups, and to the significance of the 'not said': the gaps between poems, groups or clusters that may in themselves play an important part in the developing verse-book. (Said analogously refers to the way in which late writing communicates in part 'through the blank spaces from which it has disengaged itself'.[9]) Laird says of the early poetry collection *Amores* (1916), for example, 'What is not told in the spaces within and between poems enlarges the emptiness that confronts the poet.' (*SS* 72) She also traces the developing methodologies which underlie Lawrence's procedures for ordering, selecting and revising poems within a particular volume. She examines the nature and status of

---

[5]   William S. Anderson, 'The Theory and Practice of Poetic Arrangement from Vergil to Ovid', ibid. p. 47.

[6]   Neil Fraistat, 'Introduction: The Place of the Book and the Book as Place', ibid. p. 8.

[7]   Ibid. p. 4.

[8]   Holly Laird, *Self and Sequence: the Poetry of D.H. Lawrence* (Charlottesville: The University Press of Virginia, 1988), pp. 100–101. Hereafter *SS*.

[9]   Theodore W. Adorno, *Essays on Music*, ed. Richard Leppert, with new translation by Susan H. Gillespie (Berkeley, Los Angeles and London: University of California Press, 2002), p. 566 (quoted in *OLS* 9).

each book in its completed form, considering Lawrence's psychological motivation for reordering, omitting or fragmenting particular poems or clusters used in later collections.

In Laird's view, Lawrence's restless search for himself through poetic sequence is progressive, and culminates in his 'Last Poems', which she feels is a masterpiece in sequencing, despite its incomplete, unrevised condition:

> By the time Lawrence wrote his *Last Poems*, sequential composition had become instinctive. If he had lived to publish these, it is unlikely that he would have altered them substantially from their final state in manuscript. (*SS* ix)

Implicitly adhering to the view that these last poems do, in fact, crown a lifetime's achievement, Laird argues for a cohesive sequence and divides 'Last Poems' into nine groups or clusters, each group possessing its own beginning and end. Her sense of cohesion in this collection enables her to convey an impression of finality: 'questions and criticisms alike tend to be silenced by the unusual certainty expressed in the poems. Nothing in the earlier books of poetry compares with the serene, seemingly unproblematic nature of this one' (*SS* 220). The word 'serene' is telling: it locates this interpretation of the poems within a particular model of late style, in which sublimity and peace are the legacy of pre-death works.

It seems to me, however, that this perception of the last poems as 'unproblematic' depends on an acceptance of the 'finishedness' that Laird affords 'Last Poems' when she places the notebook in the same category as completed volumes such as *Pansies* and *Nettles* (with their appropriately italicized titles):

> in his last one and a half years [Lawrence] brought three further works of poetry to a finished state, *Pansies*, *Nettles,* and *Last Poems*, and demonstrated again his ability to alter the manner of verse and book to match the occasion. (*SS* 196)

This impression of finality, however, is usefully contradicted when Laird discusses Aldington's belief that the notebook is best thought of as 'a *nearly* finished work in itself, the trial run perhaps for a long poem' (*SS* 198, my italics), and also when she writes: 'Lawrence probably would have revised *Last Poems* if he had lived to present it as a book. Any argument for internal coherence of that sequence should leave room for speculation about subsequent reshaping' (*SS* 198). A perception of 'Last Poems' as a finished volume must be qualified by an acknowledgement that Lawrence almost certainly would have made significant alterations – reordering clusters, constructing longer poems and cycles or cannibalizing the notebooks for separate, individual publications to use elsewhere. Lawrence had always made substantial changes to his volumes, and the books he completed between 1928–30 were no exception. When preparing *Apocalypse* for publication, Lawrence excised or rearranged large chunks of the text, while *Assorted Articles*, prepared in 1930, was also extensively revised. It is probable that 'Last Poems' would have been subjected to exactly this process of revision, its 'book' version differing in crucial respects from the notebook sequences, thus reflecting (for example) the evolution of the earlier *Amores* volume as it changed between manuscript and printed text.

When considering this potential for new growth and development, Laird writes '[the "Nettles" notebook] may be considered a miscellany of drafts in the background of Lawrence's more finished works [including "Last Poems"]' (*SS* 198). This allusion to the other late notebook in a hypothetical 'reshaping' of 'Last Poems' is particularly revealing, for the drafts in the 'Nettles' notebook cannot be disregarded, and it is quite possible that a volume formed by Lawrence would have amalgamated the death poems of the two manuscripts. Laird, having identified a 'break' before 'The Ship of Death' in 'Last Poems', conjectures that 'Had [Lawrence] lived longer, he might have plumped out this juncture with poems from [the "Nettles" notebook]' (*SS* 232). Such suggestions are merely speculative, and reveal the problems inherent in an attempt to fathom authorial intention and glean from the poetic sequence a methodology of revision. The conjectured 'reshaping' of poems thus introduces an entirely new dimension of complexity into the issue of sequencing involving late, unfinished poems.

The inevitable problems and confusions arising from the sequencing approach become evident if we consider one of the nine 'groups', which (according to Laird) constitute the 'Last Poems' notebook. Laird's third group begins with the poem 'Invocation to the Moon', and also includes 'Butterfly', 'Bavarian Gentians', 'Lucifer', 'The Breath of Life' and 'Silence'. She characterizes this group by saying that in these poems, the previous 'battles of thought are superseded by invocational narratives' (*SS* 225). Undeniably this is true of the first two poems, in which the moon and butterfly are directly addressed: it is also true of 'Silence', which begins with the line 'Come, holy Silence, come' (*CP* 698). Yet 'The Breath of Life' is didactic or thoughtful rather than invocational; the line 'Reach me a gentian, give me a torch!' in 'Bavarian Gentians' is clearly rhetorical; while the demand 'But tell me, tell me' in 'Lucifer' is not intended as a direct address. Paradoxically, the poem 'The Hands of God' which begins Laird's next sequence is more obviously invocational than two of the poems within the 'invocational' group, as it contains the direct appeal to divinity: 'Save me, O God, from falling … Let me never know, O God' (*CP* 699). 'The Hands of God' also engages with the fallen angel imagery, associated with humankind's degeneration into self-consciousness: 'Did Lucifer fall through knowledge? / oh then, pity him, pity him that plunge!' (*CP* 699). This appeal is obviously connected with the 'Lucifer' poem, concerned with debating the angel's loss or preservation of brightness after his fall. It seems odd to impose a group structure which severs 'The Hands of God' from two of the previous poems to which it is clearly linked in style, imagery and content.

Another complication arises from Laird's sense that the three poems 'Butterfly', 'Bavarian Gentians' and 'Lucifer' form a triad within the poem-group. She argues that 'Butterfly' and 'Bavarian Gentians' were 'obviously designed as pendants' (*SS* 226), as they were subject to revision in the 'Nettles' notebook and subsequently placed side by side in 'Last Poems'. Yet, while arguing that Lawrence scrupulously moved this pair of poems and placed them in a particular location in the 'Last

Poems' notebook, she conjectures that when revising the manuscript poems for a printed book, Lawrence would have changed the order of the poems so as to reverse the 'jarring' chronology in which October precedes September. She goes on to say that 'Lucifer' is a passionate 'enlargement' of 'Bavarian Gentians', providing an authorial gloss on the longer poem, so that 'Omitting "Lucifer" and "Butterfly" as aspects of "Bavarian Gentians" would diminish the central poem' (*SS* 228). According to this model, a juxtaposition of poems through sequencing can play the role of prose exegesis, furnishing the reader directly with the poet's own comments on his work. Clearly, aspects of 'Bavarian Gentians' are illuminated by considering its relation to the poems next to it. Yet aspects of 'Bavarian Gentians' might be equally illuminated by considering the earlier poems 'Blueness' and even 'Snake' (a comparison actually made by Laird) – or, indeed, Lawrence's writings on the Etruscans, in which his descent into their ancient tombs, lit by an acetylene lamp, is described in strikingly similar terms to the descent into Hades evoked in this late poem (see Chapter 3, p. 62).

An alternative poem-group structure for 'Last Poems' might plausibly split Laird's triad between 'Butterfly' and 'Bavarian Gentians', on the grounds that 'Butterfly' forms a neat stylistic pair with 'Invocation to the Moon', while the striking dark/blue/flame imagery of 'Bavarian Gentians' generates the 'dark-blue depths', 'layers and layers of darkness' and contrasting 'gleam' of 'Lucifer' (*CP* 697). I hope, through suggesting this new arrangement, to indicate that structuring of this kind (while extremely useful for analytical purposes) partakes of the arbitrariness of an attempt to identify clear-cut phases within a life or poetic career. When responding to late works in particular, each reader-response will involve a retrospective ordering through imposing categories and patterns, in the interests of identifying some kind of satisfying coherence. This coherence might adhere to a preconceived notion of unity, so that the book is shaped to fit a mould. Such considerations compel Annabel Patterson to ask 'To what extent does the existence of authoritative and significant order in a volume depend on the predisposition of the reader to find it or to find it absent?'[10]

Arguing for a closed system seems to run counter to Lawrence's own aims, as he said of the free-verse method which he derived from the poetry of Walt Whitman: 'It has no goal in either eternity. It has no finish. It has no satisfying stability, satisfying to those who like the immutable' (*SP* 270). The imposition of closure might be avoided through considering the way late poems are recurrently reshaped within the context of their evolving draft stages. An interpretation of 'Last Poems' that defines 'shaping' as 'reshaping' must take into account the 'Nettles' notebook and the way in which Lawrence was drawing on this wealth of material.

---

[10]   Annabel Patterson, 'Jonson, Marvell, and Miscellaneity?', in *Poems in Their Place*, p. 98.

Drafting, Reshaping and Dialogism

It is likely that Lawrence, having filled the 'Nettles' notebook, began writing poems into another – but that when necessary he referred back to the previous notebook in order to find raw material from which he could fashion his new poems. The process of revision would thus become analogous to the drafting of the last version of *Lady Chatterley's Lover* in 1928, during which Lawrence strategically referred to the previous drafts in order to rewrite and reshape the novel.[11]

My supposition that Lawrence composed parts of 'Last Poems' with the 'Nettles' notebook in front of him may be supported (although not proved) by the following observation made by Aldington and quoted by Pollnitz:

> Huxley is wrong in saying L[awrence] never corrected but re-wrote. He did re-write, but that MS vol of *Last Poems* I edited was so corrected and crossed out and interpolated I had great difficulty finding the real text.[12]

Pollnitz, after extensive perusal of the manuscripts,[13] has expressed the view that at some stage Lawrence went through the entire 'Last Poems' notebook, making substantial revisions and corrections. This proves the process of creation to have been more closely regulated than is often supposed, revealing a concern with the minutiae of individual poems, rather than simply with the impact of the notebook as a whole. The 'thicket-like appearance of some of Lawrence's manuscript pages' (*EL* 155) suggests that Lawrence was not just correcting his poems but revising, developing and recreating them, while the correlations (evident for instance in title, subject-matter and style) between drafts of poems contained within both notebooks suggest that the 'Last Poems' verse may be seen as progressing from the poem sequences begun in the earlier 'Nettles' notebook.

In order to substantiate my claims regarding Lawrence's drafting procedure, I will attempt to show that the 'God is Born' sequence with its origin in the 'Nettles' notebook indirectly occasioned some of the finest death-poetry in 'Last Poems'. The jubilant exclamation 'God is Born!' is repeated no less than ten times during the course of the poem with this title. Yet its impact was not, in the process of composition, limited to this particular poem. It gave rise to a sequence which incorporates the first extant drafts of the poems that became 'Butterfly', 'Bavarian Gentians' and 'The Ship of Death' as well as, in embryo, 'Silence' and 'Shadows'.

---

[11]   For a detailed description of the composition of the three versions of this novel, see *Lady Chatterley's Lover*, ed. Michael Squires (Cambridge: Cambridge University Press, 1993), pp. xx–xxviii. Hereafter *LCL*.

[12]   *Literary Lifelines: The Richard Aldington–Lawrence Durrell Correspondence*, ed. Ian S. MacNiven and Harry T. Moore (London: Faber, 1981), p. 16.

[13]   The notebooks are held at the Harry Ransom Humanities Research Center, University of Texas at Austin.

The original 'Butterfly' poem, which was crossed out and rewritten entirely in the 'Nettles' notebook, ended as follows:

> When I see its veined wings lifted
> as it sips at the dirt on my shoe
> my soul says at once:
> God is born![14]

The butterfly was initially a manifestation of God's grace, rather than (as it became on revision) a poignant symbol for the departing soul faced with a journey from life to death. Similarly, the initial version of 'The White Horse' was:

> The youth walks up to the white horse, to put its halter on
> and something in the still, sure pride of the lad makes me say:
> God is born! (N 128)

The lad becomes a human manifestation of the process by which God comes into being. A further progression extends these religious resonances to the title of the poem 'The State of Grace' (which later became 'Bavarian Gentians') and to the description of the flowers evoked in this poem as possessing 'dark blue godhead' (N 129). Similar terminology was also employed in the first drafting of the next poem, 'Flowers and Men', in which the honeysuckle pours out 'the breath of its godhead' (N 130).

At some point Lawrence revised these poems in the 'Nettles' notebook, and it is interesting to conjecture regarding the stage at which this process occurred. It seems likely from the coherence and consistency of the 'god' and 'godhead' revisions that he returned to these poems and corrected several of them at once, rather than altering each one after completing a first version. It is even possible that he altered these poems when faced with the task of transcribing a version of them into his later ('Last Poems') notebook. Certainly a uniform pattern of correction emerges, in which the poems are obviously 'secularized', divested of all the references to 'god' and 'godhead'. The explicitly religious terminology and suggestion is replaced by references to cosmic 'wonder' (in the over-scored 'Butterfly'), resulting in a naturalistic description of the creature that 'lifts his wings, lifts them / and sips at the dirt on my shoe' (N 128). Naturalistic description similarly ousts religious imagery in the revised versions of 'The White Horse', 'Glory of Darkness' and 'Flowers and Men'. In the former, horse and youth experience a transcendence that is no longer religious through the power of 'silence'. The title 'Glory of Darkness' replaces 'The

---

[14]   Notebook (Roberts E192) held at the Harry Ransom Humanities Research Center, The University of Texas at Austin, containing poems published in *Pansies, Nettles* and (posthumously) entitled 'More Pansies' by Richard Aldington in 1932 (now the 'Nettles' notebook: hereafter N), p. 128. This manuscript is unpaginated, but I have assigned a number to each page on which a poem by Lawrence appears.

State of Grace', the term 'glory' is later replaced by 'beauty', and 'blue godhead' becomes 'blue fringes'. In 'Flowers and Men' the miraculous essence of flowers is captured in the term 'floweriness' rather than 'godhead', while 'beauty' serves as another substitution and the honeysuckle merely pours out 'his breath', rather than 'the breath of its godhead' (N 130).

The poems I have just described (which, given a collective identity according to the sequencing approach, might be termed the 'God is Born' group) clearly served as raw material when Lawrence was creating 'Last Poems'. After completing 'Invocation to the Moon', he evidently decided to return to the 'Nettles' notebook for material, as the poem 'Butterfly' is next in sequence. One possible explanation is that 'Invocation to the Moon' was written with the poem 'Prayer' (the final poem in the 'Nettles' notebook) either as a conscious stimulus or an unconscious association, thus alerting Lawrence to the availability of other poems in the previous notebook. 'Prayer' opens with the lines:

> Give me the moon at my feet
> Put my feet upon the crescent, like a Lord!
> O let my ankles be bathed in moonlight, that I may go
> sure and moon-shod, cool and bright-footed
> towards my goal (*CP* 684)

While in this poem the moon is envisaged as providing literal support through becoming a pedestal, in 'Invocation to the Moon' it has the capacity to heal and restore physically, allowing the narrator to stand strongly again:

> Now, lady of the Moon, now open the gate of your silvery house
> and let me come past the silver bells of your flowers, and the cockle-shells
> into your house, garmentless lady of the last great gift:
> who will give me back my lost limbs
> and my lost white fearless breast
> and set me again on moon-remembering feet
> a healed, whole man, O Moon! (*CP* 696)

The ankles 'bathed in moonlight' of the earlier poem and the 'moon-remembering feet' of the other illustrate how closely they are linked in imagery and style.

Another explanation for Lawrence turning to previous draft material is that the invocatory style of the 'moon' poem proved effective in itself and hence offered a suitable mould for the recasting of an older poem. On perusal of the 'Nettles' notebook, 'Butterfly' (now existing in two versions, the earlier struck through) would have seemed suitable: the naturalistic description of the creature as well as the sense of 'wonder' it inspired could readily be transformed into a direct, invocational address. The revised 'Nettles' version already possessed an incantatory feel, achieved through the repetitions in 'lifts its veined wings, lifts them', and 'lifts his wings, lifts them' (N 128). The subsequent 'Last Poems' version, creating a vivid sense of actuality, alters these lines slightly so they become 'lifting your veined wings, lifting them? big white butterfly!' (*CP* 696) This line is preceded by an image derived from the earliest 'Nettles' version and repeated at the end of both verses of the second draft: a description of the butterfly as it 'sips at the dirt on my shoe' (*CP* 696). Then, in the 'Last Poems' version, the image becomes part of a poignant interrogative: 'Butterfly, why do you settle on my shoe, and sip the dirt on my shoe ...?' while later in the poem the butterfly is described as 'content on my shoe' (*CP* 696). The creature has become an emblem for the soul, poised on the brink of death, but content to remain in the warm garden of life, still belonging to the mortal body (for which the dirty shoe becomes an emblem). It acquires a symbolic resonance entirely absent from the earlier ('Nettles' notebook) drafts of the poem, yet employs the striking imagery clearly derived from them.

The poem 'Butterfly', then, evolves from a naturalistic description of the butterfly as embodiment of the awe-inspiring creator-God to a symbol for the departing soul faced with death but unwilling to depart from life. It seems crucial when analysing this poem not just to see it as part of a triad or as a 'Last Poems' text that has superseded all prior versions, but to place it in the context of its previous drafts, revealing ways in which Lawrence was reworking material, cross-referencing between notebooks and interpolating material into new contexts, thus changing a poem's ostensible resonances and implications.

This process is also evident on consideration of the two short poems 'Lucifer' and 'The Breath of Life', which appear in the 'Nettles' notebook and also, slightly altered, after two versions of 'Bavarian Gentians' in 'Last Poems'.[15] These poems above all others seem to prove irrevocably that Lawrence was referring back to the 'Nettles' material when working in the subsequent notebook. The first three lines of the 'Lucifer' poems in each notebook are identical, with only the minor re-ordering of the words 'he' and 'the' in the later draft. Yet a significant alteration and extension occurs, as the last two lines of the 'Nettles' poem ('He only fell out of your ken, you orthodox angels, / you dull angels, tarnished with centuries of conventionality', *CP* 614) are replaced by the following:

> In the dark-blue depths, under layers and layers of darkness,
> I see him more like the ruby, a gleam from within
> of his own magnificence,
> coming like the ruby in the invisible dark, glowing
> with his own annunciation, towards us. (*CP* 697)

Clearly the poem 'Bavarian Gentians', with its journey 'down the darker and darker stairs, where blue is darkened on blueness' (*CP* 697), has intervened

---

[15]   It remains uncertain which version contains Lawrence's most recent revisions. Keith Sagar has persuasively challenged the decision made by Aldington to print the draft that appears first in the notebook ('The Genesis of "Bavarian Gentians" ', in *The D.H. Lawrence Review*, 8.1, p. 48.

between the composition of the 'Nettles' and 'Last Poems' versions of 'Lucifer'. Perhaps Lawrence was consciously looking in the 'Nettles' notebook for a poem that would fit into the 'Bavarian Gentians' sequence, concerned with underworlds resembling Etruscan tombs and the visibility/invisibility occasioned by darkness lit by blue gentian torches. The title 'Lucifer' (identical to that of the 'Nettles' notebook poem) also helps us to a near certainty that the earlier draft was consciously adopted and adapted: a case distinct from that of the related poem 'When Satan Fell' (appearing much earlier than 'Lucifer' in 'Last Poems') whose altered title affords it a new identity.

The case of the two drafts of 'The Breath of Life' is analogous to that of 'Lucifer', as the earlier version is adopted then altered as it is recontextualized. Both drafts are cited below:

> The breath of life and the sharp winds of change are the same thing.
> But people who are fallen from the organic connection with the cosmos
> feel the winds of change grind them down
> and the breath of life never comes to nourish them. (*CP* 615)

> The breath of life is in the sharp winds of change
> mingled with the breath of destruction.
> But if you want to breathe deep, sumptuous life
> breathe all alone, in silence, in the dark,
> and see nothing. (*CP* 698)

Here, the shift is from a preoccupation with the inorganic, mechanical nature of people who have lost their connection with the cosmos to a body-centred awareness of being alive 'sumptuously' in aloneness, silence, stillness and darkness. As in the case of 'Lucifer', it is clear that 'Bavarian Gentians' (previously entitled 'Glory of Darkness'), has intervened between the composition of the two versions.

I am suggesting, then, that Lawrence is certainly using material from his previous notebook, but regenerating and reinvigorating this material, provoking new insights and new contexts in which previous ideas and images can assume a fresh significance. The apparent 'shaping' explored in Laird's sequencing must be recognized as itself a 'reshaping' of previously composed draft material. Pollnitz emphasizes the value of representing and exploring the various draft-stages through which poems pass during composition, without which the scholar forfeits a necessary intimacy with the text:

> Reading the late notebooks is also an 'intimate' experience in the sense in which Robert Hughes refers to a viewing of Auerbach's heavily reworked drawings as intimate. As part of the pleasure of looking at a drawing may come through a speculative awareness of the stages by which it reached its exhibited form, so a multiply revised Lawrence poem allows a reader of the original manuscript to

reconstruct the stages of its composition, and to read the stages as completed
drafts. (*EL* 155)

The perusal of poem drafts leads, in Pollnitz's view, to the pleasure of recognizing
clearly defined stages in a poem's composition. The complexity of the compositional
process is in part acknowledged by considering a poem in the retrospective light of
its previous successive reshapings.

Perhaps, though, even this approach (advocating the reconstruction of
completed drafts as stages) is too narrow. Pollnitz admits that there are often times
when these stages remain indefinable and elusive, reliant merely on scholarly
conjecture. It is often impossible to determine at what 'stage' revisions were made,
to establish chronology and to afford definitive, final status to one particular draft.
Such uncertainty indicates the complexity of the process by which texts evolve as
they assimilate new resonances and associations. These considerations impel one
towards a definition of Lawrentian poetic text that emphasizes unfinishedness, and
a 'constant, ceaseless creation and exchange of meaning'.[16]

In his essay 'Chaos in Poetry', Lawrence articulates his own conception of
textual instability within a book of poetry:

> Whims, and fumblings, and effort, and nonsense, and echoes from other poets,
> these all go to make up the living chaos of a little book of real poetry ... Through
> it all runs the intrinsic naiveté without which no poetry can exist, not even the
> most sophisticated ... In this act, and this alone, we truly *live*: in that innermost
> naïve opening of the soul, like a flower, like an animal, like a coloured snake, it
> does not matter, to the sun of chaotic livingness. (*IR* 115–16)

The verse-book described here is not a completed, polished entity, but rather an
attempt or exercise: a text riddled with confusion and incongruity. Lawrence's
emphasis on the chaotic nature of a 'little book' rather than individual poems
is significant, for a book or collection – like a novel – can embody textual
contradiction in a way that an individual poem cannot. In his essay 'Why the
Novel Matters', Lawrence refers to the novel as 'the one bright book of life',[17]
attributing its brightness to the multiplicity of resonances and perspectives that can
be encompassed within such an extended prose-work. A novel can be polyphonic or
multi-vocal, while a single poem tends to offer a single perspective, a single voice.
The distinction between dialogic novel and monologic poem lies at the heart of
Mikhail Bakhtin's evaluation of literary genre. In a formulation strikingly similar
to Lawrence's description of the novel, Bakhtin (in the words of his translator and
editor Michael Holquist) states:

---

[16]   Michael Holquist, *Dialogism: Bakhtin and his World* (London: Routledge, 1990),
p. 41.
[17]   'Why the Novel Matters', in *Study of Thomas Hardy and Other Essays*, ed. Bruce
Steele (Cambridge: Cambridge University Press, 1985), p. 195.

> In dialogism, the novel is the great book of life, because it celebrates the grotesque body of the world. Dialogism figures a close relation between bodies and novels because they both militate against monadism ... and the concept of a pristine, closed-off, static identity and truth wherever it may be found.[18]

Bakhtin shows how the novel is marked off from other (lesser) genres through being 'energized by forces set in motion by the give-and-take between stasis and change, the fixity of language vs. the flux of utterance, all of which animate the dialogue between self and other'.[19] The resulting multi-valence is distinguished from the characteristic uni-vocality of the other genres, including poetry, as David Lodge illustrates:

> For the 'canonized' genres – epic, tragedy and lyric – are what Bakhtin calls 'monologic': they seek to establish a single style, a single voice, with which to express a single world-view. Even if individual characters express distinct and opposing views in such a text, nevertheless an all-pervasive poetic decorum, or the regularities of rhythm and metre, ensure that the total effect is one of stylistic (and ideological) consistency and homogeneity.[20]

Poetry, according to this argument, is restricted by the limits imposed upon it by form, remaining homogeneous rather than multi-vocal.

However, it seems that in practice these genre categories are not absolute. In *The Dialogic Imagination*, Bakhtin describes the possible slippage experienced by a poetic symbol when it is made ambivalent through encountering other perspectives:

> As soon as another's voice, another's accent, the possibility of another's point of view breaks through this play of the symbol, the poetic plane is destroyed and the symbol is translated on to the plane of prose.[21]

Through this paradoxical 'novelization' of poetry, a generic confusion can occur in which (for instance) Yeats's 'Among Schoolchildren' can become 'a masterpiece in prose',[22] for 'Bakhtin never claimed that *verse* as a medium was necessarily monologic. One of his favourite sources of examples of dialogic discourse was Pushkin's verse novel, *Eugene Onegin*'.[23] Julia Kristeva emphasizes the

---

[18]   Holquist, p. 90.

[19]   Ibid. p. 181.

[20]   David Lodge, *After Bakhtin* (London: Routledge, 1990), p. 58.

[21]   Mikhail Bakhtin, *The Dialogic Imagination*, trans. Caryl Emerson and Michael Holquist (Austin: University of Texas Press, 1981), p. 328.

[22]   Lodge, p. 97.

[23]   Ibid. p. 96.

arbitrariness of the division that separates novel from poetry within dialogism by referring always to 'poetic language' in her essay on Bakhtin[24].

It is certainly arguable that even if a single poem is monologic, a *book* of verse – embodying, as it will, a multiplicity of perspectives – may plausibly be termed dialogic. This interpretation counterbalances the notion of a stabilizing unity imposed by the collecting of poems into a book:

> if the poetry book might ... be viewed as a potential hermeneutic straitjacket, fashioned to restrict the reader's movements, it might also be seen as a form through which poets can supplant or destabilize the meaning of one poem by that of others, freeing the reader to pursue any number of interpretive paths. And the cost of this freedom is the troublesome recognition that our articulation of any pattern in a book will inevitably be at the expense of other, perhaps equally conceivable, schemes.[25]

This seems particularly true of a book of free-verse poetry by Lawrence, which struggles to achieve the formlessness of spontaneity, eschewing rigid, gem-like, fixed verse and (according to its author) making a virtue of its own whims and fumblings. The fact that such a book will also encompass 'echoes from other poets' opens up an even broader range of interpretative possibilities.

Late Intertexts[26]

> The utterance is like a spasm, naked contact with all influences at once. (*SP* 270)

According to this quotation, a writer is openly and promiscuously receptive to every text and experience surrounding him/her at the moment of composition, resulting in the 'chaotic livingness' (cited above) of a book of verse. The term 'spasm' is problematic, however, in suggesting pure spontaneity of expression immune from deliberate revision and conscious artistry. The spontaneity/revision paradox had been prevalent throughout Lawrence's 1919 essay 'Poetry of the Present', in

---

[24] Julia Kristeva, 'Word, Dialogue and Novel', in *The Kristeva Reader*, ed. Toril Moi (Oxford: Blackwell, 1986).

[25] Fraistat, p. 10.

[26] For a full discussion of the wide-raging implications of this term see *Intertextuality: Theories and Practices*, ed. Judith Still and Michael Worton (Manchester: Manchester University Press, 1990). Useful definitions are given, for example, by John Frow ('Intertextuality and Ontology', p. 46) and Michael Riffaterre ('Compulsory Reader Response: the Intertextual Drive', pp. 57–8). See also Anthony H. Harrison, *Victorian Poets and Romantic Poems: Intertextuality and Ideology* (Charlottesville: University Press of Virginia, 1990), p. 11.

which he argues that new poetry, such as that of Whitman, is distinguishable from 'finished', consummate poetry of the past because it embodies textual incongruity or chaos:

> there is another kind of poetry: the poetry of that which is at hand: the immediate present ... The strands are all flying, quivering, intermingling into the web, the waters are shaking the moon. (*SP* 267)

The web image is used rather oddly here, in order to create the sense of an utterly spontaneous creative drive in which the utterance is pulsating restlessly with life rather than existing as a carefully regulated artefact. In reality, a spider's web must be carefully and intricately spun into the required pattern in a way that seems to contradict the arbitrary nature of spontaneous intermingling. Consequently, the image is an apposite embodiment of the paradox inherent in Lawrence's poetics. The strands of a poem may seem to be arbitrarily and instinctively intertwined, yet the effect is achieved through a *cultivated* spontaneity, whose underlying pattern gives integrity to the larger structure.

Nonetheless, the idea of a poem which, at the moment of composition, is nakedly exposed to all influences simultaneously is both interesting and functional. It suggests that a draft will be intertextually full and resonant, implying a kind of contact that is immediate, uncalculating and indiscriminate. When discussing late works in particular, it is important to consider whether this process of broadening through intertextual (and extra-textual) borrowing is likely to be heightened or diminished. Lateness is often associated with a retreat into isolation and autonomy – the proverbial ivory tower – where it is possible to consolidate: to makes sense of a life through recasting it in a work of art. This inward-looking withdrawal might entail a retreat from external forces rather than an intensified receptivity. Paradoxically, however, the study of late works – particularly within the fields of music and the visual arts – often points to an intertextual broadening in last years, rather than a rejection of external influences, in order to articulate a staunchly personal final vision. It is interesting to note, too, the extent to which artists turn to other late-style works in the attempt to write their own.

The Tempest is omnipresent in literature as a particularly influential late work. Three lines from this play – 'Nothing of him that *doth* fade / But *doth suffer a sea-change* / *Into something* rich and strange[27] – surface in revised form within the 'Nettles' notebook:

> And those that do descend have got to suffer a sense-change
> into something new and strange. (*CP* 667)

Lawrence borrows the concept of 'sea change' – which becomes 'sense change' – to hint at the possibility of a new consciousness within modern man that will elevate

---

[27]   William Shakespeare, *The Tempest*, I. ii. 402–404.

him above a devalued, mechanized society. Significantly, also, the two lines from *The Tempest* were the two lines inscribed upon Shelley's tomb, and Lawrence expressed a strong sense of affinity with this man of action who died heroically. The poem 'The Ship of Death' might be interpreted as a version of the drowning of Shelley,[28] and *The Tempest* could be seen to underlie the image of journeying across the last of seas that permeates a number of the latest mythological poems in the two notebooks.

Lawrence's allusion to *The Tempest* in his late work is by no means anomalous. Henry James and Joseph Conrad both turned to *The Tempest* in order to mark a late moment,[29] while notable actors such as Sir John Gielgud have seen their appearances within this monumental play as a highly significant landmark in their late careers.[30] The Polish film-maker Krzysztof Kieślowski predicated his last film in the *Three Colours* sequence (*Trois Couleurs: Rouge*, 1994) upon the idea and tradition of *The Tempest*, creating a Prospero-like figure in the judge who plays God and settles scores, while adopting a secluded island setting and incorporating a redemption theme.[31]

Many notable composers appear to have broadened intertextually in their last years. Mozart's late works, for instance, reveal the influence of Italian opera while Beethoven's late style draws on a greater number of precursive works (notably those of Handel and Bach) than ever before.[32] Another composer who drew on Bach's music was Gioacchino Rossini, whose late work *Péchés de Vieillesse* (*Sins of Old Age*) in particular owed a significant debt to his precursors and encompasses a panoply of styles.[33] Richard Wagner was a particular admirer of the challenging style evident in Beethoven's last decade, from 1816–26, and this admiration is evident in his last opera *Parsifal*.[34] In the first canticle of his last opera, *Death in Venice*, Benjamin Britten sets the poem 'Death of St Narcissus', finding an

[28]   See Bethan Jones, 'Shaping, Intertextuality and Summation in D.H. Lawrence's *Last Poems*', unpublished PhD thesis (University of Nottingham, 1998), Chapter 2, pp. 76–97.

[29]   Gordon McMullan, paper entitled 'How Old is Late? Late Shakespeare, Old Age, *King Lear*', presented at the conference *Rethinking Late Style*, King's College, London (16–17 November 2007).

[30]   Ibid.

[31]   Philip Horne, 'The Late Krzysztof Kieślowski', paper presented at the conference *Rethinking Late Style*.

[32]   John Deathridge, 'Late Style as Fiction: the Case of Strauss's *Four Last Songs*', paper presented at the conference *Rethinking Late Style*.

[33]   Philip Gossett, 'How can there be a "late style" when there is no "middle"? Reflections on Rossini's *Péchés de Vieillesse*', paper presented at the conference *Rethinking Late Style*.

[34]   William Kinderman, 'Late Style in Beethoven and Wagner: A Reassessment', paper presented at the conference *Rethinking Late Style*.

appropriate poetic catalyst among T.S. Eliot's lesser-known works.[35] In the visual arts, the late Picasso (with his legendary visual memory) identified with late Rembrandt's self-portraits and particularly with Degas; the paintings of this period are characterized by echo, parody and allusion.[36] Interestingly, examples of such allusive broadening in late or last years are harder to find in literature, although William Golding, in his late 'Sea Trilogy',[37] provides one striking instance. Often, the allusiveness of late fiction or poetry lies in its ever-widening frame of reference rather than more conscious and conspicuous references to precursive texts or authors. Lawrence's late poems are richly (and perhaps unusually) intertextual in both senses: they consciously engage with a plethora of literary and other sources while testifying to a lifetime of accumulated knowledge.

As well as identifying a process of intertextual assimilation that may have increased during lateness, it is necessary to take into account the intratextual dimension, involving self-borrowing.[38] Successful ageing artists and writers might select, optimize and adapt aspects of their previous writing: late writing enters into dialogue with the entirety of a writer's own oeuvre, defining a 'last' self with reference to the reclaimed past. Said indicates that Mozart's late opera *Cosi Fan Tutte* possesses an 'echoic form' and 'is not only structured by the ensembles but looks back to earlier works and is full of "thematic reminiscences" ' (*OLS* 62). In writing *Death in Venice*, Britten 'devises a music for the opera that draws on his past work as well as on non-European sources' (*OLS* 159). I have illustrated in Chapter 1 that Lawrence was producing a volume of collected poems in 1928; drawing on his previous Etruscan and anthropological works when writing his last poems and travel book; and expanding a previously written review of Frederick Carter's book on Revelation into his last full-length work in 1929.

A text may be consciously reworked or 'reshaped' by its author, as in the case of Lawrence's manipulation of text within the 'Nettles' and 'Last Poems' notebooks. It will also simultaneously constitute a reshaping of multiple intertexts, entering a continuum in which it is itself reworked and rewritten. When considering the composition of poems and collections it seems necessary to range beyond poem-grouping and even the cross-referencing between notebooks that I have advocated above. In subsequent chapters I will therefore consider the late poems in relation to a wide range of texts, including works of literature read and assimilated by

---

[35] Linda and Michael Hutcheon, 'Rethinking Late Style: Age and Disability (Benjamin Britten)', paper presented at the conference *Rethinking Late Style*.

[36] Elizabeth Cowling, 'Picasso's Late Style or Late Styles?', paper presented at the conference *Rethinking Late Style*.

[37] This trilogy, entitled *To the Ends of the Earth*, incorporates the late novels *Rites of Passage* (1980), *Close Quarters* (1987) and *Fire Down Below* (1989).

[38] For definitions of 'intratextuality' see, for example, Mary Orr, *Claude Simon: The Intertextual Dimension* (Glasgow: University of Glasgow French and German Publications, 1993), p. 183 and Ann Jefferson, 'Autobiography as Intertext: Barthes, Sarraute, Robbe-Grillet', in *Intertextuality: Theories and Practices*, ed. Still and Worton, pp. 110–11.

Lawrence from 1927 to his death in 1930, as well as works written by him during this period. In establishing influential texts read and used by Lawrence I will engage with the empirical evidence available, citing correspondence in order to create plausible connections. Although the works by Lawrence discussed all derive from his three last years, my aim is to indicate that this is not a clear-cut 'phase' that remains distinct from the experiences and works that preceded it. Rather, I wish to illustrate that creative interests and insights evolve and accrue across a lifespan, deepening into a resonant form of expression that may be categorized retrospectively as 'late style'.

Chapter 3
Etruscan Connections

Lawrence in Etruscan Places

> What would I not give
> To bring back the rare and orchid-like
> Evil-yclept Etruscan? (*CP* 297)[1]

On 19 March 1927, Lawrence left the Villa Mirenda (near Florence, Italy) and embarked on an 'Etruscan pilgrimage'[2] with his friend Earl Brewster. After meeting up in Ravello, Lawrence and Brewster drove to Sorrento, before beginning their investigations at the Villa di Papa Giulia in Rome.[3] In early April they visited tombs at Cerveteri, Tarquinia, Vulci and Volterra, and Lawrence's imaginative response to these places would resonate throughout his late works. Almost immediately after his return to the Villa Mirenda he wrote Part I of his story *The Escaped Cock*, which was 'suggested by a little Easter toy of a cock escaping from a man, seen in a shop-window in Volterra the week before Easter after looking at Etruscan tombs—' (*VG* xxvi and n. 24). In this recollection of the story's origin, written considerably later on a page bound in before the manuscript of Part II, Lawrence confuses his own fictional account with its stimulus, as (according to Brewster) the Easter toy actually represented a 'white rooster escaping from an egg', rather than a man.[4] Yet there is no confusion over the fundamental influence of the Etruscan experience on this fascinating and controversial tale.

Having worked on Part I of *The Escaped Cock* between 13 and 28 April, Lawrence then turned his attention to the travel book that became *Sketches of Etruscan Places* (hereafter *Sketches*). A few months later, in October 1927, he composed the unfinished piece '[Autobiographical Fragment]' (*LEA* 49–68): a resurrection narrative (like *The Escaped Cock*) that again owes a profound debt to the impact of the Etruscans on Lawrence during that year. The ongoing implications of this influence become evident on consideration of last poems such as 'The Ship of Death' and letters penned as late as 21 November 1929 (*L* vii 569–70).

---

[1] From 'Cypresses' in *Birds, Beasts and Flowers* (1923).

[2] Earl and Achsah Brewster, *Reminiscences and Correspondence* (London: Secker, 1934), p. 122.

[3] 'The National Museum of Antiquities was built under Pope Giulio III and is commonly called "Villa Giulia" ' (*SEP* xxx n. 27).

[4] Brewster, p. 123.

Lawrence's assimilation of the Etruscan experience in 1927 might be taken as a landmark in designating a late phase – yet there is convincing evidence pointing to an earlier imaginative engagement. Since 1912–14, he had been fascinated by the inhabitants, the landscape and the atmosphere of Italy:

> One must love Italy, if one has lived there. It is so non-moral. It leaves the soul so free. Over these countries, Germany and England, like the grey skies, lies the gloom of the dark moral judgement and condemnation and reservation of the people. Italy does not judge. (*L* i 544)

He had lived in Italy and written extensively about it, notably in *Twilight in Italy, Sea and Sardinia* and the poetry volume *Birds, Beasts and Flowers*. In *Sea and Sardinia*, written in 1921, Lawrence refers to the 'conscious genius' characterizing every part of Italy, which he associated in particular with the early Mediterranean gods:

> Man has lived there and brought forth his consciousness there and in some way brought that place to consciousness, given it its expression, and, really, finished it. The expression may be Proserpine, or Pan, or even the strange 'shrouded gods' of the Etruscans or the Sikels, none the less it is an expression.[5]

It was the 'shrouded', mysterious nature of the Etruscans – as though they were harbouring a fascinating secret – that became so compelling to Lawrence in his last years.

Lawrence's stay in Italy in 1920 provoked the interest in the Etruscans he displayed in 'Cypresses', published in *Birds, Beasts and Flowers* (1923). Simonetta de Filippis asserts that this poem 'shows clearly how Lawrence had already traced the main elements which he later developed into the more complex and conscious vision offered in *Sketches of Etruscan Places*' (*SEP* xxiii).[6] In order to account for the immediate inspiration for Lawrence's writing of this poem, she quotes Rosalind Baynes's recollection that 'Sometimes [Lawrence] came to Fiesole where I was now living, climbing by a steep track up through the olives and along under the remains of Fiesole's Etruscan walls … It was here several … poems were suggested—"Cypresses," for example'.[7] Filippis indicates that 'Cypresses' was written 'in September 1920 at Fiesole (Tuscany)' (*SEP* xxiii) although Pollnitz has questioned this dating, suggesting instead that the poem was composed during

---

[5]   D.H. Lawrence, *Sea and Sardinia*, ed. Mara Kalnins (Cambridge: Cambridge University Press, 1997), pp. 116–17.

[6]   I am indebted to Simonetta de Filippis for the biographical and intertextual account of Lawrence's evolving interest in the Etruscans given here: see her 'Introduction' in *SEP* xxi–lxxiii.

[7]   Edward Nehls, *D.H. Lawrence: A Composite Biography*, vol. ii (Madison: University of Wisconsin Press, 1958), pp. 49–50.

Lawrence's visit to Florence in August–September 1921, by which time his interest in the Etruscans had strengthened.[8] Filippis refers to a letter written by Lawrence to his mother-in-law on 10 September 1921, in which a physical parallel is once again drawn between the Tuscan cypresses and the Etruscan race:

> This is Tuscany, and nowhere are the cypresses so beautiful and proud, like black-flames from primeval times, before the Romans had come, when the Etruscans were still here, slender and fine and still and with naked elegance, black haired, with narrow feet. (*L* iv 84)

The terminology closely reflects that of 'Cypresses', while the sense that an Etruscan 'secret' is contained within the trees is similarly expressed in a letter written six weeks later to Catherine Carswell (who had recently visited Tuscany), in which Lawrence asks: 'will you tell me *what* then was the secret of the Etruscans, which you saw written so plainly in the place you went to? Please don[']t forget to tell me, as they really do rather puzzle me, the Etruscans' (*L* iv 105).

Carswell's visit to Tuscany was obviously one source of Lawrence's preoccupation with the Etruscans. Yet Filippis suggests an intertextual interest once again reaching back to Lawrence's youthful reading:

> Lawrence's readings in his formative years may have awakened his curiosity in Etruscan culture. In 1908, for instance, as Jessie Chambers recalls, he 'was very impressed by Balzac's *La Peau de Chagrin*'. At the beginning of the novel, the hero observes 'an Etruscan vase of finest clay, the nut-brown maiden dancing before the god Priapus, to whom she joyously waved her hand'. In December 1915 Lawrence read *The Golden Bough* and was very much taken by Frazer's account of tree-spirits in chapter IX, 'The Worship of Trees', where central Etruria and its 'rich fields' are mentioned. (*SEP* xxiii)

In this early intertext by Balzac a named god – Priapus – is brought into conjunction with the shadowy Etruscan race and its unnamed gods, through being depicted on a vase; analogously, Priapus is used to create an image at the end of Lawrence's poem 'Name the Gods' (in the 'Nettles' notebook, *CP* 651): a poem advocating a refusal to name them. The reference to James Frazer is significant, showing that Lawrence's concern with the Etruscans was bound up with his more general interest in primitive peoples, and with the multiple mythologies and races described both

---

[8] In addition to detailed textual evidence to substantiate this claim, Pollnitz indicates that Lawrence's interest in the Etruscans, and his identification of cypress trees with the Etruscans, appears to have been stronger in 1921. This is shown in *L* iv 84 and 105, and in a related passage from *Aaron's Rod* – a novel which Lawrence was revising as late as October 1921 – see *Aaron's Rod*, ed. Mara Kalnins (Cambridge: Cambridge University Press, 1988), p. 265 and pp. xxviii–xxx).

by Frazer and Edward B. Tylor.[9] In the 'Foreword' to *Fantasia of the Unconscious* (1922), Lawrence classes the Etruscans with the rest of the 'pagan world':

> I honestly think that the great pagan world of which Egypt and Greece were the last living terms; the great pagan world which preceded our own era once had, I believe, a vast and perhaps perfect science of its own, a science in terms of life. In our era this science crumbled into magic and charlatanry. But even wisdom crumbles ... Then came ... the world flood ... The refugees ... fled ... and some, like Druids or Etruscans or Chaldeans or Amerindians or Chinese, refused to forget, but taught the old wisdom, only in its half forgotten, symbolic forms.[10]

At this stage Lawrence categorized the Etruscans with the Greeks, in his assertion that 'We are really far, far more life-stupid than the dead Greeks or the lost Etruscans',[11] although later – in *Sketches* – he was to develop a crucial distinction between these two civilizations.

It is unsurprising that Lawrence's return to Florence in 1926 created a resurgence of interest in the Etruscans. His desire to 'roam round in Umbria for a little while, and look at the Etruscan things, which interest me' (*L* v 416), as well as his first contact with an Etruscan town and museum, led to his enthusiastic decision early in April 1926 to write 'a book about Umbria and the Etruscans: half travel-book, scientific too' (*L* v 412). This decision led Lawrence to cast around for suitable texts that would provide relevant background information, and he read both widely and thoroughly (in English and Italian) in order to prepare for the visit and for the writing of his book. Lawrence also considered that he might 'stay at Perugia for a couple of months and get material' (*L* v 415): presumably historical. When informing Martin Secker of his plans for the Etruscan book, he added a request for literary sources that could be of use:

> We might go to Perugia, and I might do a book on Umbria and the Etruscan remains ... It would be half a travel book – of the region round Perugia, Assisi, Spoleto, Cortona, and the Maremma – and half a book about the Etruscan things, which interest me very much. – If you happen to know any good book, modern, on Etruscan things, I wish you'd order it for me. I've only read that old work, Dennis' – *Cities and Cemeteries of Etruria*. (*L* v 413)

---

[9]   Edward B. Tylor, *Primitive Culture* (London: John Murray, 1903). See Chapter 5 for a full discussion of Tylor's influence on Lawrence's writing during this period.

[10]   'Foreword: An Answer to Some Critics', in *Psychoanalysis and the Unconscious and Fantasia of the Unconscious*, ed. Bruce Steele (Cambridge: Cambridge University Press, 2004) p. 63.

[11]   Chapter VII, *Fantasia of the Unconscious*, Ibid. p. 118.

On 29 April he informed Secker: 'I'm reading Italian books on the Etruscans – very interesting indeed. I'll join Vieusseux's library here – they will have more things' (*L* v 444). Subsequently he wrote:

> Secker has been urging me to write a travel book: and I don't want to do an ordinary travel book, just of places. So I thought I might stay here [at the Villa Mirenda] two months or so, and prepare a book on the Etruscan cities – the dead Etruscans ... That would be in June – at present I'm reading the Italian books on the Etruscans, getting the idea into shape. (*L* v 448–9)

It is interesting that Lawrence employs the term 'shape' here, to describe the intertextual process of producing an 'idea' of the Etruscans from the material provided by his literary sources. He felt this shaping of his ideas and preconceptions to be an obligatory task, even when he was at times reluctant to apply himself to it: 'At present I am supposed to be reading up about my precious Etruschi!' (*L* v 447).

Lawrence appeared to oscillate between enthusiasm for the book and a profound disillusionment regarding his reading public: 'Why write books for the swine, unless one absolutely must!' (*L* v 483) and 'I get such a distaste for committing myself into "solid print," I am holding off. Let the public read what there is to read' (*L* v 496). Nevertheless, Lawrence continued to read what there was to read on the Etruscans, and formulated his opinions partly in response to the texts he encountered.

He ranged far beyond George Dennis's *1 and Cemeteries of Etruria,* which he may well have read as early as 1920[12] and had certainly read by 1925, as he left a copy in America and had later to request another.[13] He also read a book on the Etruscans by Theodore Mommsen, perhaps *The Early Inhabitants of Italy,* in May 1926 (*DH* 102); Pericle Ducati's *Etruria Antico* (*DH* 102); Fritz Weege's *Etruskische Malerei* (*DH* 104); and D. Randell-Marivers's *Villanovans and Early Etruscans* (*DH* 105). These specified titles constitute only a small proportion of the books he actually read, as is indicated (for instance) by Aldington's recollection that he had 'a dozen standard works on the subject' sent to him in preparation for a visit from Lawrence during the summer of 1926.[14] As late as November 1929, Lawrence was receiving 'an Etruscan book' along with other unspecified books sent to him by Max Mohr (*DH* 110).[15]

---

[12] Keith Sagar, *A D.H. Lawrence Handbook* (Manchester: Manchester University Press, 1982), p. 101. Hereafter *DH*.

[13] See Lawrence's letter to Martin Secker of 29 April 1927 (*L* vi 45).

[14] Edward Nehls, *D.H. Lawrence: A Composite Biography*, vol. iii (Madison: University of Wisconsin Press, 1959), pp. 84–5.

[15] In his 'Introduction' to the 1986 Italian edition simply entitled *Etruscan Places*, Massimo Pallottino discusses the 'romance' inherent in writers' conception of Etruria, generating an intertextual chain identifiable with a larger cultural and historical 'Etruscan

Lawrence engaged in a dialogue with these various sources, not treating them as scientific material, but using them as a spring-board for his own ideas. He pitted his own sense of the 'aliveness' and physicality of the Etruscans against any negative (and in his view superficial) judgements regarding their worth:

> Mommsen hated everything Etruscan, said the germ of all degeneracy was in the race. But the bronzes and terra cottas are fascinating, so alive with physical life, with a powerful physicality which surely is as great, or sacred, ultimately, as the *ideal* of the Greeks and Germans. (*L* v 465)

Filippis describes how Lawrence 'damned with faint praise' Fritz Weege's *Etruskische Malerei* and Pericle Ducati's *Etruria Antica* (*SEP* xxviii), though the reproductions in the former seemed to interest him. Lawrence proceeded to say that 'I got photographs too from Alinari – and on the one from the *Tomba dei Tori*, the two little improper bits, 'un poco pornographico', as brave as life. Amusing!' (*L* vi 50). Weege may have inspired Lawrence's decision to include photographs and illustrations in his own book, something that he came to believe was essential to the book's success; yet Weege's writing itself failed to stimulate him. Filippis asserts that Ducati's book also failed to affect Lawrence profoundly: like many of the other books he found it 'neither particularly original nor stimulating' (*SEP* xxviii). She goes on to say that 'Lawrence dismissed the so-called authoritative books on the subject as "dreary, repetition and surmise", partly because their traditional, historical interpretation was based on a viewpoint so radically different from his own' (*SEP* xxviii). In fact, what Lawrence found lacking in the scholars he read was an *idea* about the Etruscans:

> [Fell is] very thorough in washing out once more the few rags of information we have concerning the Etruscans: but not a thing has he to say. It's really disheartening: I shall just have to start in and go ahead, and be damned to all authorities! There really is next to nothing to be said, *scientifically*, about the Etruscans. Must take the imaginative line. (*L* v 473)

Lawrence's decision to 'be damned to all authorities' and to 'take the imaginative line' is crucial to an understanding of *Sketches,* and also to the intra-textual process by which the Etruscans infiltrate other late texts, such as *Last Poems*, '[Autobiographical Fragment]', *The Escaped Cock* and *Lady Chatterley's Lover*. The Etruscan culture appealed to Lawrence because it was enigmatic, and therefore receptive to poetic or fictional manipulation. In this instance, Lawrence felt, the

---

quest'. See *Etruscan Places*, ed. Massimo Pallottino, second edition (London: Olive Press, 1994), pp. 11–27.

scholars were on unstable ground, so that the imaginative approach would be equally valid, and certainly a good deal more interesting.[16]

Return of the Etruscans: 'Cypresses' and 'Last Poems'

In literary terms, the Etruscans may be said to have 'returned' to inhabit Lawrence's writing of 1927–30. Figuratively, they may be said to underlie the actual 'return' described in the 'mythological' poems at the very start of the 'Last Poems' notebook. It might seem paradoxical to assert that the poem that begins the notebook – 'The Greeks are Coming!' – engages with the Etruscan civilization. Yet (as I will suggest in later chapters), Lawrence takes 'hints' from diverse cultural and mythological writings, amalgamating all sorts of unnamed gods, and allowing the named Olympians to remain fluid, so they can retain their pre-Homeric characteristics (see Chapter 6, pp. 135–7). In this way the Olympians of 'Last Poems' have Greek names, yet seem to possess some of the key attributes that Lawrence derived from the Etruscan culture he believed in many ways to be superior to that of Greece.

The co-existence of Greek and Etruscan cultures in Lawrence's thinking is evident on juxtaposition of the earlier 'Cypresses' with a group of the 1929 poems, revealing extraordinary similarities. In 'Middle of the World', the 'return' of the mythological protagonists is described as follows:

> I see descending from the ships at dawn
> slim naked men from Cnossos, smiling the archaic smile
> of those that will without fail come back again,
> and kindling little fires upon the shores
> and crouching, and speaking the music of lost languages. (*CP* 688)

The Etruscans of 'Cypresses' too are described as 'subtly-smiling', possessing 'The smile, the subtle Etruscan smile still lurking / Within the tombs' (*CP* 297). They are also referred to as 'Going with insidious, half-smiling quietness / And some of Africa's imperturbable sang-froid / About a forgotten business' (*CP* 297).

---

[16]   In his 'Introduction' to the Italian *Etruscan Places,* Massimo Pallottino situates both Dennis and Lawrence within a 'romantic' or 'poetic' conception of the Etruscans, generated by an intertextual lineage and a wider cultural phenomenon. In this edition he includes an essay by Giovanni Kezich entitled 'Lawrence in Etruria: *Etruscan Places* in context', in which Kezich explores Lawrence's book as the 'literary acme' of a tradition that appropriates the Etruscans in a self-indulgent and manipulative way (see, for instance, *Etruscan Places*, ed. Pallottino, p. 168). The perception of the Etruscans as a 'godsend' to Lawrence in this sense (Richard Aldington, 'Introduction' to *Apocalypse*, London: Secker, 1932, pp. xxvi–vii) has been widely held, and fails to acknowledge the extent and profundity of his research and insights.

They come over the sea from a distance and their 'quietness' is interpretable with reference to Lawrence's concept of 'insouciance'.[17] The term 'forgotten' is significant: the Etruscan civilization has been forgotten by the modern world, while the Etruscans are prone to forgetfulness as they perform actions spontaneously, without cerebral exertion.

In their easy physicality and insouciance, the Etruscans of 'Cypresses' bear a good deal of resemblance to the mythological protagonists of the 1929 poems, who are identifiable by their laughter rather than by words:

> So now they come back! Hark!
> Hark! the low and shattering laughter of bearded men
> with the slim waists of warriors, and the long feet
> of moon-lit dancers. (*CP* 689)

In 'Cypresses' the Etruscans are 'slender, tender-footed / Long-nosed men of Etruria'; they are also 'sensitive-footed' and 'Naked except for fanciful long shoes' (*CP* 296). Their dancing is made indicative of the blood-being that distinguishes the rhythms of instinct from deliberate intellectual effort: they act according to the 'Dusky, slim marrow-thought of slender, flickering men of Etruria' (*CP* 297). The words 'flickering' and 'flicker' are conspicuous in the 'Nettles' notebook poem 'Be it So', describing a moment in which 'the gods' are made manifest in a human being: 'O, if a flame is in you, be it so! / When your flame flickers up, and you flicker forth in sheer purity' (*CP* 674). Similarly, the poem 'Two Ways of Living and Dying' describes 'that purity / that flickered forth in the best hours of life, / when the man was himself, so a god in his singleness' (*CP* 676), while 'Conceit' ends with the lines: 'Now let me be myself, / now let me be myself, and flicker forth, / now let me be myself, in the being, one of the gods' (*CP* 674). The term 'flickering' suggests vivid, ever-changing life: the antithesis of fixed, mechanical non-existence.

The Etruscan 'dark thought / For which the language is lost' (*CP* 296) relates to the 'music of lost languages' (*CP* 688) spoken by the crouching men from Cnossos in the late poem 'Middle of the World'. In 'Cypresses' the mystery resulting from the loss of the Etruscan language facilitates a critique of the contemporary in which the implicit values of our language are questioned – 'are our words no good?' – and:

> Nay, tongues are dead, and words are hollow as hollow seed-pods,
> Having shed their sound and finished all their echoing
> Etruscan syllables,
> That had the telling. (*CP* 296)

---

[17]   See Lawrence's short article 'Insouciance' (*LEA* 95–7).

Modern language is seen as hollow, lacking the 'sound' that can create resonance beyond meaning. In contrast with verbal communication, the narrator of '[Autobiographical Fragment]' is able to understand the language of the Newthorpe inhabitants as a dog hears and understands, and is not reliant on the literal definitions of words (*LEA* 60).

In 'Cypresses', the notion of evil becomes untrustworthy because of the way in which a conqueror's value-laden language has replaced all others:

> For as to the evil
> We have only Roman word for it,
> Which I, being a little weary of Roman virtue,
> Don't hang much weight on. (*CP* 297)

The ludicrous attribution of evil or viciousness to the Etruscans is suggested when Lawrence satirically labels their cypress trees 'Vicious dark cypresses':

> Vicious, you supple, brooding, softly-swaying pillars of dark flame.
> Monumental to a dead, dead race ... (*CP* 297)

The incongruity achieved here through the juxtaposition of the term vicious with the vivid description of the cypresses' beauty creates a similar effect to the rhetorical question 'is the gentian savage, on her tall stem?' (*CP* 684): both invite a redefinition of the key term ('savage'/'vicious') involved in the process of cultural determinism.

It seems absurd to ascribe such human attributes as savagery and viciousness to a gentian flower or a cypress tree, and by poetic extension it becomes ridiculous to refer in this way to the dead, lost Etruscan race. Lawrence's description of the 'slender, flickering men of Etruria, / Whom Rome called vicious' (*CP* 297) provokes a reversal in which viciousness is attributed not to the Etruscans but to the Roman race that destroyed them:

> There is only one evil, to deny life
> As Rome denied Etruria
> And mechanical America Montezuma still. (*CP* 298)

Montezuma, of course, was (and is) frequently represented as a monster of evil tyranny. A modern analogy is used to suggest that the Etruscan 'delicate magic of life' has been lost and never yet regained – it remains buried – for modernity is still intent on the same process of repression that characterized the Roman subjugation of the Etruscan race. In *Sketches* Lawrence's championing of the Etruscans against the Romans is expanded and treated with greater conviction, perhaps in response to the Italian political situation of 1927–28, when the country was increasingly dominated by a repressive fascist state.

'Cypresses' indicates, therefore, that the meaning of life has been lost, and as a consequence it advocates an imaginative 'return' through the decipherment of a shrouded secret:

> They say the fit survive,
> But I invoke the spirits of the lost.
> Those that have not survived, the darkly lost,
> To bring their meaning back into life again... (*CP* 298)

In this poem the Etruscan secret is allowed to remain 'wrapped inviolable' in the cypress-trees; it was not until 1927 that Lawrence made a really concerted attempt to penetrate to the depths of this tantalizingly obscure civilization. Given his early fascination, fuelled by a visit to Etruria in April 1927 and his writing of the travel book *Sketches* in the succeeding months, it is unsurprising that Lawrence used Etruscan culture to bring a new layer of meaning into his poetry of 1929. This would account for the close connections I have demonstrated between 'Cypresses' and the group of mythological poems at the front of the 'Last Poems' notebook. The Etruscans had grown to play a crucial role in Lawrence's writing of the late 1920s; his language referred back to his earlier work but with greater purpose and a new sense of urgency.

Etruscan Arrival and Origins: Last Travel Book and Last Poems

Sketches, written during the months following Lawrence's visit to the Etruscan tombs in April 1927 (though not published as a volume until 1932[18]), connects in a number of useful and interesting ways to the late poems. In *Sketches*, for instance, Lawrence describes the way in which Etruscan ships came from a number of different locations to the Italian shores:

> this is the Tyrrhenian sea of the Etruscans, where their shipping spread sharp sails, and beat the sea with slave-oars, roving in from Greece and Sicily, Sicily of the Greek tyrants; from Cumae, the city of the old Greek colony of Campagnia, where the province of Naples now is; and from Elba, where the Etruscans mined their iron-ore. The Etruscans sailed the seas. (*SEP* 25–6)

The sailing of the seas by the Etruscans is attributed to the spirit of 'restlessness' that 'seems to have possessed the Mediterranean basin' so that 'ancient races began shaking ships like seeds over the sea. More people than Greeks, or Hellenes, or Indo-Germanic groups, were on the move' (*SEP* 26). The seed image is striking, and in keeping with Lawrence's association of the Etruscans in particular with

---

[18]   *Etruscan Places* was published by Martin Secker in England and by Viking in the USA. Previously, individual chapters had appeared in *Travel* (see *SEP* xiii–xiv).

'floweriness' and germination, relating to his depiction of their villages as transient: made of wood and therefore disintegrating as flowers grow and die (see *SEP* 32).[19]

The proliferation of ships suggested by the random seed-shaking is echoed in the lines 'And every time, it is ships, it is ships, / it is ships' (*CP* 687) in 'The Greeks are Coming!'. In the subsequent poem, 'The Argonauts', the ships are specifically 'Odysseus' ships', but Odysseus – and the other gods – form merely part of a continuum of journeying, experienced by all the restless races that set sail in ancient times for Italy:

> Probably ships did come – even before Ulysses. Probably men landed on the strange flat coast, and made camps, and then treated with the natives. Whether the newcomers were Lydians, or Hittites with hair curled in a roll behind, or men from Mycenae or Crete, who knows. Perhaps men of all these sorts came, in batches. (*SEP* 26)

The phrase 'men of all these sorts', in conjunction with 'all sorts of gods' (in the poem with that title and elsewhere in the 'Nettles' notebook), indicates that the 'heroes' of 'Last Poems' are an amalgam of disparate races and diverse mythologies, both preserving and forfeiting specific attributes and associations according to the poet's will. Certainly the men who come in batches and are seen 'descending from the ships at dawn', or respectfully 'treat[ing] with the natives', bear enough resemblance to the Etruscan voyagers described in *Sketches* to demonstrate their common poetic or symbolic origin.

In 'The Greeks are Coming!' the voyagers arrive in 'ships of Cnossos' and also 'Aegean ships', that have come out of 'the eastern end' (*CP* 687). This suggestion of Eastern derivation may be related to the passages in *Sketches* in which Lawrence engages with a key debate within George Dennis's *Cities and Cemeteries of Etruria*. Dennis asserts that the origin of the Etruscans has been attributed to the Greeks, the Egyptians, the Phoenicians, the Canaanites, the Libyans, the Cantabrians or Basques, the Hyksos (or Shepherd-Kings of Egypt) and even the Celts.[20] Yet Dennis himself has a firm view on this matter, referring to the 'oriental character of the civil and religious polity, the social and domestic manners' (*CC* 18); to the 'oriental origin' of their divination and augury; and to 'evidence of extant monuments' indicating 'a close analogy between the Etruscan religious creed and those of oriental nations' (*CC* 19). He also points to the 'doctrine of good and evil spirits attendant on the soul', suggesting that they 'held the dualistic principle of oriental creeds', and observes that 'Their luxurious habits were so strictly oriental, that almost the same language is used in describing them and those of the Lydians' (*CC* 21).

---

[19]   Cf. Lawrence's essay 'Flowery Tuscany' (*SEP* 223–43).

[20]   George Dennis, *Cities and Cemeteries of Etruria*, vol. 1 (London: J.M. Dent, 1907), p. 16. Hereafter *CC*.

Lawrence, responding in part to the debate as expounded by Dennis and in part relying on intuition, formulates a tentative explanation. While resolving that Italy must already have been inhabited when the newcomers arrived, he asserts:

> The newcomers, whether they were few or many, seem to have come from the east, Asia Minor or Crete or Cyprus. They were, we must feel, of an old, primitive Mediterranean and Asiatic or Aegean stock. The twilight of the beginning of our history was the nightfall of some previous history, which will never be written. Pelasgian is but a shadow-word. But Hittite and Minoan, Lydian, Carian, Etruscan, these words emerge from shadow, and perhaps from one and the same great shadow come the peoples to whom the names belong. (*SEP* 26–7) [21]

The suggestion of Aegean origin in 'The Greeks are Coming!', the specific reference to the 'Minoan distance' in 'Middle of the World' and the use of 'eastern end' all contribute to the supposition that the 'Last Poems' heroes are emerging from the same great shadow as the Etruscans of *Sketches*.

Yet the following passage from *Sketches* offers a slightly different interpretation of the arrival of the Etruscans in Italy:

> But whatever little ships were run ashore on the soft, deep, grey-black volcanic sand of this coast, three thousand years ago, and earlier, their mariners certainly did not find those hills inland empty of people … Even before the fall of Troy, before even Athens was dreamed of, there were natives here. And they had huts on the hills, thatched huts in clumsy groups most probably; with patches of grain, and flocks of goats and probably cattle. (*SEP* 26)

The men arriving in 'Last Poems' step into the midst of a culture that Lawrence describes as pre-existing. Just as the Etruscans come in their ships and find someone already there, so the slim, naked men from Cnossos discover a society of Minoan gods and Gods of Tiryns 'softly laughing and chatting, as ever' (*CP* 688). The attitude of the newcomers, the strangers, is purely respectful: men and gods interact amicably, as is emphasized by the poem in which Dionysos – 'young and a stranger' – leans on a gate, listening to the soft talking and laughing 'in all respect' (*CP* 688). In this way of thinking, then, Lawrence uses his imagined landing of the Etruscans as a model for the return of the gods and heroes – with their Greek names – evoked in the mythological poems at the front of the 'Last Poems' notebook.

A final extract has some bearing on the significance of an ostensibly Greek return, but one in which the Etruscans are implicated. This citation suggests that

---

[21]   Lawrence used his 'shadow word' when depicting 'Pelasgic faces uncovered', in the poem 'Sicilian Cyclamens'.

it is only after the coming of the Greeks that the silent Etruscan can be revealed to the world:

> Then, as the Greeks came crowding into colonies in Italy, and the Phoenicians began to exploit the western Mediterranean, we begin to hear of the silent Etruscans, and to see them. (*SEP* 28)

Perhaps the Greek names used in the poems imply a moment of discovery in which an entire past civilization is brought to light and life, resulting in an interaction characterized by mutual respect rather than the exploitation evident in the Romans' destructive response to their predecessors.

While Lawrence is at times merging and amalgamating disparate gods and cultures (such as the Etruscan and the Greek), in *Sketches* he is also concerned with highlighting the distinction between the 'floweriness' of the Etruscan way of life, and the more ostensibly impressive art and architecture of the Greeks:

> [The ease and friendliness of the Etruscan tombs] must be partly owing to the peculiar charm of natural proportion which is in all etruscan things of the unspoilt, unRomanticised centuries… The Greeks sought to make an impression… The Etruscans, no. The things they did, in their easy centuries, are as natural and as easy as breathing. (*SEP* 19)

The 'breast breathing freely and pleasantly' (*SEP* 19) resulting from contact with the Etruscan artefacts is the antithesis of the 'impression' made by Keats's Grecian Urn, which leaves the heart 'high-sorrowful and cloyed', and provokes 'A burning forehead, and a parching tongue'.[22] The Etruscan ease may be identified even in the 'little sentences freely written in red paint or black, or scratched in the stucco with the finger, slanting with the real etruscan carelessness and fulness of life, often running downwards, written from right to left… debonair inscriptions' (*SEP* 18). The same abundance of vitality is evident in their small temples, which were:

> alive with freely-modelled, painted figures in relief, gay dancing creatures, rows of ducks, round faces like the sun, and faces grinning and putting out a big tongue, all vivid and fresh and unimposing. The whole thing small and dainty in proportion, and fresh, somehow charming instead of impressive. (*SEP* 32)

Significantly, Lawrence makes a link between these temples and those of the 'early Greeks', which evidently escape being 'ponderous' like the later Grecian and Roman constructions:

---

[22] John Keats, 'Ode on a Grecian Urn', in *John Keats: The Complete Poems*, ed. John Barnard (London: Penguin, 1988), p. 345.

> Myself, I like to think of the little wooden temples of the early Greeks and of
> the Etruscans: small, dainty, fragile, and evanescent as flowers. We have reached
> the stage where we are weary of huge stone erections, and we begin to realise
> that it is better to keep life fluid and changing, than to try to hold it fast down
> in heavy monuments. Burdens on the face of the earth, are man's ponderous
> erections. (*SEP* 32)

There is humour in this distinction, when it is considered that some of the few
surviving relics of the Etruscans are literally 'stone erections': the variously
sized phallic symbols of stone that were placed at the entrances of tombs. Yet
these stones, with their intimate connection with procreation and regeneration are
utterly different from the 'huge stone erections' (such as the Parthenon) which
characterize later Grecian architecture. Lawrence expresses his desire for 'things
that are alive and flexible, which won't last too long and become an obstruction
and a weariness' (*SEP* 33): the flower growing out of the earth is a more satisfying
image than the marble of a magnificent building.

Life in Death: the Tombs at Tarquinia

Lawrence employs key scenes and images taken from the tomb walls at Tarquinia
in his analysis of the customs, lives and deaths of the Etruscans. According to his
interpretation, the vital Etruscan dancing in life is paralleled by festivities that take
place after death, presented consequently as a continuation:

> And death, to the Etruscan, was a pleasant continuance of life, with jewels and
> wine and flutes playing for the dance. It was neither an ecstasy of bliss, a heaven,
> nor a purgatory of torment. It was just a natural continuance of the fulness of life.
> Everything was in terms of life, of living. (*SEP* 19)

Terms typically attributed to the Etruscans, such as 'ease', 'naturalness' and
'spontaneity', as well as the 'free-breathing' sensation experienced by the observer
of Etruscan things, are applied specifically to a visitor's experience of the tombs:

> The tombs seem so easy and friendly, cut out of rock underground. One does
> not feel oppressed, descending into them ... There is a simplicity, combined
> with a most peculiar, free-breasted naturalness and spontaneity in the shapes
> and movements of the underworld walls and spaces, that at once reassures the
> spirit. (*SEP* 19)

The 'naturalness' of the tombs is seen as a consequence of the acceptance of death:
something envisaged by Lawrence as one of the most attractive features of the
Etruscan civilization. Dennis refers to 'the great reverence for the dead, which the
Etruscans possessed in common with the other nations of antiquity', and asserts

that it was this reverence that prompted them 'to store their tombs with these rich and varied sepulchral treasures, which unveil to us the *arcana* of their inner life' (*CC* 3). Lawrence would probably have differed in believing that the Etruscan 'reverence for the dead' was a distinct and distinguishing attribute, rather than merely symptomatic of a 'common' trend (although he might have classed them with the Egyptians in this respect). In fact, it is important to emphasize both that Lawrence learned from Dennis and that he deviated from him profoundly in his assessment of the tombs' content.

The reverence and affection for the dead was, in Lawrence's conception, reflected in the Etruscan landscape, in which the acropolis and necropolis would co-exist on parallel hills, so that the living could look easily across:

> And within the walls they liked to have one inner high place, the arx, the citadel. Then outside, they liked to have a sharp dip or ravine, with a parallel hill opposite. And on the parallel hill opposite, they liked to have their city of the dead, their necropolis. So they could stand on their ramparts and look over the hollow where the stream flowed among its bushes, across from the city of life, gay with its painted houses and temples, to the near-at-hand city of their dear dead, pleasant with its smooth walks and stone symbols, and painted fronts. (*SEP* 13–14)

The term 'dear' creates a sense of closeness and affection: it suggests a reciprocity and touch that normally characterizes relationships between living human beings. The necropolis is envisaged as a 'city' like the acropolis, and is described as 'pleasant' (suggesting simplicity and ease) rather than sad or oppressive. Lawrence stresses the attributes of the tombs that relate to everyday life: for instance, 'By the doorway of some tombs there is a carved stone house, or a stone imitation chest with sloping lids like the two sides of the roof of an oblong house.' (*SEP* 20) Each tomb is depicted as a 'home', and can be entered and experienced retrospectively, as both Dennis and Lawrence attempted to do.

Lawrence establishes proximity with the Etruscan figures depicted in the Tarquinian tombs through describing their feasting as if he were a contemporaneous observer:

> The walls of this little tomb are a dance of real delight. The room seems inhabited still by Etruscans of the sixth century before Christ; a vivid, life-accepting people, who must have lived with real fulness. On come the dancers and the music-players, moving in a broad frieze towards the front wall of the tomb, the wall facing us as we enter from the dark stairs, and where the banquet is going on in all its glory. (*SEP* 47–8)

The desired involvement indicated by the use of the present tense – 'on come the dancers' – reveals the wish to participate also evident in 'Bavarian Gentians', in which the poet desires the status of invited guest:

> Give me a flower on a tall stem, and three dark flames,
> for I will go to the wedding, and be wedding-guest
> at the marriage of the living dark. (*CP* 960)[23]

It is through such involvement that the categories of life and death can become blurred, a blurring that Lawrence establishes as the natural result of the Etruscan habit of portraying vivid life-scenes in the houses of the dead:

> The scene is natural as life, and yet it has a heavy archaic fulness of meaning.
> It is the death-banquet; and at the same time it is the dead man banqueting in
> the underworld; for the underworld of the Etruscans was a gay place. While the
> living feasted out of doors, at the tomb of the dead, the dead himself feasted in
> like manner, with a lady to offer him garlands and slaves to bring him wine,
> away in the underworld. (*SEP* 46)

Just as the acropolis and necropolis rest on parallel hills, so parallel festivities take place in the upper world and the underworld.

Analogously, in the tombs at Cerveteri, the dead are imagined to be 'sleeping as if in life' (*SEP* 17), which suggests the kind of peacefulness of repose resulting from ease and the inevitability of reawakening precisely envisaged in the poem 'Pax':

> Sleeping on the hearth of the living world
> yawning at home before the fire of life
> feeling the presence of the living God
> like a great reassurance
> a deep calm in the heart ...
> in the house of life. (*CP* 700)

In this poem Lawrence asserts the desire for continuing life that throughout *Last Poems* thwarts any attempt to accept 'oblivion' (the 'wonder-goal') as the be-all and end-all. At the close of the long draft poem 'Ship of Death' (in the 'Nettles' notebook), a hint at 'procreation' or re-emergence from the 'deepest and longest of seas' supersedes the apparent peace and fulfilment offered by sinking into oblivion (*CP* 962–4). Although oblivion is described in 'All Souls' Day' as a 'sweet home' (*CP* 721) it cannot possess the vividness of the 'house of life' (or of an Etruscan tomb-home) with all its vitality. Significantly 'Phoenix' – the final poem in the 'Last Poems' notebook – sees the sponging out or cancellation resulting from death as merely the antecedent to change. The death poems merge life and death, just

---

[23]   My quotations from 'Bavarian Gentians' in this chapter derive from the second version of the poem within 'Last Poems', rather than the preceding draft that is most widely known and most frequently anthologized.

as the Etruscans (in Lawrence's creation of them) blurred these two categories, so that they became parallel or easily consecutive experiences.

Both the 'hearth of the living world' and the idea of 'home' – used so frequently with regard to the Etruscan tombs – are crucial in the 'Nettles' and 'Last Poems' notebooks. In the blurring of life and death, hearth and home are seen as natural goals for the dead, as in the poem 'In the Cities':

> In Minos, in Mycenae
> in all the cities with lion gates
> the dead threaded the air, lingering
> lingering in the earth's shadow
> and leaning towards the old hearth. (*CP* 704)

Here, the comfortable co-existence of the living and the dead is seen as a more general 'ancient' phenomenon than Lawrence's writings on the Etruscans would suggest. Such a co-existence is also evident in Lawrence's depiction of the imagined 'return' of Hermes in the poem 'Maximus' when he comes in and sits down 'by the hearth' (*CP* 692).

The dead who are allowed to lean on old hearths are the antithesis of the recent dead who are homeless because modern man cannot welcome them back into life, nor prepare for them a death-ship with its complement of objects from hearth and home:

> Oh, now they moan and throng in anger, and press back
> through breaches in the walls of this our by-no-means impregnable existence
> seeking their old haunts with cold, ghostly rage
> old haunts, old habitats, old hearths,
> old places of sweet life from which they are thrust out
> and can but haunt in disembodied rage. (*CP* 722–3)

The 'houseless dead' of modern times are described by Lawrence as catastrophically hostile, linked to the more abstract negative force evoked in 'Evil is Homeless'. In such a poem, home is reified, while homelessness is seen as a greyness interestingly epitomized in a vision of 'grey Dante, colour-blind / to the scarlet and purple flowers at the doors of hell' (*CP* 711). Dante's greyness stands in contrast to the vivid light/dark and heaven/hell dichotomies evoked in 'Doors' and 'Evil is Homeless', while the homelessness associated with the colour grey contrasts with those (like the Etruscans) who can inhabit both realms of dark and light at once: 'like Persephone, or Attis / there are souls that are at home in both homes' (*CP* 711). This citation illuminates Persephone's role in 'Bavarian Gentians', for she embodies the ease of transition between the two dwelling-places of the upper and lower worlds.

'Bavarian Gentians', a poem relevant here in terms of preoccupation and imagery, is in fact a version of the descent into an Etruscan tomb, or 'underworld home'. Lawrence's experience of descent is described in *Sketches* as follows:

> The lamp begins to shine and smell, then to shine without smelling: the guide opens the iron gate, and we descend the steep steps down into the tomb. It seems a dark little hole underground: a dark little hole, after the sun of the upper world! (*SEP* 44)

In the journey to Hades described in 'Bavarian Gentians', the poet-narrator leaves the 'heavy white draught of the day', also described as 'white-cast' and as 'Demeter's yellow-pale day', in order to descend into the underworld, aided by a 'torch-flower' rather than an acetylene lamp:

> Reach me a gentian, give me a torch!
> let me guide myself with the blue, forked torch of a flower
> down the darker and darker stairs, where blue is darkened on blueness
> down the way Persephone goes, just now, in first-frosted September
> to the sightless realm where darkness is married to dark … (*CP* 960)

As I have suggested, one fascinating aspect of the myth for Lawrence was that Persephone could inhabit two worlds in oscillation, thus embodying the cyclic pagan process of seasonal death and rebirth. This feeling of inhabiting the upper and lower worlds can be experienced fleetingly on visiting many of the Etruscan tombs at Tarquinia in succession, until the dark realm of the underworld seems to possess the predominant and most vivid reality:

> There are many tombs. When we have seen one, up we go, a little bewildered, into the afternoon sun, across a tract of rough, tormented hill, and down again to the underground, like rabbits in a warren. The hill-top is really a warren of tombs. And gradually the underworld of the Etruscans becomes more real then the above day of the afternoon. One begins to live with the painted dancers and feasters and mourners, and to look eagerly for them. (*SEP* 49)

In the experience of visiting and exploring, the Etruscan life/death balance becomes a physical experience, even for modern man. Such balance underlies the poem 'Song of Death', in which it is asserted that 'without the song of death, the song of life / becomes pointless and silly' (*CP* 723), as well as 'When Satan Fell', in which 'hell and heaven are the scales of the balance of life / which swing against each other' (*CP* 710).

Furnishing a Poem: 'The Ship of Death'

'The Ship of Death' is the most obviously 'Etruscan' late poem, as it takes an explicitly Etruscan artefact as its primary symbol; by implication, too, the short poems following in 'Last Poems' (which initially belonged to the 'Ship of Death' draft in the 'Nettles' notebook) may be said to be of predominantly Etruscan origin.[24] The central image derives from Lawrence's description of a 'little bronze ship of death' among the other sacred treasures of the dead in one tomb:

> Facing the door goes the stone bed on which was laid, presumably, the Lucuomo and the sacred treasures of the dead, the little bronze ship of death that should bear him over to the other world, the vases of jewels for his arraying, the vases of small dishes, the little bronze statuettes and tools, the weapons, the armour: all the amazing impedimenta of the important dead. Or sometimes, in this inner room, lay the woman, the great lady, in all her robes, with the mirror in her hand, and her treasures, her jewels and combs and silver boxes of cosmetics, in urns or vases ranged alongside. Splendid was the array they went with, into death. (*SEP* 17)

In another passage Lawrence describes the 'little bronze figures, statuettes, animals, bronze ships, of which the Etruscans put thousands in the tombs, [which] became the rage with the Roman collectors' (*SEP* 21).

These passages are interesting when it is recognized that the death ship seems to have been an imaginative Lawrentian construct as much as a common Etruscan artefact. Lawrence could not have seen 'thousands' of death ships in the museums, for there were scarcely any in existence. In a tour of the Etruscan sites I was only able to identify one bronze ship taken from the tombs, and this one was an imitation of a Sardinian trading vessel, found in a tomb that Lawrence did not see, though housed in the Etruscan section of the Museo Archeologico in Florence, which he visited (*SEP* xxvi n.19). Equally, there is no mention of a bronze ship in the standard literature discussing Etruscan relics. It seems that Lawrence was engaging in his predictably eclectic myth-making and combining Etruscan custom with the Egyptian tradition of placing a ship in the tomb, to ferry the soul across the sea of death.

Egyptian death ships were not made of bronze, but they are typically large enough to fill with the necessary impedimenta, equipping the voyaging soul for its journey. Certainly these articles, as well as the bronze utensils and other objects

---

[24] The poems 'The Houseless Dead' and 'Beware the Unhappy Dead' derive from the long draft version entitled 'Ship of Death': the draft that was written into the 'Nettles' notebook but was later revised and copied into 'Last Poems' as 'The Ship of Death'. The latter was split into sections, and much of the original material was taken out, then used to create a series of shorter poems with their own titles.

placed in the Etruscan tombs, must have provoked the 'accoutrements' described in 'The Ship of Death':

> A little ship, with oars and food
> and little dishes, and all accoutrements
> fitting and ready for the departing soul ...
>
> Now launch the small ship ...
> with its store of food and little cooking pans
> and change of clothes ... (*CP* 718–19)

In order to furnish this little ship, Lawrence is figuratively furnishing or enriching his own mythological frame of reference. In so doing he creates an image that combines practicality and precision with affection, echoing an Etruscan response to their 'dear dead'. The reiterated exhortation 'Pity the poor dead' in the early draft ('Ship of Death', *CP* 962) is an attempt to establish affinity and reciprocity, leading to the kind of impulse that compelled the Etruscans to equip their tombs so lavishly, with such designs and such accoutrements as would seem more obviously serviceable to the living.

In 'The Ship of Death' the ship is referred to as an 'ark of faith' (*CP* 719), while in the draft version the core of oblivion is described as 'like the foldings and involvings of a womb' (*CP* 963), 'womb-like convoluted shadow' and the 'womb of silence in the living night' (*CP* 964). The womb-ark association is also explicable in terms of an Etruscan image:

> The stone house, as the boy calls it, suggests the Noah's Ark without the boat-part: the Noah's Ark box we had as children, full of animals. And that is what it is, the Ark, the arx, the womb. The womb of all the world, that brought forth all the creatures. The womb, the arx, where life retreats in the last refuge. The womb, the ark of the covenant, in which lies the mystery of eternal life, the manna and the mysteries. There it is, standing displaced outside the doorway of etruscan tombs at Cerveteri. (*SEP* 20)

Interestingly, the single bronze Etruscan ship in the Florence museum has bronze animals as decoration around the rim. Certainly the 'ark of the covenant' (*Sketches*) and the 'ark of faith' ('The Ship of Death') are linked, while the womb in which 'lies the mystery of eternal life' may also suggest the sea into which the soul's 'life retreats in the last refuge' (being sponged out, made nothing) before emerging and experiencing rebirth.

The rebirth envisaged combines dawn and twilight, creating a colour-scheme analogous to the vivid evocation of landscape and light in 'Twilight in Italy' (1916).

In his earlier travel book, Lawrence describes, for instance, 'the wonderful, faint, ethereal flush of the long range of snow … It was dawning in exquisite, icy rose upon the long mountain-summit opposite'.[25] In 'The Ship of Death' the description is as follows:

> Wait, wait, the little ship
> drifting, beneath the deathly ashy grey
> of a flood-dawn.
>
> Wait, wait, even so, a flush of yellow
> and strangely, O chilled wan soul, a flush of rose. (*CP* 719–20)

The dawn evoked can provide both warmth and peace to the re-born soul, yet it is simultaneously 'cruel': inevitably painful and bewildering. In '[Autobiographical Fragment]' a man tells the narrator that 'It is perhaps cruel to awaken … even at a good moment' (*LEA* 67), while the waking protagonist of *The Escaped Cock* experiences overriding pain, nausea and unspeakable disillusion at coming back to life. The urge for resurrection in the stories and poems regularly entails a desired continuance of life that oscillates with a yearning for the utter peace of oblivion in which the reawakening soul cries to sleep (or be nothing) once again.

'The Ship of Death' reveals the problematic nature of an attempt to make a 'bruise or break of exit' from this life – just as the poem 'Butterfly' stresses the difficulty of leaving the warm, walled garden of our earthly existence, submitting to the wind that drives us into the cold unknown. The poem 'Difficult Death' asserts this problem unequivocally – 'It is not easy to die, O it is not easy / to die the death' – while also stressing the need to 'build your ship of death' in order to drift towards dark oblivion (*CP* 720–21). However, this poem ends with an assertion of rebirth: 'Maybe life is still our portion / after the bitter passage of oblivion' (*CP* 721). The 'passage' between life and death is seen as possible when envisaged in Etruscan terms, aided literally and metaphorically by the impedimenta of the tombs. This emphasis on transition highlights the significance of doors, gates, exits and entrances both in relation to the tombs and in the late poetry.

Lawrence's association of the life/death transition with the Etruscans is suggested by his depiction of the 'leopards or panthers of the underworld Bacchus, guarding the exits and the entrances of the passion of life' (*SEP* 49), when describing 'The Tomb of the Leopards'. In his depiction of the tombs he also describes the 'rock doorway, rather narrow, and narrowing upwards, like Egypt', and the 'inner doorway' leading to the 'last chamber, small and dark and cumulative' (*SEP* 17). The poem 'Doors' evokes such dark doors of the underworld:

---

[25] *Twilight in Italy and Other Essays,* ed. Paul Eggert (Cambridge: Cambridge University Press, 1994), p. 111.

> Life has its palace of blue day aloft
> and its halls of the great dark below,
> and there are the bright doors where souls go gaily in:
> and there are the dark doors where souls pass silently
> holding their breath, naked and darkly alone
> entering into the other communion. (*CP* 711)

The dark doors of the silent Etruscans are suggested by the references to quietness, darkness and nakedness; the imagery also emphasizes the contrast between the bright upper world and the Hades-like world below (setting for the 'halls' of 'Bavarian Gentians'). A further parallel is suggested in the first stanza of this poem, by the reference to the 'double Phallus of the devil himself / with his key to the two dark doors' (*CP* 710). In *Sketches* Lawrence refers specifically to the double-coned stone phalluses found at the entrances to certain tombs; while the entrances of course have their own dark doors through which one gains entry to the inner chambers.

As well as the actual doorways providing access, the tombs often possess a false door, painted on one wall. This artificial entrance may have symbolized the passage of the dead into the Etruscan equivalent of Hades, thus creating an ease of return in which the soul, if compelled to leave the tomb and seek an exit, could enter again and reinhabit the tomb-house. In this context, the return of the slender soul to its 'house' again at the end of 'The Ship of Death' may be subject to a new interpretation. Critics have often seen the soul's movement back into its house as the metaphorically charged progression of a disembodied spirit back into the body ('house'), thus achieving a 'peace' of heart resulting from the wholeness in which the two halves of the Cartesian dichotomy are fused. This interpretation is justified, particularly as the body is described as a bruised apple (perhaps suggesting a previous fruit-like wholeness). However, the Etruscan tomb with its impedimenta suggests that the 'house' described in the poem is a physical location: a place with rooms, cooking pans and food rather than a metaphor for the empty shell of a soulless body. The slender soul in 'The Ship of Death' may not merely indicate a Cartesian split: it is not just a soul in the spiritual sense but a soul in the colloquial sense of 'the poor soul!' (that is, person). The soul at the end of the poem undergoes a return similar to that experienced by the heroes of the mythological poems: it steps back physically into an old home (perhaps leaning towards a familiar hearth) which may be envisaged as an Etruscan tomb-home or as the kind of house described in 'Pax' or 'Maximus'.

The poem 'Silence', like 'Doors', considers the implications of a silent passing – only this time gates rather than doors provide access:

> For now we are passing through the gate, stilly,
> in the sacred silence of gates
> in the silence of passing through doors,
> in the great hush of going from this into that,
> in the suspension of wholeness, in the moment of division within the whole! (*CP* 699)

In 'Invocation to the Moon' the re-entry into a lunar mansion is through 'the gate of your silvery house' (*CP* 696), while in '[Autobiographical Fragment]' the narrator, before he lies down in his small cave, desires to achieve a new birth of some kind by passing through a gate into another sphere of existence:

> And in this still, warm, secret place of the earth I felt my old childish longing to pass through a gate, into a deeper, sunnier, more silent world. (*LEA* 57)

The above may be taken as a paradigm for Lawrence's desire to find access to an alternative vision of life through imaginative connection with a previous culture.

During his Etruscan trip of April 1927, Lawrence literally passed through the iron gates at the mouth of every tomb and the 'lion-gates' of each ancient city, while figuratively, through the imagination, he descended into the deeper, sunnier world of the 'silent Etruscans'. They had fascinated him for a long time, but during his last years the ancient civilization that celebrated death as a natural continuation of life and treated its dead with tender solicitude must have possessed a heightened appeal. The 'shadow' over the Etruscans, obscuring them from the light of assured scientific knowledge, allowed Lawrence to mould them into a race utterly conducive to the prose and poetry of his late style. In *Sketches* of 1927 and the crucially related mythological poems of 1929, Lawrence achieved an imaginative passage by inviting the Etruscans to 'return' and inhabit his vision.

Chapter 4
Beyond the Chatterley Machines

Lady Chatterley's Lover can be considered a correlative to *Last Poems*, *Sketches of Etruscan Places* and the subsequent *Apocalypse* in being the latest composition within a particular genre. Lawrence's last novel exists in three separate versions, illustrating the process of creation and revision in a manner analogous to the discernible progression of late poems through distinct draft stages. In terms of subject-matter and imagery there are a number of recurrences within the last poems and last novel, despite the fact that only one poem in the 'Nettles' notebook engages explicitly with the issues surrounding the novel's publication and reception (I will discuss this poem in some detail below). It has frequently been observed that *Lady Chatterley's Lover* is as radical in its portrayal of class and industry as it is in breaking sexual taboos; both novel and verse-books generate a web of interconnected imagery associated with the machine. In this chapter, therefore, I aim to explore the symbolic ramifications of the travel icons and images linked, inevitably, with Lawrence's critique of industrialization, as well as his recipes for transcendence of the impoverished modern world. I will explore the kinds of 'motion and emotion' associated with the industrial machine, its robotic human operator and the 'wanderers' who manage to remain immune. I will proceed to examine the concepts of obsessive, aimless tourism and the evocation of mythological and archaic civilizations in contradistinction to nullifying modernity. Finally, I will consider journeying (particularly in 'Last Poems') in more figurative terms, discussing poems that evoke the soul's passage between life and death, envisaged as a boat journey, a lapse into oblivion or as the flight of a butterfly.

First, however, I will establish a precise compositional chronology by outlining the development of the novel through its draft stages. Lawrence had visited the English Midlands in the summer of 1926, and around 22 October he began work on what he first envisaged as a short novel. Writing quickly, he had completed the first draft of a full-length book by 25 November. In December he began a complete rewrite, composing at a slower rate; in February he laid it aside but in March decided to 'go over it again' (*L* vi 21). By this time, the novel was becoming '*absolutely* improper' (*L* v 638), resulting in Lawrence's uncertainty about how to proceed with it. After a period of illness, and having formulated a tentative plan for publishing the novel, Lawrence began rewriting it again circa 26 November 1927 and completed the final version on 8 January 1928. By this time, he considered it pure and tender, but 'the most improper novel in the world!' (*L* vi 238). After a number of problems and complications, Lawrence published the novel with an old-fashioned Florentine printshop – the Tipografia Giuntina – receiving his copy on 28 June 1928. Subsequent to the emergence of a number of pirated editions, Lawrence located a Paris bookseller named Edward R. Titus, who printed 3,000 copies of the novel, to be sold at only 60 francs. Significantly, Lawrence composed a foreword for this edition to expose the fraudulent practice of the pirates: this was subsequently expanded into 'A Propos of *Lady Chatterley's Lover*', 'a sort of key to the whole novel' (*L* vii 531). Establishing his methodology in 'A Propos', Lawrence wrote:

> And these notes, which I write now almost two years after the novel was finished, are not intended to explain or expound anything: only to give the emotional beliefs which perhaps are necessary as a background to the book. (*LCL* 333–4)

Composed initially between 26 March and 3 April 1929, the essay was probably extended in October, so that it became precisely contemporaneous with many of the poems within the two last notebooks.

The chronology outlined above indicates that parallels between last novel and late verse might plausibly be established. I will be principally concerned here with the third draft of the novel, as it is the latest version and therefore closest to the composition of the poems, although I will allude to the first and second versions where necessary. The progression from the writing of the novel's three versions (1926–28) to the late poetry notebooks (1929) might, in fact, suggest that the poems would engage with the concerns of Lawrence's last novel but take them further, thus possessing greater authority as 'last words' or thoughts. They might be seen as little 'penseés' encapsulating a brief, monologic epiphany: a fleeting, final comment on such crucial issues raised in the novel as class barriers, mob mentality, the destructive power of the machine, organic connection, touch, tenderness and the need to be alone. But, as always with Lawrence, it is necessary to resist this neat kind of categorization and imposed closure, particularly as the 'A Propos' essay extends Lawrence's writing on these issues into late 1929, and has been seen as articulating his 'final thoughts on male–female relationships in the modern world'.[1] The late poems and Chatterley drafts, therefore, might be seen as existing within an intratextual continuum, while the juxtaposition of poetry and prose is mutually enlightening in exposing both concurrence and contradiction.

The single 'Nettles' notebook poem that takes *Lady Chatterley's Lover* as its explicit subject is 'To Pino':

> O Pino
> What a bean-O!
> when we printed Lady C.!
>
> Little Giuntina
> couldn't have been a
> better little bee!

---

[1]   *Lady Chatterley's Lover*, ed. Michael Squires (London: Penguin, 1994), p. xvi. Hereafter 2*LCL*.

When you told him
perhaps they'd scold him
for printing those naughty words

All he could say:
'But we do it everyday!
like the pigeons and the other little birds!'

And dear old lady Jean
'I don't know what you mean
by publishing such a book

We're all in it, all my family
me and Ekkehart and Somers and Pamelie—
You're no better than a crook—!'

'Wait, dear Lady Jean, wait a minute!
What makes you think that you're all in it?
Did you ever open the book?

Is Ekke Sir Clifford? it's really funny!
And you, dear Lady Jean, are you Connie?
So open the book and look!—'

But off she went, being really rattled
and there's a battle that's still to be battled
along with the others! what luck! (*CP* 668–9)

Lawrence is thought to have sent a manuscript containing an abridged version of this poem to Giuseppe ('Pino') Orioli (1884–1942) either on 28 July or 19 August 1929.[2] Pino was the Florentine bookseller and friend of Lawrence who assisted with the publication of the first edition of *Lady Chatterley's Lover* and successfully managed the novel's sale and distribution. The tone of the poem is set with the printers' slang term 'bean-o!' (an abbreviation of 'Beanfeast' meaning 'good time' or 'celebration'). The subsequent use of the affectionate diminutive – 'Little Giuntina' – locates the poem precisely, alluding to the Florentine printers of *Lady Chatterley's Lover*, or 'Tipografia Giuntina', who did not have enough type to set the whole novel, and whose inadequate command of English resulted in a barrage of errors.

Stanzas three and four, highly specific in origin, are best explained through reference to the following passage from 'A Propos':

---

[2]   See *L* vii 393–4 and *L* vii 432–3.

one paper wrote pitying the poor printer who was deceived into printing the book. Not deceived at all. A white-moustached little man who has just married a second wife, he was told: Now the book contains such and such words, in English, and it describes certain things… What does it describe? he asked. And when told, he said, with the short indifference of a Florentine: O! ma! But we do it every day! (*LCL* 334)

The poem's characters, satirized for their egocentricity in seeing themselves as the originals for the novel's protagonists, are equally traceable despite the false names that publicly veil their identities. '[D]ear lady Jean', for instance, is based on Lady Ida Sitwell (1869–1937), whom the Lawrences had visited at her *castello* in Montefugo on 2 June 1926.[3] Unbeknown to her at the time, Lady Ida served as a model for the character of Sir Clifford's aunt, Lady Eva Rolleston, in *The First Lady Chatterley*. Ekkehart, Somers and Pamelie were, respectively, Sir George Reresby Sitwell (1868–1943), Osbert Sitwell (1892–1969) and Edith Sitwell (1887–1964), though Lawrence may have borrowed the name Ekkehart from Eckart ('Ecki' or 'Ekkie') Petterich, a friend of Aldous and Maria Huxley. Lawrence had liked Osbert and Edith Sitwell when they visited him at the Villa Mirenda on 23 May 1927, although he felt 'upset and worried' for Osbert in particular (*L* vi 65). In September 1928, Lawrence would write to Orioli referring to the Sitwells' discovery that they were 'in' *Lady Chatterley's Lover*: 'The Sitwells, of course want to be important at any price, poor souls' (*L* vi 579).[4] If Lady Ida had not read the novel (as 'Lady Jean' has not), her informant that her 'whole family' were satirized in a *roman à clef* was probably the common friend who also informed Lawrence of her outrage: namely Orioli.[5]

The poem, ironically, draws a veil over the actual identities of the people targeted for satire: it remains elusive as a result of its own self-imposed mode of censorship. Nonetheless, it engages directly with the characters and issues of Lawrence's last novel, focusing particularly on the misguided, misinformed responses to it, just as 'A Propos' does in prose. Yet while it is bitter at root and reflects a genuine grievance, the tenor of this poem remains flippant and playful – even superficial. It is the more subtle linguistic and semantic echoes within other

---

[3]   See *L* v. 468; 473–4.

[4]   In *Façades* (London: Macmillan, 1978), pp. 222–32, John Pearson traces Lawrence's contact with both generations of the Sitwells and argues persuasively that he drew on Osbert's traits to remodel the character of Sir Clifford Chatterley in the novel's final version.

[5]   In 1933, Osbert Sitwell was cabled by filmmakers seeking to use the Sitwells' Derbyshire seat, Renishaw, for a film of *Lady Chatterley*, and responded that the request was as 'gross as it is libellous'; in 1957, he continued to maintain that it was 'unlikely' that Renishaw was Wragby. Although this correspondence is not conclusive evidence, it is highly likely that Osbert read the novel around 1933, while Edith may have read the 1960 Penguin edition.

late poems, reflecting the ideas and preoccupation of the preceding novel, that prove more fruitful and challenging to investigate. There is a considerable acreage of common ground, and at the heart of it can usually be found a machine.

Wheels, Hubs and Automobiles

> There are masses, and there are classes
> but the machine it is that has invented them both. (*CP* 641)

Both *Lady Chatterley's Lover* and the 'Nettles' notebook poems frequently engage in a critique of the mechanized, desensitized society they portray. Connie voices her sense of a 'grey, gritty hopelessness' arising from the ugliness of the industrial masses and the 'upper classes as she knew them' (*LCL* 153). This paucity does not appear to be limited to the upper echelons: Mellors's Colonel has told him that 'the English middle classes have to chew every mouthful thirty times because their guts are so narrow' (*LCL* 217).[6] In 'A Propos', Lawrence emphasizes the pernicious effect of class division, which impedes genuine warmth of human contact: 'Class hate and class-consciousness are only a sign that the old togetherness, the old blood-warmth has collapsed, and every man is really aware of himself in apartness.' (*LCL* 332) Lawrence extends the trajectory of this insight, asserting that such a 'fall' into individualism will permeate the entire gamut of social strata, beginning with the cultured classes. He alleges that the working classes cling on to the blood-warmth more tenaciously, but ultimately suffer the same loss as their social superiors. Clifford is cited as someone who has 'lost entirely all connections with his fellow-men and women, except those of usage' (*LCL* 333).

The gutlessness identified within modern society is seen as a side-product of mechanization, resulting in a dangerous symbiosis: while the (upper and middle) 'classes' are identified as the brains of the machine, the 'masses' are the machine's arms and legs. Imagery of fusion and manipulation dominate many of the 'industrial' late poems, while others emphasize the irony inherent in the role-reversal through which man has become subservient to the product of his own invention. Money is closely associated with the machine as another root of considerable evil, inciting the industrial hordes to acts of malice. Mellors refers to the 'mass-will of people, wanting money and hating life' (*LCL* 300) – exemplified by the young ones who 'scoot about on motor-bikes with girls' (*LCL* 300), whose greed results in their attempt to get hold of the necks of those who truly want to live, in order to 'squeeze the life out' of them (*LCL* 300).

In the 'Nettles' notebook, one particular machine – the car – acquires the associations of greedy consumerism and the 'inhuman robotisation of thought and

---

[6] The bourgeoisie is explicitly condemned in the poem 'How Beastly the Bourgeois is' in *Pansies* (*CP* 430–31). See also *LCL* 38.

gesture fostered by an insensitive cash culture'.[7] Lawrence alludes to the 'money-smelling man in a motor-car' (*CP* 645) who cannot be recognized as a neighbour or fellow man, and also to the slyly feline Rolls Royce whose purr communicates its owner's propensity to 'lick the cream off property' (*CP* 664).

The motor car becomes emblematic of the modern urge to move obsessively without direction, adopting motion in order to combat a fear:

> People go on walking when they have nowhere to go.
> People keep it up, because they daren't stop. (*CP* 657)

It is the wheel, however, that becomes the paradigm for a kind of paradoxical movement within stasis, and which Lawrence also adopts as a metaphor for the 'ego' of modern man. The wheel is condemned in a series of explicit formulations, such as 'Wheels are evil' (*CP* 716), 'the wheel starts the principle of all evil' and 'the wheel is the first principle of evil' (*CP* 712). These formulations become interesting when expanded in such a way as to enact poetically the futile yet relentless non-movement of the wheel on its hub:

> And men that sit in machines
> among spinning wheels, in an apotheosis of wheels
> sit in the grey mist of movement which moves not
> and going which goes not
> and doing which does not
> and being which is not:
> that is, they sit and are evil, in evil,
> grey evil, which has no path, and shows neither light nor dark,
> and has no home, no home anywhere. (*CP* 711–12)

The syntactical reversal in 'moves not' which situates the negative at the end of the line, as well as the reiteration in 'movement which moves not / and going which goes not / and doing which does not / and being which is not' combine to emulate the rhythmically monotonous turning of a wheel. The associated image of grey uniformity is also linked to the notion of directionlessness: there is 'no path', and hence no capacity for progression or movement beyond the fixed point. In short, there is no scope for wandering: 'the wheel goes round, but it never wanders. / It stays on its hub.' (*CP* 713)

In *Lady Chatterley's Lover*, Clifford is the paradigm of 'men who sit in machines', and Lawrence indicates a symbiotic fusion of man and wheelchair in order to reveal his total dependence. In moments of high-spirited defiance of his condition, Clifford is able to exclaim: 'I ride upon the achievement of the mind of man, and that beats a horse' (*LCL* 179), yet this conceit is catastrophically

---

[7]   Stephen Rowley, 'The Quest for a Nucleate Trope in Lawrence's Poetry: Organic Becoming and Inorganic Collapse', *Etudes Lawrenciennes*, 30 (2004), p. 7.

undermined in the remainder of the chapter through the failure of the chair and Clifford's resulting humiliation. His progress is explicitly satirized in the following mock-heroic rhetoric, in which the chair is seen not as a horse but as a ship:

> Oh last of all ships, through the hyacinthine shallows! oh pinnace on the last wild waters, sailing in the last voyage of our civilisation! Whither, oh weird wheeled ship, your slow course steering—!! Quiet and complacent, Clifford sat at the wheel of adventure: in his old black hat and tweed jacket, motionless and cautious. Oh captain, my Captain, our splendid trip is done! Not yet though! (*LCL* 185)

The allusion to Whitman[8] (absent from the two previous versions of the novel) is overt and effective, mocking the tentative Clifford as he negotiates a path through the flowers within his own wood. The fact that he is ironically motionless while in motion suggests the fixity of a wheel that spins endlessly on its hub, never progressing or wandering. Unease about the performance of the chair makes Clifford 'rigid with anger' (*LCL* 189) or provokes in him a 'fixed face' (*LCL* 42). The logical conclusion of this restriction to free movement is the breakdown of the chair, which occurs in Chapter 13 when Clifford attempts to drive up a rough slope without assistance from Mellors or Connie. At this point above all others, Clifford becomes a living embodiment of the 'movement which moves not / and going which goes not / and doing which does not / and being which is not' cited above.

In this poem, the association of wheels with a lack of meaningful movement is extended to the human ego. Clifford obstinately refuses to allow Mellors to assist the chair when it is proceeding with some difficulty, resulting in a further breakdown and the need for Mellors to strain himself physically. While Clifford's stubborn exertion of his will is understandable given the frustration he experiences at his own dependence, it is bound up with selfishness and class snobbery: the deep-seated belief that Mellors is expendable as he is paid to serve.

In the poem 'Death is not Evil, Evil is Mechanical', it is the wheel's inability to wander that extends to the human ego, again envisaged as in endless motion yet fixed:

> Only the human being, absolved from kissing and strife
> goes on and on, without wandering
> fixed upon the hub of the ego
> going, yet never wandering, fixed, yet in motion (*CP* 713)

---

[8]   The first line of Walt Whitman's poem 'O Captain! My Captain!' repeats the words of the title, then proceeds 'our fearful trip is done': see *The Complete Poems*, ed. Francis Murphy (London: Penguin, 1975), p. 359. In versions 1 and 2 the chair is a 'strange ship' with Clifford as captain at its helm, but the citation from Whitman does not appear: see *The First and Second Lady Chatterley Novels*, ed. Dieter Mehl and Christa Janssohn (Cambridge: Cambridge University Press, 1999), pp. 88 and 414.

The 'fixity' of the ego that uses 'all life only as power, as an engine uses steam or gas' (*CP* 635) stems partly from a refusal to acknowledge the complexity and duality inherent in the mortal condition, in which one is (for example) 'a mixture of yea and nay', 'a rainbow of love and hate' and 'a wind that blows back and forth' (*CP* 714). Denial results in the wheel-condition that indicates a figurative metamorphosis into mechanization or nullity:

> And thou shalt begin to spin round on the hub of the obscene ego
> a grey void thing that goes without wandering
> a machine that in itself is nothing
> a centre of the evil world-soul. (*CP* 714)

The poem 'The Evil World-Soul' picks up on the association made in the last line cited above and expands it into an entire poem. In this poem, the wheel-machine is seen to possess a soul that is both individual and part of a larger evil:

> Every wheel on its hub has a soul, evil,
> it is part of the evil world-soul, spinning. (*CP* 713)

The world-soul is seen as a power 'which wishes to blaspheme the world into greyness, / into evil neutrality, into mechanism' (*CP* 712). Similarly, in the poem 'Departure' the 'evil will in many evil men' makes an evil world-soul, which purposes 'to reduce the world to grey ash' (*CP* 716). The evil 'world-soul' envisaged here is dangerous as it is an actively harmful force, possessed of a will-to-destruction.

Throughout this poem sequence, ego and machine are inextricably joined, the joining envisaged in horrifyingly literal terms, with the iron entering the soul, the machine entangling the brain, steel twisting the loins of man and electricity exploding his heart (*CP* 629). There is also a lament (explicit or implicit, depending on the context), for the passivity of man, who submits to a process of mechanized manipulation, again envisaged in very vivid and visual terms. In the poem 'What is a Man to Do?', repetition is this time used to convey the paradox of vigorous yet manipulated energy: 'they dance, dance, dance this dry industrial jig of the corpses entangled in iron / and there's no escape, for the iron goes through their genitals, brains and souls' (*CP* 631). Analogously, in 'City-Life' people are described as having hooks in their faces, in the manner of snagged fish: there is, in fact, an explicit reference to a 'malignant fisherman' on an 'unseen shore' (*CP* 632). The term 'unseen' is itself sinister, yet more sinister still is the following reference to the invisible wires of steel, as though these humans have become macabre puppets dancing to the industrial tune. As well as being manipulative, the machine is seen as predatory, parasitic or even vampiric: 'The machine has got you, is turning you round and round / and confusing you, and feeding itself on your life' (*CP* 642). The turning of a fixed wheel has become the disorientation of a blindfolded human spun on the spot and unable to regain a sense of direction or perspective.

The citations above hint at a split attitude towards humankind, perceived as both the culpable creator of the machine and its pitiable victim. This particular manifestation of the characteristically Lawrentian love/hate dichotomy is clearly evident in both verse-notebook and novel. Seeing a group of steel-workers from Sheffield – men she describes as 'weird distorted smallish beings' – Connie reflects, 'Ah God, what has man done to man? What have the leaders of men been doing to their fellow men?' (*LCL* 153). Connie's cry is directly echoed in the poem 'What have they done to you—?'[9] in which the workers have been exploited while their bosses pocket the money. This poem ends with the lines:

> Oh look at my fellow-men, oh look at them
> the masses! Oh, What has been done to them? (*CP* 631)

The term 'fellow men' is used in the poetry (with or without irony) to indicate affinity or repudiation. In 'We Die Together', the narrator feels bound up inextricably with the fate of the mill hand in Leeds, and by implication, with the rest of the industrial masses. Yet in 'Love thy Neighbour—', the masses are seen as too intrinsically vile to be loved or even acknowledged as human.[10]

It is probably the resented affiliation – the 'Salvator Mundi' impulse (see *WL* 130) – rather than the hatred that provokes such vehement, violent poems as 'The Triumph of the Machine' and 'Humanity Needs Pruning'. Rather than the unseen, malignant and manipulative fisherman, 'The Triumph of the Machine' evokes a heavy and brutal force 'roll[ing] us hither and thither', in contrast with the 'unrolling of ferns' and the 'white tongues of the acanthus lapping at the sun' (*CP* 623). The machine – with its guiding human perched aloft – is presented as catastrophically inimical to nature, as in the episode from *Lady Chatterley's Lover* (Chapter 13) previously discussed. After ploughing along the paths of 'mashed flowers' (*LCL* 187), Clifford's chair 'came to her end amid a particularly promising patch of bluebells' (*LCL* 188), which subsequently becomes 'wrecked and trampled' (*LCL* 189). Like Clifford in his chair, the machine of the poem charges through the natural world leaving an indiscriminate trail of destruction in its wake. The difference is that nature is passive in the novel episode, while in the poem it becomes irate and retaliatory. Clifford is merely aware, as he drives, that 'The larks were trilling away over the park' (*LCL* 180), while in the poem the lark (like the other creatures emblematic of uncorrupted human souls) has the capacity to turn to violence in order to stop the machine: 'The trilling lark in a wild despair will trill down arrows from the sky' (*CP* 624). The poem dramatizes a future moment of crisis in which the destruction of the natural world has reached its apotheosis, catalyzing an automotive apocalypse in which 'traffic will tangle up in a long-drawn-out crash of collision / and engines will rush at the solid houses'

---

[9]   Many poem titles end with a long dash in the manuscript, often omitted by Pinto and Roberts. These reinserted punctuation points occur as silent emendations in this study.

[10]   For a fuller discussion of this poem see Chapter 6, p. 119).

(*CP* 624). At the end of the poem we are left with a smoky ruin of iron continuing to pollute the middle earth.

However, in spite of the carnage and its aftermath, the lark is 'trilling, angerless again' (*CP* 625) while the lambs frisk and frolic. The poem is conspicuous in suggesting that there are some who remain uncorrupted: people who will not become an 'engine of flesh' (*CP* 635), but who will find some way of evading the grip of the 'vast maw of iron' (*CP* 630). Among the 'streams that stream white-faced, in and out / in and out when the hooter hoots' (*CP* 628), there are the 'gentle passengers / of growing life' (*CP* 675) who must 'slip aside' or 'slip out' (*CP* 642) – albeit hesitantly, falteringly or wincingly. Often these individuals are traumatized, frail and tentative (as well as precious), feeling their way as though dimly sighted (*CP* 665) and with a propensity to remain under cover: 'Only here and there a pair of eyes, haunted, stares out as if asking: / Where then is life?' (*CP* 625).

Against the indiscriminate pluralism of the mechanized hordes, then, is shored the uniqueness of the few who are true advocates of life and warmth. Such an individual is described by Lawrence as the 'single' man or woman, as distinct from the masses or classes. In 'What is a Man to Do?' (previously cited), a series of rhetorical questions expose a despairing picture of the modern masses in their maniacal industrial jigging. One re-formulation of the interrogative title is 'what is a *single* man to do?' (*CP* 631, my italics), while a further question demands 'Then must a single man die with them, in the clutch of iron?' (*CP* 632). The term 'single' (ironically) is doubly charged, indicating the rarity of the individual who is hostile to the masses, while also emphasizing his or her uniqueness. The problems encountered by a 'single' person in society are exhibited by Mellors, who is constantly oppressed by the intrusion of the outside world into his privacy. In exasperation he says: 'If only there weren't so many other people in the world' (*LCL* 118). This longing also finds expression in the short poem actually entitled 'There Are Too Many People':

> There are too many people on earth
> insipid, unsalted, rabbity, endlessly hopping
> They nibble the face of the earth to a desert. (*CP* 606)

It is this sense of excess – as well as the distinction between the superfluous masses and the invaluable 'single' person – that clearly underlies the radical (if unpalatable) notion of thinning out humanity in order to preserve an essential quality of life. After this purge, the 'single' person might have the capacity to bud or blossom, to adopt the language of organic growth that Lawrence so frequently employs in this context.

Organic Connection and Being Alone

The poem 'Humanity Needs Pruning' is the most savage and extreme voicing of the desire for discriminate purging:

> Humanity needs pruning
> It is like a vast great tree with a vast great lot of sterile, dead, rotting wood
> and an amount of fungoid and parasitic growth.
> The tree of humanity needs pruning, badly,
> it needs thoroughly pruning, not as in the late war, blasting
> with unintelligent and evil destruction
> but pruning, severely, intelligently and ruthlessly pruning.
>
> The tree of human existence needs badly pruning
> or the whole tree will fall rotten. (*CP* 677)

This is an extreme poem, responding to what are certainly perceived to be extreme circumstances. Rather than the ceaseless, pointless motion conveyed in the image of the masses 'endlessly hopping', this poem employs a metaphor of corruptive growth ultimately resulting in inertia through rottenness. Modern man is envisaged as sterile: merely dead or rotten wood on the tree of life, having lost his 'organic connection' with the cosmos. This view is explicitly articulated in 'A Propos':

> This is what is the matter with us. We are bleeding at the roots, because we are
> cut off from the earth and sun and stars, and love is a grinning mockery, because,
> poor blossom, we plucked it from its stem on the tree of Life, and expected it to
> keep on blooming in our civilised vase on the table. (*LCL* 323)

In the essay, Lawrence also writes: 'Vitally, the human race is dying. It is like a great uprooted tree, with its roots in the air. We must plant ourselves again in the universe.' (*LCL* 330) This formulation finds its poetic counterpart in 'The Uprooted', in which modern, mechanized people, severed from life, are 'crying like plants whose roots are cut' (*CP* 610).

Metaphors of compromised or corrupted organicism are rife within the 'Nettles' notebook, one very explicit instance being the poem 'Fallen Leaves',[11] in which the natural and the mechanistic are set at opposite poles:

> There is the organic connection, like leaves that belong to a tree
> and there is the mechanical connection, like leaves that are cast upon the earth.
>
> Winds of heaven fan the leaves on the tree like flames and tunes,

---

[11]   Lawrence reviewed S.S. Kotelianski's translation of V.V. Rozanov's *Fallen Leaves*: see *IR* 347–51 and lxxxv–lxxxvi.

but winds of heaven are mills of God to the fallen leaves
grinding them small to humus, on earth's nether mill-stone. (*CP* 615)

The concept of 'organic connection' is fundamental, and its significance in the poems might in part be attributable to its prior use in specific instances within *Lady Chatterley's Lover* (this phrase does not appear in versions one or two of the novel[12]). Most explicitly, Tommy Dukes laments Clifford's retreat from the physical into the mental life with the words 'You've severed the connection between the apple and the tree: the organic connection.' (*LCL* 37) Dukes argues that knowledge is physiological as well as cerebral, and asserts the necessity of living in organic wholeness, in order to avoid the kind of fatal severance he has observed in his friend. Clifford is not alone within their intellectual group in this respect: rather, he exemplifies a common trait of the social stratum within which he operates. Hammond, in spite of his wife and two children, is 'much more closely connected with a type-writer' (*LCL* 32), suggesting that his ultimate allegiance is to the mental life and the machine.

Clifford is an extreme example of a man who has forfeited both organic connection and human touch. His paralysis is the external manifestation, rather than the cause, of a 'cold spirit of vanity, that had no warm human contacts' (*LCL* 72), with the consequence that he is 'not in actual touch with anything or anybody' (*LCL* 16). Like Hammond, he compensates for his lack of human warmth and contact with cerebral pursuits, such as the writing of the stories that initially receive such acclaim. Ironically, Clifford's sister Emma attributes to these stories the capacity to counteract an age of waste and nullity, *restoring* an organic connection with the past. She believes that within modern society 'There was no organic connection with the thought and expression which had gone before' (*LCL* 17), and that Clifford's stories might provide new impetus, proving a landmark for the future. As the novel progresses, we become aware of the futility inherent in this misplaced optimism and family pride. After the initial thrill of the story-writing and subsequent public accolade, Connie sees the stories as frighteningly vacuous. They are merely the extension of Clifford's spoken utterances, which she has described in her moments of despair as 'the hosts of fallen leaves of a life that is ineffectual' (*LCL* 50). In a developed version of this organic image, reminiscent of the leaves being ground to pieces on earth's millstone in the poem 'Fallen Leaves', 'all the brilliant words seemed like dead leaves, crumpling up and turning to powder, meaning really nothing, blown away on any gust of wind' (*LCL* 50).

---

[12]   The term 'organic' does appear in version two, but it is used principally in relation to society rather than humankind's connection with the cosmos: 'Vitally, organically, in the old organic sense of society, there were no more classes. That organic system had collapsed. So she need not have any class-mistrust of Parkin, and he need have none of her', in *The First and Second Lady Chatterley Novels*, ed. Mehl and Janssohn, p. 500.

Connie, languishing at Wragby, 'knew she was out of connection: she had lost touch with the substantial and vital world' (*LCL* 20). In Connie's case this lack of rootedness might be attributed to her solitude and lack of genuine human touch: a situation of course rectified by contact with Mellors, and her symbolic retreat into the natural environment of the wood. Interestingly, Clifford articulates an alternative (Nietzschean) vision of escape into personal fulfilment – a surprisingly poetic indictment of the individual surging above the submerged industrial hordes. This extract (clearly developing an extremely similar passage in versions one and two[13]) occurs in a letter to Connie when she is away in Venice:

> But sometimes the soul does come up, shoots like a kittiwake into the light, with ecstasy, after having preyed on the submarine depths... our immortal destiny is to escape, once we have swallowed our swimmy catch, up again into the bright ether, bursting out from the surface of Old Ocean, into real light. Then one realises one's eternal nature. (*LCL* 266)

Caliban-like, Clifford's letter finds a rather poignant way of evoking the emergence of an individual from among the masses, reversing the endless downward fall that both novel and verse-books see as the fate of modern, mechanized society. However, as is often the case with Clifford, this flight of fancy is bound up with issues of class snobbery, while the language might be considered affected or conceited. The phrase 'preyed on' is also potentially sinister, hinting at the exploitative, repressive relationship between landowner and workers.

While Clifford is content with an image of individual transcendence, Mellors gropes toward a collective vision. He experiences fleeting moments in which he can believe that the touch he shares with Connie might become a life-principle, if the faint sparks of the working men could be fanned into a flame (see *LCL* 206, 219 and 314). In these rare moments of optimism, he echoes the belief expressed in the poem 'Future Relationships':

> The world is moving, moving still, towards further democracy.
> But not a democracy of idea or ideal, nor of property, nor even of the emotion of brotherhood.
> But a democracy of men, a democracy of touch. (*CP* 611)

The poem 'Future States' expresses the same kind of optimism, asserting 'Once men touch one another, then the modern industrial form of machine civilisation will melt away' (*CP* 611). Tommy Dukes, less tentative in his hope than Mellors, defines his vision of the future in similar terms:

---

[13]   Ibid.: see version one, p. 127 and version two, p. 502.

> Give me the resurrection of the body ... But it'll come, in time—when we've
> shoved the cerebral stone away a bit, the money and the rest. Then we'll get a
> democracy of touch, instead of a democracy of pocket. (*LCL* 75)

Connie doesn't understand the phrase 'democracy of touch', but it comforts her 'as
meaningless things may do' (*LCL* 76). It is striking that the phrases 'resurrection
of the body' and 'democracy of touch' have been introduced for the first time into
the latest version of the novel.

Both verse-book and novel, through brief glimpses of a possible future, convey
a vision of the way in which an individual's transfiguring gleam might invigorate
the masses into awareness and action. Both texts, however, reflect a deep awareness
of the struggle entailed in the attempt to make such singularity plural. Mellors is
more frequently cynical than optimistic, while numerous poems from the 'Nettles'
notebook enact a pendular swing towards solitude as the key to self-fulfilment.
In 'The Uprooted', it is not the presence of other people that will result in the re-
establishment of organic connection, but the reacquisition of self through solitude.
The poem ends:

> The thing to do is in solitude slowly and painfully put forth new roots
> Into the unknown, and take root by oneself. (*CP* 610)

This emphasis on solitude or aloneness – an unquestionable preoccupation in the
late poems – is surprisingly prevalent in *Lady Chatterley's Lover*, a novel about
the importance of touch and tenderness. Mellors's existence as 'A man very much
alone, and on his own' (*LCL* 60), with a 'flickering detachment' (*LCL* 286), is a
necessary prerequisite for any new relationship. His repudiation of society as a
result of cynicism regarding mechanized humankind has led him to the conviction
that 'if he could not be left alone, he would die' (*LCL* 88). In the poem 'Image-
making love', the best state of all is 'Nakedly to be alone, unseen', which is 'a relief
like death' (*CP* 601). The poem essentially reflects a rejection of the 'trespassed
contacts' that Mellors fears when his master's wife invades his space in the wood
and demands a key to the hut. The poem 'People' celebrates the way in which
humans command respect when it is possible to see 'their aloneness alive in them'
(*CP* 602).

Mellors clings to a deep-rooted faith in the necessity of his own aloneness, yet
indicates that it might be compatible with fleeting moments of contact:

> But he, the keeper, as the day grew, had realised: it's no good! It's no good trying
> to get rid of your own aloneness. You've got to stick to it—all your life. Only at
> times, at times, the gap will be filled in. At times! But you have to wait for the
> times. Accept your own aloneness and stick to it, all your life. And then accept

the times when the gap is filled in, when they come. But they've got to come. You can't force them. (*LCL* 145)[14]

Positioned near the half-way point of the novel, when Connie is merely one of a conjectured, plural 'they', this indictment might be seen as a mere half-truth, later contradicted by Mellors's commitment to Connie and their child. Equally, it might point to the kind of fluctuating contact evident in their period of separation and chastity at the novel's close. Such an oscillation is advocated in the poem 'Desire', with the proviso that the poem locates the yearning for contact in the past, as a retrospective urge:

Ah, in the past, towards rare individuals
I have felt the pull of desire:
Oh come, come nearer, come into touch!
Come physically nearer, be flesh to my flesh—

But say little, oh say little
And afterwards, leave me alone.
Keep your aloneness, leave me my aloneness. (*CP* 602)

Arguably, Mellors equates to the quiet, inscrutable lover who comes into transient touch but resists talking about it, although the poem's voice also echoes that of Birkin, in his bid to establish a star-equilibrium that goes deeper than the 'love' demanded by Ursula in her reiterated pleas for reassurance (see, for example, *WL* 154). Certainly the paradox of touch and aloneness is one that resonates conceptually and dramatically throughout Lawrence's work, particularly during these late years: the protagonist of *The Escaped Cock* sails away at the close of the tale after impregnating the priestess of Isis, fearful of her mother's displeasure and further complications (*VG* 162–3). The late fragment 'The Man Who Was Through with the World' (*VG* 237–40) describes one man's attempt to retreat from society as a hermit – but, like 'The Man Who Loved Islands', indicates the futility of this venture. In a letter of 19 May 1927 to his sister Ada, Lawrence rejected his earlier desire for 'turning hermit' and 'hiding away the rest of my days' (*L* vi 63), asserting instead: 'I shall go out into the world again, to kick it and stub my toes. It's no good my thinking of retreat' (*L* vi 71–2).

Ultimately, Mellors realizes that the thing he has to do is come into tender touch with Connie, without forfeiting his dignity or pride (*LCL* 279). The poem 'Men and Women' epitomizes Mellors' perspective: 'Men and women should learn tenderness to each other / and to leave one another alone' (*CP* 620). This poem remains poised, balancing its central paradox, while others adopt a more extreme

---

[14]   References to Mellors/Parkin as alone resonate throughout versions one and two of the novel. In version two, the word 'alone' occurs over 200 times.

position in their assertion that desire has irrevocably died, so that aloneness remains the only true state of being. The poem 'Desire', cited above, ends:

> I used to say this in the past—but now no more.
> It has always been a failure.
> They have always insisted on love
> And on talking about it
> And on the me-and-thee and what we meant to each other.
>
> So now I have no desire any more
> Except to be left, in the last resort, alone, quite alone. (*CP* 602)

One poem title – 'Delight of being alone' – testifies to the magnitude of this craving for isolation in which it is possible to elude both intimate human contact and mechanized man in general. This state of receptive aloneness is frequently associated with stillness: the antithesis of frenzied movement, restless tourism and aimless travel.

'Everything has been seen to death'

I have previously indicated that the 'masses' are associated in the 'Nettles' notebook with the mechanical 'jigging' of their dance, and with the motor car, which epitomizes restless, directionless travel. The propensity of the hordes to move and travel for the sake of evading themselves and their own petty sphere of reality is reflected in the extraordinary number of allusions to modes and methods of travel. Wheels, Dunlop tyres, engines, traffic streams, automobiles, trams, ferries (P&O and Orient liners in particular) and even perambulators are ubiquitous in these late poems. Equally prevalent are allusions to travel, travellers, travelling and 'trafficking', with one specific reference to the travel agency Thomas Cook pointing to a preoccupation with tourism.

The 'tourist' poems, as I will call them, might be identified as a sub-group within the 'Nettles' notebook, though they do not function as a connected, chronological sequence. Like the poems previously discussed, they illustrate the disjunction between the dulled, desensitized masses and the wincing, shy individual, unique and vulnerable in his or her singleness. The latter is, of course, in the minority. In one formulation, a woman washing herself under a tap evokes a 'glimmer of the presence of the gods', like lilies or water-lilies (*CP* 651). The tap image in fact serves to illustrate the contrast between the shy, glimmering individual and the sea-soaking hordes, as is evident in the ironic poem 'Sea-Bathers':

> Oh the handsome bluey-brown bodies, they might just as well be gutta-percha,
> and the reddened limbs red india-rubber tubing, inflated,
> and the half-hidden private parts just a little brass tap, robinetto,
> turned on for different purposes. (*CP* 625)

While the penis becomes a multi-purpose tap, the over-sunned limbs are the inner tube of a tyre – an image that, in the related poem 'Forte dei Marmi', becomes the measure of the tourists' ignorance:

> But the blatant bathers don't know, they know nothing;
> the vibration of the motor-car has bruised their insensitive bottoms
> into rubber-like deadness, Dunlop inflated unconcern. (*CP* 625)[15]

Connie feels that the Lido in Venice, 'with its acres of sun-pinked or pyjamaed bodies, was like a strand with an endless heap of seals come up for mating' (*LCL* 258). Later, in *Apocalypse*, the 'modern sunbathers' become 'disintegrated by the very sun that bronzes them' (*A* 77); this disintegration is occasioned by the sun exhibiting its hostility to the nervous, personal consciousness in humankind. In the poem 'Forte dei Marmi', however, the hard-bottomed insensitivity of the bathers is seen as a direct result of the car's motion.

Such insensitivity might also be attributed to Clifford (particularly given that he is permanently fixed above wheels, while his paralysis literally occasions a lack of sensation below the waist). Connie actually employs terminology analogous to that of 'Forte dei Marmi' in describing Clifford: in version two he has 'tough indiarubber bowels'[16] while in version three he is 'stupidly insentient, tough and india-rubbery where other people were concerned' (*LCL* 194). This insight follows the conversation in which Connie vents her anger at Clifford's selfish exploitation of Mellors after the breakdown of his wheelchair (discussed above). Yet the most explicit use of this tyre image in the novel occurs in a passionate speech in which Mellors condemns not only the upper echelons of society but his own working class, the common people:

> Their spunk's gone dead—motor-cars and cinemas and aeroplanes suck the last bit out of them. I tell you, every generation breeds a more rabbity generation, with indiarubber tubing for guts and tin legs and tin faces. Tin people! It's all a steady sort of bolshevism—just killing off the human thing, and worshipping the mechanical thing. (*LCL* 217)

In the aphoristic poem 'There Are Too Many People' (cited earlier in this chapter), the term 'rabbity' is used to designate the parasitic tendencies of modern man who destroys the natural world ('nibble[s] the face of the earth to a desert') and hops about in restless, manic motion. In the prose passage, a vivid conceit (one scarcely compatible with the rabbit image) is employed in order to reflect the robotization of humankind, which has acquired internally the attributes of a tyre ('indiarubber

---

[15] Interestingly the image of rubber tubing, associated with the car tyre in the poems, is applied in the novel by Mellors when describing a debased, abstract modern art – which he describes as 'tubified and titivated up' (*LCL* 287).

[16] *The First and Second Lady Chatterley Novels*, ed. Mehl and Janssohn, p. 488

tubing') and externally the characteristics of a machine ('tin legs and tin faces'). It is notable, too, that this process of dehumanization is explicitly occasioned by the experience of travel, through reference both to the motor car and the aeroplane.

Such associations provoke the resistance to tourism evident in the late poems. While one might speculate that the journeying entailed in tourism would correlate with the wandering through which mechanistic fixity is eluded, the poems generally contradict this view. Only in one poem – 'Food of the North' – is the desire to travel evident; this is provoked by disillusionment with the north and a longing for the olive trees of the south. This poem is anomalous and might be contrasted with 'Tourists', which consists of the lines: 'There is nothing to look at any more. / Everything has been seen to death' (*CP* 660). More explicitly still, the poem 'Travel is Over' advocates not-looking over the strained effort of over-conscious sight:

> I have travelled, and looked at the world and loved it.
> Now I don't want to look at the world any more,
> there seems nothing there. (*CP* 662)

These three lines precisely reflect Connie's perspective when she leaves Wragby towards the end of the novel in order to travel in Europe with her sister Hilda. Her disillusionment begins at their first stop, London, where the people are 'spectral and blank', despite their appearance of being 'brisk and good-looking' (*LCL* 254). While London is 'barren', Paris is epitomized by a 'now-mechanical sensuality' (*LCL* 254); it is sad and worn-out, 'weary of the tension of money, money, money' (*LCL* 254). It is also perceived as lacking the capacity for disguise, being 'not sufficiently Americanised or Londonised to hide its weariness under a mechanical jig-jig-jig!' (*LCL* 254): a formulation correlating with the, 'robot jig-jig-jig' of the poem 'As Thyself—!' (*CP* 645). While the charming Frenchwomen have a greater degree of sensuality than their 'jigging English sisters' (*LCL* 255) they are, in Connie's view, dry, wilful and even less capable of tenderness. She is also depressed by the number of oddly dressed Americans and 'dreary', 'hopeless' English tourists (*LCL* 255).

While Paris instils in Connie a sense that 'the human world was just getting worn out' to the point where she becomes 'shrinking and afraid' (*LCL* 255), like the anonymous woman of the poem 'As Thyself—!', who is 'shrinking / from the robot contact on every hand!' (*CP* 645), Connie finds equally that Switzerland, the Tyrol and Italy are entirely lacking in vitality. She acknowledges objectively that the road trip itself is 'quite nice' (*LCL* 255) but feels an utter inability to connect with it, or to care about the landscape. This indifference is initially perceived as reflecting a weakness within herself: 'Why don't I really care? Why am I never really thrilled?' (*LCL* 255). Yet this sense of failure modulates into defiance, reflecting her cynicism regarding the nullifying tourist venture: 'I just don't care for landscape any more. Why should one stare at it? ... I refuse to.' (*LCL* 255)

Such ruminations lead to a more explicit condemnation of travel and tourism in general, in which the natural world is seen as the victim of human exploitation:

> [The travellers] wanted to get enjoyment, perforce, like squeezing blood out of a stone. Poor mountains! poor landscape! it all had to be squeezed and squeezed and squeezed again, to provide a thrill, to provide enjoyment... This tourist performance of enjoying oneself is too hopelessly humiliating: it's such a failure. (*LCL* 255–6)

Her experience of the tourist sham precisely reflects the attitude expressed in the poems 'Tourism' and 'Travel is Over'.

Ironically, Connie realizes with some surprise that she thinks of Wragby, and even her life with Clifford, as more 'real' than the numerous sights she sees in the course of her travels. The appeal of Wragby at the moment is simply that she is not required to perform there. She can 'go about and be still' (*LCL* 256): a stillness that is deeply appealing in its contrast with the endless roving of tourism. In the late poems, stillness is frequently associated with the capacity to be receptive, resulting in a profundity of connection and awareness. The poem 'Travel is Over' ends by offering such an alternative to the relentless effort of seeing entailed in tourism:

> In not-looking, and in not-seeing
> comes a new strength
> and undeniable new gods share their life with us, when we cease to see. (*CP* 662)

As the antithesis of frenzied travelling, then, these poems move towards a conception of passive, receptive assimilation, making a vicarious experience of motion – motion operating beyond the self – possible. This condition of being is envisaged as a kind of balance: a cosmic attunement like that of Heraclitus' bow and lyre.[17] The novel explores ways in which such balance can be achieved by Connie and Mellors in the wood, through tenderness and sexual renewal, while in the poems, attunement results from the capacity to experience numerous gods in transit. In both cases, the potential recipient of the transformative experience is required to be receptive to the unknown.

Forces of Renewal

In his introduction to *Lady Chatterley's Lover,* Michael Squires argues that 'the novel's voices carry forward Lawrence's eloquent defence of the forces of renewal, these forces shaping a kind of moral fable' (*2LCL* xxxi). He identifies the sexual

---

[17] John Burnet, *Early Greek Philosophy* (London and Edinburgh: Black, 1892). pp. 136–7. Hereafter *EGP.*

ecstasy experienced by Connie as an illustration of her willingness to become open to a number of forces driving from within:

> Connie's cries yield at last a 'life-exclamation', an affirmation, a vindication ... of the human value of opening oneself to the unknown, unexpected, unleashed forces that roil unconquerable in the self. These forces drive the self toward renewal and away from mechanical deadness. (*2LCL* xxx)

Lawrence sets the revitalizing power of sex against the deadening influence of the machine. Furthermore, in the 'A Propos' essay, the sex between Connie and Mellors is placed in contrast with the debased sexuality that typifies stale relationships within the modern world: 'now the act tends to be mechanical, dull, and disappointing, and only fresh mental realisation will freshen up the experience' (*LCL* 308). The term 'freshen' is of particular significance here, emphasizing the constant replenishment provided by sex that is 'the balance of male and female in the universe, the attraction, the repulsion, the transit of neutrality, the new attraction, the new repulsion, always different, always new.' (*LCL* 323) Balance is achieved through flux and change: an enabling 'transit' through oscillating, even contradictory, states of being.

Any profound connection between man and woman is shown to be dependent on the ability to establish a wider connection with the cosmos or universe, through adhering to cosmic rhythm and the 'ritual of the seasons' (*LCL* 329) In 'A Propos', Lawrence writes:

> the greatest need of man is the renewal forever of the complete rhythm of life and death, the rhythm of the sun's year, the body's year of a life-time, and the greater year of the stars, the soul's year of immortality. This is our need, our imperative need. It is a need of the mind and soul, body, spirit and sex: all. It is no good asking for a Word to fulfil such a need. No Word, no Logos, no Utterance will ever do it.' (*LCL* 329)

The emphasis on cosmic connection with the sun and stars is very close to that of Lawrence's last book, *Apocalypse*, begun only a month after 'A Propos', and which I will discuss fully in Chapter 7. In *Apocalypse*, Lawrence laments mankind's loss of the sun, moon and other planets, which have become mere 'thought-forms' (*A* 50) through a debased response to them. The sun has become a 'ball of blazing gas' (*A* 51–2)[18] while the moon is 'pock-marked' (*A* 52): both have lost their profound associations reaching back to pagan times. 'A Propos' reflects precisely this view, attributing the cause of this impoverishment directly to the machine:

> the machine has killed the earth for us, making it a surface, more or less bumpy, that you travel over. How, out of all this, are we to get back the grand orbs of

---

[18]   Cf. the poem 'Stoic', in which the sun is a 'pyre of blazing gas' (*CP* 702).

the soul's heavens, that fill us with unspeakable joy? How are we to get back Apollo, and Attis, Demeter, Persephone, and the halls of Dis? How even see the star Hesperus, or Betelgeuse. (*LCL* 331)

In the poem 'The Wandering Cosmos' (discussed in Chapter 5, p. 98), Betelgeuse is cited as a 'wandering' star: an instance of the cosmic 'footstep onwards' (*CP* 713) that signifies progression and is the antithesis of wheel-like stasis. The passage just cited expresses the urgent need for a re-establishment of contact, a reclaiming both of the ancient (or pagan) myths and the liberated motion of wandering heavenly bodies. While 'A Propos' provides tentative answers through reference to sexual renewal, ritual and seasonal rhythms, the late poems suggest other ways in which profound contact with the unknown may be established. Like the essay, the poem 'Old Men' prioritizes 'fluidity' and 'living change' which are shored against the robotic fixity of the wheel (*CP* 662). Yet while the essay and novel associate such renewal with sexuality, the poem merely attributes these characteristics to 'The gods, who are life' (*CP* 662). While the essay and novel address the issue of getting back the 'grand orbs of the soul's heavens' and *Apocalypse* is concerned with the reacquisition of stars such as Hesperus and Betelgeuse, the poems confront the question 'How are we to get back Apollo, and Attis, Demeter, Persephone, and the halls of Dis?' In *Last Poems*, Lawrence imaginatively regains a plethora of deities, including named gods (such as Persephone), often perceiving them as embodiments of living change through being in transit. In turning to the archaic or the mythopoeic, then, Lawrence is able to articulate a vision of travel or trafficking that transcends the machine and reveals a profound receptivity to the unknown.

Within the poem 'In the Cities', the modern world, symbolized by the air thickened and muddied by traffic fumes, is contrasted with the ancient cities in which the wheel does not play a part:

In the cities
there is even no more any weather
the weather in town is always benzene, or else petrol fumes
lubricating oil, exhaust gas.

As over some dense marsh, the fumes
thicken, miasma, the fumes of the automobile
densely thicken in the cities.

In ancient Rome, down the thronged streets
no wheels might run, no insolent chariots.
Only the footsteps, footsteps
of people
and the gentle trotting of the litter-bearers. (*CP* 703)

While the modern cities are characterized by weatherless, contaminating smog – by-product of the turning of wheels – the ancient citizens undertake only a 'gentle' trotting, the term 'footstep' functioning as a paradigm for unmechanized progression. Moving beyond this specific instance, the late poems evoke a condition of receptivity in which it is possible to hear 'goddesses trafficking mysteriously through the air' (*CP* 655). In the opening 'Last Poems' sequence, such a deistic 'return' becomes more explicit – more fully dramatized – through the sighting of a number of named gods in transit. 'The Greeks are Coming!' (*CP* 687) heralds the arrival of 'ships a-sail from over the rim of the sea' containing 'men with archaic pointed beards', while in the next poem, the sea becomes 'the Argonauts' sea' (*CP* 687), with Odysseus at the helm. In 'Middle of the World' (*CP* 688) a 'slim black ship of Dionysos' is singled out and vividly evoked, while in 'Maximus' (*CP* 692), Hermes puts in an appearance. These returning gods are variously Greek, Minoan or gods of Tiryns, with additional attributes of the Egyptian and the Etruscan (see Chapter 3). They are described at one point as 'moon-lit dancers' (*CP* 689), revealing them to be revellers in the natural and the cosmic like the dancers of '[Autobiographical Fragment]', rather than the puppets made to dance by the steel strings and hooks of the machine.

Even in these mythological poems the modern world intrudes, creating a contrast between the buoyant archaic vessels and the polluting steam-driven ferries. In 'The Greeks are Coming!' a passing ocean liner is described as a 'small beetle walking the edge' (*CP* 687), leaving a trail of black smoke behind. 'Middle of the World' has its own allusions to these 'smoking ships': those of P&O, the Orient Line and all the 'other stinkers' (*CP* 688). These ships move like 'clock-work' across the Minoan distance, indicating compromised, mechanical, meaningless travelling rather than the progress of ancient vessels.

Nonetheless, in this late verse the sea becomes a profound emblem for the possibilities of progressive journeying, and in 'Last Poems' in particular it is envisaged as providing a passage from life to death. 'The Ship of Death' is the most obvious – or at least extended – poem to allude to here: the poem to which L.D. Clark gives prominence in *The Minoan Distance*. He identifies it as exemplification of 'what travel meant to Lawrence's life and work', indicating the extent to which Lawrence envisaged his life as a literal and symbolic voyage.[19] The death-journey is perceived here as a kind of wandering, as it is specified that there is 'nowhere to go', no port to aim for: the ship and soul are merely subsumed into oblivion before it is possible for re-emergence, after which the ship can wing its way home. In 'Butterfly', the soul undertakes a different, air-borne journey in its progression from the warm, walled garden of our existence to the unknown beyond. 'Bavarian Gentians' witnesses yet another journey, this time envisaged in specifically mythological terms, in which a gentian flower lights the way to Hades.

---

[19]   L.D. Clark, *The Minoan Distance: the Symbolism of Travel in D.H. Lawrence* (Tucson: University of Arizona Press, 1980), p. 411.

The death poems are poems of passage, charting a final journey: the 'great adventure of death, where Thomas Cook cannot guide us' (*CP* 677). More generally, through ships, footsteps and other kinds of trafficking, Lawrence explores ways of portraying journeying as un-wheel-like. Through allusions to the 'sacred silence of gates' and the 'silence of passing through doors', he conveys a sense of progression, 'going from this into that' (*CP* 699) which is the antithesis of the 'going which goes not' enacted by the wheel. Yet within these visions of progression and transition is the sense that the residue of modernity will remain. Smash the machine and the debris of it lurks and contaminates the middle-earth. Look for an ancient ship and you might see a P&O ferry. There is also the sense that transition itself may be reliant on a contradiction, given that it is a 'core of stillness' that facilitates receptivity to the movement of trafficking gods. In 'Shadows', the narrator is 'walking still' with god; his life is 'moving still' with the dark earth. These oxymoronic formulations indicate that while Lawrence rejects the wheel, prising it off its axle, his vision of wandering is reliant on an analogous paradox.

In terms of language use and frame of reference, *Lady Chatterley's Lover* is, in some areas, more closely linked to the late poems than to its earlier drafts. Phrases such as 'organic connection', 'resurrection of the body' and 'democracy of touch' (absent from versions one and two) indicate this affinity, as do the specific usages of terms such as 'tourist' and 'renewal' in novel and poems. Both continue to articulate the profound dissatisfaction with mechanization and industry evident within the 'Industrial Magnate' chapter of *Women in Love* and many other earlier works. In these late texts, however, Lawrence extends the implications of his critique of the machine to encompass travel and tourism more generally, expressing a less commonly voiced disillusionment with adventure. Through metaphors of compromised organicism and the severing of cosmic connection, he reveals the paucity of a modern world almost devoid of touch and tenderness, also indicating ways in which mechanization may be eluded or surpassed:

> Connie and Mellors ... shape their code of morality not *out* of their culture's materials but *apart* from them; they are hostile to impediments, averse to what is counterfeit, appalled by what is cheap, whether of body or mind. At the same time they retain their humanity and their personal integrity by demanding to be re-rooted in the most regenerative experience possible – the sexual. (*2LCL* xxx–xxxi)

In his last novel, the 'solution' proposed entails the definition or redefinition of self *against* – or beyond the bounds of – society.

While the re-rooting of Connie and Mellors is achieved through sexual awakening (associated with seasonal renewal), the poems of 1929 offer a way of re-rooting through isolation, stillness and receptivity. Yet these separate forces of renewal are not mutually exclusive, given that receptive stillness exists as one phase within the ritual or routine of coming together and moving apart. Squires observes that 'As Connie and Mellors retreat from the "outer world of chaos"

(*LCL* 10) into the protected "sanctuary" of the wood (*LCL* 20), Lawrence stresses silence and stillness' (*2LCL* xxiii–xxiv). They find one of the 'peaceful oblivious places / where the angels used to alight' (*CP* 725), repudiating the machine and becoming receptive to the unknown. In the novel the unknown is revealed as the regenerative force of touch and tenderness; in the poems it entails the visitation of multiple trafficking gods, so that 'touch' is less tangible:

> Who is it that softly touches the sides of my breast
> and touches me over the heart
> so that my heart beats soothed, soothed, soothed and at peace? (*CP* 652)

The soothing presence of this poem is 'no man' and 'no woman' for the narrator is alone; here, the receptive act results in contact with a spiritual essence or manifestation that exists 'according to the soul's desire' (*CP* 652). While Lawrence's last novel celebrates human touch, the late poems shift this touch onto a spiritual or mythopoeic plane through invoking multiple gods.

Chapter 5
Elements of the Pre-Socratics

Not Reading the Same Text Twice

> Though this discourse is true evermore, yet men are as unable to understand
> it when they hear it for the first time as before they have heard it at all. For,
> although all things happen in accordance with the account I give, men seem as if
> they had no experience of them, when they make trial of words and works such
> as I set forth, dividing each thing according to its nature and explaining how it
> truly is. But other men know not what they are doing when you wake them up,
> just as they forget what they do when asleep.[1]

Lawrence discovered the fragments penned by a number of pre-Socratic
philosophers in John Burnet's *Early Greek Philosophy*, which he read and re-
read at various times throughout his life. His final re-reading of Burnet occurred
in 1929, so the book is particularly interesting in relation to the poems that were
being composed during his last year. The Burnet volume provides an example
of a plural text incorporating fragments which were collected and arranged into
a whole, like Aldington's edition of *Last Poems* or Said's *On Late Style*. Burnet
had cast his net wider, however, given that the works of several pre-Socratics
were collated within a single volume. The work is also multiple in that (during
Lawrence's lifetime) the book existed in three widely differing editions, and it is
certain that he was familiar with at least two of these. *Early Greek Philosophy* was
a crucial work whose impact is clearly evident when reading late Lawrence, but
(like the Etruscan influence) it furnished material which was gradually assimilated
over time.

He read the book for the first time in 1915 having obtained a copy from Bertrand
Russell, who lent him either the first edition of 1892 or the second of 1908 (see *CP*

---

[1] Heraclitus, fr. 2 in John Burnet, *Early Greek Philosophy* (London and Edinburgh:
Black, 1892), p. 133 (*EGP*), When quoting from Burnet I normally derive the text from the
1892 edition, while also citing the third edition (1920) equivalent in a footnote if there are
significant differences. In the third edition this quotation reads:

Though this Word is true evermore, yet men are as unable to understand it when they hear
it for the first time as before they have heard it at all. For, though all things come to pass in
accordance with this Word, men seem as if they had no experience of them, when they make
trial of words and deeds such as I set forth, dividing each thing according to its kind and
showing how it truly is. But other men know not what they are doing when awake, even as
they forget what they do in sleep. (*3EGP* 133)

995). This book made such an impression on Lawrence that he felt compelled to revise his own philosophical writing in the light of the newfound insights:

> I have been wrong, much too Christian, in my philosophy. These early Greeks have clarified my soul. (*L* ii 364)

> I shall write all my philosophy again. Last time I came out of the Christian Camp. This time I must come out of these early Greek philosophers. (*L* ii 367)

Lawrence's philosophical essay 'The Crown', written in 1915, indeed proceeds from the standpoint of the early Greek philosophers, and of Heraclitus in particular. This essay reveals that Lawrence, unlike those who 'know not what they are doing when you wake them up' was able to respond initially to Heraclitus' philosophy with an 'act of attention' (*IR* 113). Yet he was not content with an initial response, a single reading. Rather, Lawrence returned to the book regularly: he had a copy in America in 1922–3 and left it there; he bought a copy in London in 1926; he then had to ask for it again in 1929 (in a letter of 10 October), during work on his last book, *Apocalypse* (most of which was composed just after Lawrence had stopped writing poems into the two late poetry notebooks):

> Do you still have that book *Early Greek Philosophy* which I bought when I was last in London? if so, would you send it me, I want to do some work on the Apocalypse, and consult it. If you haven't got it, no matter. (*L* vii 518)[2]

The depth of his engagement with the pre-Socratics after this re-reading is suggested by Mara Kalnins in her essay 'Symbolic Seeing: Lawrence and Heraclitus'. After acknowledging the extent to which Lawrence's initial reading of Burnet in 1915 influenced his 'doctrine of duality',[3] Kalnins goes on to suggest that 'his interpretation of the ideas he found there underwent a striking change in 1929, the final year of his life, a change which, significantly, was precipitated by his re-reading of Burnet and the work of Heraclitus and the pre-Socratics in that year'.[4] In her introduction to *Apocalypse*, too, Kalnins emphasizes the significance of this book in the 'shaping' of Lawrence's thoughts:

---

[2]   In October 1929, Lawrence almost certainly read the third edition (1920). In my concluding chapter I discuss the significance of this edition in relation to the short prologues composed by Lawrence for inclusion in the Cresset Press edition of *Birds, Beasts and Flowers* (1930).

[3]   Mara Kalnins, 'Symbolic Seeing: Lawrence and Heraclitus', in *D.H. Lawrence: Centenary Essays*, ed. Mara Kalnins (Bristol: Bristol Classical Press, 1986), p. 173.

[4]   Ibid.

Burnet's philosophical study, therefore, was of the greatest importance in shaping Lawrence's thoughts about human nature and the cosmos.[5]

It is likely that he returned to this key text with the intention of rediscovering crucial insights and incorporating them in *Apocalypse*, which was to constitute yet another re-writing of his philosophy. In 1929, after his re-reading, it seems that Lawrence was able to 'make trial' of the 'words and works ... set forth' by Heraclitus, engaging intuitively with them and relating them to his own insights and experience. Literally and figuratively Lawrence avoided reading the same text twice: in 1929 (and probably 1926, as it is likely that the text he possessed then was sent to him three years later) he had the third edition rather than the earlier editions read in 1915 and (probably) 1922. His reading of Burnet later in life – at a new stage in his thinking – meant that the text would have acquired a very different significance.

The pre-Socratic philosophers Anaximander, Heraclitus, Empedocles, Anaxagoras and Pythagoras are of particular relevance when considering the 'philosophy' articulated in *Last Poems,* and the way in which Burnet functioned as intertext. Kalnins's reference to the vision of man in relation to the cosmos conveyed by Lawrence is particularly significant in this context. I have indicated in Chapter 4 how the wandering/wheel antithesis is one that is prevalent throughout *Last Poems*, functioning as a critique of modern man in his relation to the machine. One benefit of side-stepping the relentless advance of the machine by remaining genuinely alone, 'escaping the petrol fumes of human conversation / and the exhaust-smell of people', is that it becomes possible to 'feel the living cosmos softly rocking' (*CP* 646). In several instances, illustrative of Lawrence's cosmopoetics,[6] planetary motion contrasts with mechanistic fixity. Such cosmic motion accomplishes a progression onwards or forwards, rather than a static spinning. It functions as a macrocosmic correlative to the microcosmic wandering evoked in the poems discussed in Chapter 4, in which tentative 'single' beings elude the spinning wheels emblematic of industrial nullity.

Anaximander's Wheels

It is possible to acquire insight into Lawrence's engagement with the fragments incorporated in Burnet's book by considering the late poem 'Astronomical Changes' and Lawrence's other poems concerned with the 'wandering cosmos' in relation to the theories of Anaximander. In 'Astronomical Changes' Lawrence engages specifically with change that is occasioned by the movement of the heavens, explaining this change in terms of the zodiacal signs:

---

[5] *Apocalypse*, ed. Mara Kalnins (London: Penguin, 1995), p. 16. Hereafter *2A*.

[6] I borrow the term directly from Fella Bouchouchi's article 'D.H. Lawrence's Cosmopoetics' in *Etudes Lawrenciennes* no. 30 (2004), pp. 71–81.

The whole great heavens have shifted over, and slowly pushed aside
the Cross, the Virgin, Pisces, the Sacred Fish
that casts its sperm upon the waters, and knows no intercourse;
pushed them all aside, discarded them, make way now for something else.

Even the Pole itself has departed now from the Pole Star
and pivots on the invisible,
while the Pole Star lies aside, like an old axle taken from the wheel.
(*CP* 616)

He is alluding here to the 'Procession of the Equinoxes', discovered by the Greek astronomer Hipparchus in the second century bc and now known to follow a 26,000-year cycle. This astronomical phenomenon describes the Earth's 'wobble' about its polar axis creating the illusion that even the 'fixed' stars are moving because (for instance) the North Pole no longer points to the Pole Star. Astrologically, the change described here is the process of human perception mirroring the heavenly bodies as they appear to move from Pisces into Aquarius.[7] This change is also indicative of a religious shift from the era of Christianity signified by Pisces or 'Jesus of the watery way', to 'something else'. It is a movement beyond the Cross, the Virgin and the wasted sperm of the Sacred Fish to a condition that the poem does not specify, but which might be imagined in terms of the poem 'Whales Weep Not!'. In this poem, the 'wonder of whales' is created by the strong phallus bridging the male and female bodies, and the coldness associated with the Sacred Fish finds its antithesis in the 'dark rainbow bliss' experienced in the procreative act (*CP* 694). The astrological shift, then, signifies the movement from a Christian doctrine of spiritualism to a more pantheistic sense-consciousness (in Lawrence's terms) foregrounding physical experience.

In *Apocalypse*, Lawrence relates the heavenly wheels specifically to paganism, and describes how this pagan association oddly appears in the Bible. It appears in Ezekiel rather than in Revelation itself, for 'In John of Patmos, the "wheels" are missing. They have been superseded long ago by the spheres of the heavens' (*A* 83). Describing Ezekiel's 'great vision', Lawrence writes:

the Kosmokrator stands among the wheels of the heavens, known as the wheels of Anaximander, and we see where we are. We are in the great world of the pagan cosmos. (*A* 82)

Lawrence elaborates on this vision of the heavens, describing its originator, Anaximander, as 'almost the very first of the ancient Greek thinkers, [who] is

---

[7]   For Frederick Carter's discussion of planetary motion and the shift from Pisces into Aquarius see *The Dragon of the Alchemists* (London: Elkin Mathews, 1926; hereafter *DA*), pp. 38–41 and *The Dragon of Revelation* (London: Desmond Harmsworth, 1931), pp. 19–20.

supposed to have invented this "wheel" theory of the heavens in Ionia in the sixth century B.C.' (*A* 83).

Anaximander's heavenly wheels are described in the following passage, quoted in Burnet's *Early Greek Philosophy*, in which Anaximander's theory is expounded by Hippolytos and Aetios:

> The heavenly bodies are wheels of fire separated off from the fire which encircles the world, and surrounded by air. And they have breathing-holes, certain pipe-like openings through which the heavenly bodies are seen ...
>
> Anaximander said the stars were hoop-like compressions of air, full of fire, breathing out flames at a certain point from orifices. The sun was highest of all, after it came the moon, and below these the fixed stars and the planets.
>
> Anaximander said the sun was a ring twenty-eight times the size of the earth, like a cart-wheel with the felloe hollow and full of fire, showing the fire at a certain point, as if through the nozzle of a pair of bellows. (*EGP* 69–70)[8]

This passage, as well as Anaxagoras' perception of the thunder and lightning causing 'a flash by contrast with the darkness of the cloud' (*EGP* 70), obviously lies behind Lawrence's response to the wheel-conception of the heavenly bodies in *Apocalypse*:

> Strange and fascinating are the great revolving wheels of the sky, made of dense air or night-cloud and filled with the blazing cosmic fire, which fire peeps through or blazes through at certain holes in the felloes of the wheels, and forms the blazing sun or the pointed stars. All the orbs are little holes in the black wheel which is full of fire: and there is wheel within wheel, revolving differently. (*A* 82)

It is interesting that when Lawrence considers the motion of the heavenly wheels he has to refer to their motion as 'complex' as well as 'orderly', and to accentuate this complexity by picturing many a sub-stratum of wheels: 'wheel within wheel, revolving differently'. He is probably adding a later understanding of revolving spheres here: one which enables him to avoid creating the visual impression of a wheel – or group of wheels – turning continually and unswervingly in an orderly,

---

[8] In the third (1920) edition the equivalent passages read as follows:

The heavenly bodies are a wheel of fire, separated off from the fire of the world, and surrounded by air. And there are breathing-holes, certain pipe-like passages, at which the heavenly bodies show themselves ...

The heavenly bodies were hoop-like compressions of air, full of fire, breathing out flames at a certain point through orifices ...

The sun was a wheel 28 times the size of the earth, like a chariot-wheel with the felloe hollow, full of fire, showing the fire at a certain point through an orifice, as through the nozzle of a pair of bellows. (*3EGP* 66–7)

predetermined rotation. In 'Astronomical Changes' it is exactly such an orderly rotation that the Pole manages to evade. The Pole has departed from its fixed point or axle and now 'pivots on the invisible': a movement that suggests progression. The Pole Star (fixed, unlike the wandering planets which deviate from a set course) is left as merely the 'old axle taken from the wheel': the superseded emblem of a rigidity from which the Pole has been liberated.

In many of the *Last Poems*, Anaximander's 'wheel theory' and the concept of 'wandering', liberated heavenly bodies are seen as irreconcilable:

> Oh, do not tell me the heavens as well are a wheel.
> For every revolution of the earth around the sun
> is a footstep onwards, onwards, we know not whither
> and we do not care,
> but a step onwards in untravelled space,
> for the earth, like the sun, is a wanderer. (*CP* 713)

Here, the wandering of the heavenly bodies has the 'strange' fascination that in *Apocalypse* Lawrence attributes to the 'revolving wheels of the sky'. The poem, appropriately entitled 'The Wandering Cosmos', begins in a declamatory style reminiscent of the pre-Socratic fragments. It launches a direct challenge to the notion of planetary motion as cyclical and hence wheel-like, asserting instead that the revolution of the earth around the sun must be seen as a step onwards: a step that remains undefined and spontaneous, as the term 'wandering' suggests. While either the Robot or the wheel is identified as the unit of evil in earlier poems, here we might identify the cosmic footstep as the unit of life.

Heraclitus and Living Change

> The gods, who are life, and the fluidity of living change
> leave the old ones fixed to their ugly, cogged self-will
> which turns on and on, the same, and is hell on earth. (*CP* 662)

Lawrence's views on the duality and fluidity inherent in life were profoundly influenced by Heraclitus, the pre-Socratic philosopher to whom he responded most enthusiastically. On his initial reading of Burnet, Lawrence had been impressed by Heraclitus to the extent that he vowed to 'write out Herakleitos [*sic*], on tablets of bronze' (*L* ii 364).[9] In this letter to Bertrand Russell, written circa 14 July 1915, Lawrence offers a political alternative to Russell's socialism, involving the establishment of an 'aristocracy of people who have wisdom', governed by a 'Ruler' or 'Kaiser' (*L* ii 364). Lawrence casts Heraclitus in this role, perceiving

---

[9] This seems to indicate a process of engraving rather than simply inscription – '*in* tablets of bronze' –, perhaps in the manner of Blake's designs.

him as a new equivalent to the ancient religious prophet or seer like Moses. He then proceeds to write out parts of Heraclitus, albeit on paper rather than tablets of bronze, choosing fragments which reflect and support his anti-democratic campaign:

> 'And it is law, too, to obey the counsel of one.'[10]
>
> 'For what thought or wisdom have they? They follow the poets and take the crowd as their teacher, knowing not that there are many bad and few good. For even the best of them choose one thing above all others, immortal glory among mortals: while most of them are glutted like beasts.'[11]
>
> 'They vainly purify themselves by defiling themselves with blood.'[12]
>
> 'If you do not expect the unexpected, you will not find it. For it is hard to [be] sought out, and difficult.'[13] (*L* ii 364–65)

In this letter Lawrence does not only quote Heraclitus directly, but also slips into the style of the fragments in order to articulate his own thoughts, which, like those of Heraclitus, chop and change between different preoccupations:

> Also we must unite together, not work apart.
>
> I am rid of all my christian religiosity. It was only a muddiness. You need not mistrust me. In fact you don't.
>
> In a fortnight now I shall come to town.
>
> Murry, on the Sunday, was himself again ...
>
> It is only the unexpected can help us now. (*L* ii 365)

Lawrence responds overtly to the inherent wisdom of Heraclitus' discourse, yet in adopting the style of these fragments he reveals that his intertextual response has been artistic as well as conceptual or ideological. He is not content simply to read, attempt to decipher and assimilate: he must engage at a deeper level in order to participate in the experience of this mode of writing.

It is unsurprising that Lawrence was struck by these fragments, which have the appeal of the enigmatic Blakean aphorisms found, for instance, in 'The Marriage of Heaven and Hell'. The mysterious nature of the fragments is emphasized by Burnet:

---

[10] Heraclitus, fr. 110 (*3EGP* 140).

[11] Heraclitus, fr. 111 (*3EGP* 140).

[12] Heraclitus, fr. 129, 130 (*3EGP* 141).

[13] Heraclitus, fr. 7 (*3EGP* 133).

> The style of Herakleitos [*sic*] is proverbially obscure, and got him the nickname
> of 'the Dark' in antiquity. He employs images without any indication of the point
> of comparison (*EGP* 131)[14]

Burnet refers to Heraclitus' use of irony, oxymoron and word-play as well as the
oracular style which tends to lead to semantic confusion. He points to a veiled
meaning, perhaps because Heraclitus wanted to avoid accusations of impiety
(Schuster's suggestion) or because he wanted to hide his opinions from the
'profane vulgar' (Teichmüller's view: *EGP* 131–2). If this is the case, then the
fragments may have appealed to Lawrence as texts needing to be deciphered: a
kind of unsealing in which visionary implications are discovered and revealed.

Burnet also gives an alternative explanation of the text's enigmatic quality:

> The truth is simply that there was as yet no such thing as a clear scientific prose
> style. Herakleitos [*sic*] could not find any but metaphorical language in which to
> express the new thoughts which had taken possession of his mind. (*EGP* 132)[15]

It may be true that if Heraclitus 'does not go out of his way to make his meaning
clear, neither does he hide it' (*EGP* 132). The meaning or meanings may not
be veiled, but the stylistic restraints experienced by the author and his refusal
to engage in conscious clarification mean that the text requires active – perhaps
creative and imaginative – interpretation. Heraclitus' appeal for Lawrence did not
only lie in his obscurity, however, but in the implication of the 'words and works'
set forth in his fragments: particularly those which relate to the cosmos and to human
consciousness. Heraclitus' conception of both cosmos and consciousness is reliant
on the paradoxical belief that 'Oneness' arises from the co-existence of opposite
tensions, while stability is the product not of stillness but of constant motion, or
'flux'. According to Heraclitus, the apparent stability of the cosmos stems from the
simultaneously occurring 'upward' and 'downward' paths, in which one element is
constantly changing and becoming another. Earth takes the upward path, changing
to water, to air and then to fire, while fire is simultaneously taking the 'downward
path' and replenishing the supply of earth (*EGP* 153–4). Although the quantities
of each element may vary slightly, the balance is not significantly disturbed, and
no single element can exceed its measure. As long as the upward and downward
paths remain in polarity, the elements are held within limits, and there will never be
universal collapse.

---

[14]   In the third edition the passage reads 'The style of Herakeitos [*sic*] is proverbially
obscure, and, at a later date, got him the nickname of "the Dark" ' (*3EGP* 132). The next
sentence from the first edition is omitted.

[15]   In the third edition Heraclitus' obscurity is attributed rather to a consciously
adopted oracular style, and to a 'headstrong temperament', which 'sometimes led him into
incompleteness and inconsistencies of statement' (*3EGP* 132).

Lawrence's idea of the 'fluidity of living change' – the alternative to robotic fixity – may originally have derived from the Heraclitean conception of the cosmos in flux. Heraclitus' emblem for the paradox of 'flux within stability' is an ever-flowing, ever-changing stream or river:

> You cannot step twice into the same rivers; for fresh waters are ever flowing in upon you. (*EGP* 136; *3EGP* 136)[16]

Ostensibly a river is always in the same place, with little deviation except from a particular water-level. Yet it is constantly moving, flowing inexorably onwards: it appears to be changeless, yet it is perpetually changing. The river is paradoxically 'moving still': an oxymoron that Heraclitus applies not only to the *elemental* 'flux within stability', but also to the process of flux as it is embodied within humankind.[17] In flowing onwards while simultaneously 'wandering' (streamlets are said to wander or meander), the river might be considered to adhere to the Heraclitean paradox expressed in Fragment 83: 'It finds rest in change' (*EGP* 139).[18] Rather like the shoal described in 'The Flying-Fish' in which the porpoises are constantly moving and changing position within an apparently unaltering outer shape,[19] the water flowing between river-banks has ceaseless motion without the appearance of alteration, and is constantly self-replenishing.

In the poem 'False Democracy and Real', Lawrence uses the image of a running stream to designate those who remain distinct from the industrialized masses by looking – and flowing – towards 'the gods':

> The few must look into the eyes of the gods...
> and the stream is towards the gods, not backwards, towards man. (*CP* 650)

'The gods' here symbolize the 'marvellous rich world of contact and sheer fluid beauty' ('fluid' being a significant word) which can be attained when 'man has escaped from the barbed-wire entanglement / of his own ideas and his own mechanical devices' (*CP* 667). Through awareness of the gods it is possible to

---

[16] The abbreviation *3EGP* indicates the third edition of Burnet's book (1920).

[17] In his analysis of the Heraclitean fragments, Burnet quotes the 'obviously Heraclitean' sentence 'All things are passing, both human and divine, upwards and downwards by exchanges', and interprets it as follows:

We are just as much in perpetual flux as anything else in the world. We are and are not the same for two consecutive instants ... The fire in us is perpetually becoming water, and the water earth; but, as the opposite process goes on simultaneously, we appear to remain the same (*3EGP* 151–2).

[18] In the third edition fr. 83 reads 'It rests by changing' (*3EGP* 139).

[19] D.H. Lawrence, 'The Flying-Fish', in *St Mawr and Other Stories*, ed. Brian Finney (Cambridge: Cambridge University Press, 1983), p. 221.

experience 'a going outward into the worlds of *becoming*, of ceaseless change and transformation'.[20]

In the essay 'Poetry of the Present' (1919) Lawrence had associated the fluidity of 'becoming' with poetry that is alive, spontaneous and flexible in its capturing of the 'immediate present, the Now':

> Here, in this very instant moment, up bubbles the stream of time, out of the wells of futurity, flowing on to the oceans of the past. The source, the issue, the creative quick. (*SP* 268)

The virtue of poetry of the present (as expressed in this essay) is that it exists in creative flux: it ought to be transient and flexible rather than permanent and rigid. Lawrence wrote of the *Pansies* poetry collection: 'I offer a bunch of pansies, not a wreath of *immortelles*', and warned his readers not to 'nail the pansy down. You won't keep it any better if you do' (*SP* 291). His late aphoristic poems, rather like the Heraclitean fragments as well as Pascal's *Pensées,* La Bruyère's *Caractères* and La Rochefoucauld's *Maximes*[21] are brief, enigmatic and mutually contradictory, in keeping with the unimpaired flowing or meandering of creative composition.

The poem 'Change' asserts the necessity of a passage through the 'waters of oblivion' before it is possible to become essentially 'different':

> Do you think it is easy to change?
> Ah, it is very hard to change and be different.
> It means passing through the waters of oblivion. (*CP* 727)

Here, the waters clearly relate to the 'sea of change' described in the long draft poem 'Ship of Death' (in the 'Nettles' notebook), deriving from the mythological river Styx. In this poem, it is necessary to be dipped into oblivion in order to emerge or be reincarnated, so that 'the whole thing starts again' (*CP* 720). Similarly the poem 'Phoenix' states the need to be 'dipped' into oblivion (as Achilles was immersed in the Styx and left invulnerable except for the undipped heel) before change can ensue:

> Are you willing to be sponged out, erased, cancelled,
> made nothing?
> Are you willing to be made nothing?
> dipped into oblivion?
>
> If not, you will never really change. (*CP* 728)

---

[20]   James M. Pryse, *The Apocalypse Unsealed* (New York: J.M. Pryse, 1910), p. 13. Hereafter *AU*.

[21]   See Chapter 2, pp. 13–14.

Oblivion is again envisaged as the 'sea of change', which may be related to the Heraclitean river embodying the paradox of 'rest within change'.

In 'Shadows' the 'changing phases of man's life' occasion 'snatches of lovely oblivion, and snatches of renewal' (*CP* 727). Life's changing phases are seen to be determined by the cyclical or diurnal course of nature – earth's lapse and renewal – so that sickness oscillates with regenerated health. This oscillation enables the narrator to be sent forth on a new morning, 'a new man', while in 'The Ship of Death' the resurrected body emerges 'strange and lovely' (*CP* 720) as if it has experienced a Shakespearean sea-change into 'something new and strange'.[22]

The lapse/renewal and sickness/health dichotomies are representative of the duality that Lawrence stresses in *Last Poems* and elsewhere: 'All existence is dual, and surging towards a consummation into being'.[23] In his emphasis on duality (and on strife in particular) he follows Heraclitus, who taught that all creation is dual but emerges from a primary absolute. Lawrence's emphasis on 'strife' as resulting from the creative tension of contraries is evident in 'The Crown' and in late poems such as 'Strife':

> When strife is a thing of two
> each knows the other in struggle
> and the conflict is a communion
> a twoness.
>
> But when strife is a thing of one
> a single ego striving for its own ends
> and beating down resistances
> then strife is evil, because it is not strife. (*CP* 714)

Here, strife 'of two' paradoxically unites through conflict, while strife 'of one' merely indicates disharmony within an ego-bound, aggressive individual. In the short prose prologue to the 'Reptiles' section of *Birds, Beasts and Flowers* (discussed at length in Chapter 9), Lawrence quotes Heraclitus' fragment 'Homer was wrong in saying: "Would that strife might perish from among gods and men!" He did not see that he was praying for the destruction of the universe; for, if his prayer were heard, all things would pass away' (*EGP* 136; *3EGP* 136). This fragment, and also Heraclitus' statement that 'It is opposition that brings things together' (*EGP* 137),[24] link Heraclitus with Anaximander, Empedocles and Aristotle, who also stress the potentially positive or creative power of strife. Aristotle, for instance, asserts that

---

[22] See Chapter 2, pp. 41–2.

[23] D.H. Lawrence, 'Reflections on the Death of a Porcupine', in *Reflections on the Death of a Porcupine and Other Essays*, ed. Michael Herbert (Cambridge: Cambridge University Press, 1988), p. 359.

[24] In the third edition fr. 46 reads 'It is the opposite which is good for us' (*3EGP* 136).

'while Strife is assumed as the cause of destruction, and does, in fact, destroy the Sphere, it really gives birth to everything else in so doing' (*EGP* 246; *3EGP* 233); while he also says that Empedocles 'holds that the world is in a similar condition *now in the period of Strife* as formerly in that of Love' (*EGP* 249; *3EGP* 234–5).

Anaximander highlights the functioning of strife and opposition specifically within and between the elements:

> Anaximander was struck, it would seem, by the opposition and strife between the things which go to make up the world; the warm fire was opposed to the cold air, the dry earth to the liquid sea. (*EGP* 51)[25]

Similarly Empedocles considers the way in which Strife brings about the birth of sun, earth, sky and sea, while enabling them to remain distinct as a 'mixture':

> [The elements] differ as far as possible in their origin and mixture and the forms imprinted on each, being altogether unaccustomed to come together, and very hostile, under the influence of Strife, since it has wrought their birth. (*EGP* 227)[26]

The elements thus represent the opposition or balance in the cosmos that Lawrence had considered to be so significant since first reading Burnet in 1915, and which finally became the focus of his 'elemental' poems, for which the fragments of Empedocles in Burnet provide the key source.

Empedocles and the Four Roots

Lawrence's poem 'The Four' indicates the nature and significance of the elements he perceives as omnipresent:

> To our senses, the elements are four
> and have ever been, and will ever be
> for they are the elements of life, of poetry, and of perception,
> the four Great Ones, the Four Roots, the First Four
> of Fire and the Wet, Earth and the wide Air of the world.
> To find the other many elements, you must go to the laboratory

---

[25] In the third edition this passage reads: 'Anaximander started, it would seem, from the strife between the opposites which go to make up the world; the warm was opposed to the cold, the dry to the wet.' (*3EGP* 53–4)

[26] In the third edition this passage is printed as part of fragment 22: 'Those things, again, that differ most in origin, mixture and the forms imprinted on each, are most hostile, being altogether unaccustomed to unite and very sorry by the bidding of Strife, since it hath wrought their birth.' (*3EGP* 209)

and hunt them down.
But the Four we have always with us, they are our world.
Or rather, they have us with them. (*CP* 706)

While his reference to the 'other many elements' reveals a broader scientific awareness, Lawrence indicates that 'the Four' are the sources of all life and creativity. They have the capacity to dictate or order our lives, accepting or rejecting us: 'they have us with them'. The reference to the four elements as the four 'Roots' is one directly derived from Empedocles:

> The elements or 'roots of all things' which Empedokles [*sic*] assumed were the four which have since become traditional, Fire, Air, Earth, and Water. (*EGP* 240)[27]

According to Burnet, Empedocles was 'quite confident that his "four roots" were an exhaustive enumeration of the elements': a conviction that derives from 'his belief that they sufficiently accounted for all the qualities presented by the world to the senses; Fire accounted for light and heat, Water for darkness and cold, Earth for solidity and hardness' (*EGP* 244).[28] Empedocles describes 'how, out of Water and Earth and Air and Fire mingled together, arose the colours and forms of all those mortal things that have been fitted together by Aphrodite' (*EGP* 227; *3EGP* 215–16). The significance of the elements, as far as mankind is concerned, is emphasized by his assertion that 'by these do men think and feel pleasure and pain' (*EGP* 232; *3EGP* 220).

Burnet quotes Aristotle's statement, made twice, that Empedocles treats his four elements in fact as only two, setting fire in opposition to all the rest. As Burnet asserts, this conclusion has no grounds whatsoever when considering Empedocles' general theory of the elements. Burnet assumes that Aristotle is merely referring to Empedocles' theory of the origin of the world, in which Fire plays the leading role as a source of motion: this would be expected, for it does so in all early cosmologies (*EGP* 244; *3EGP* 231). It is Heraclitus, rather, who places the greatest emphasis on Fire, identifying it as a primary substance at the heart of all existence:

---

[27] In the third edition this passage reads: 'The "four roots" of all things (fr. 6) which Empedocles assumed—Fire, Air, Earth, and Water—seem to have been arrived at by making each of the traditional "opposites"– hot and cold, wet and dry –into a *thing* which is real in the full Parmenidean sense of the word.' (*3EGP* 228)

[28] This appears in condensed form in the third edition (*3EGP* 231). The quotation continues: 'We have no record of the qualities ascribed to Air, except that it receives the epithet "bright." '

> This order, which is the same in all things, no one of gods or men has made;
> but it was ever, is now, and ever shall be an everliving Fire, fixed measures of it
> kindling and fixed measures going out. (*EGP* 135)[29]

He also asserts in Fragment 22 that 'All things are exchanged for Fire, and Fire for all things' (*EGP* 135; *3EGP* 135) and in Fragment 26 that 'Fire will come upon and lay hold of all things' (*EGP* 135).[30]

The significance of fire in Lawrence's late poems is evident in 'Phoenix', in which the mythic bird is burnt alive, but the burning only results in re-emergence from the flames and renewal of the phoenix's youth:

> The phoenix renews her youth
> only when she is burnt, burnt alive, burnt down
> to hot and flocculent ash. (*CP* 728)

The conflagration is a source not of destruction but of revitalization. In the poem 'Death', fire is necessary to soften the obstinate men and women who possess 'hardened souls' and resist their own demise:

> their hardened souls are washed with fire, and washed and seared
> till they are softened back to life-stuff again, against which they hardened themselves.
> (*CP* 663)

As in 'Phoenix', continuation or reawakening is implied here, this time by the softening of stubborn resistance that the fire accomplishes.

The phrase 'washed with fire' hints at a crucial dualism, referred to sometimes as 'fire and the wet', which informs many of the 'elemental' *Last Poems*. Water in these poems usually takes the form of salt-water – the sea – whose constant capacity for replenishment is emphasized in the poem 'Kissing and Horrid Strife':

> But still I know that life is for delight
> and for bliss
> as now when the tiny wavelets of the sea
> tip the morning light on edge, and spill it with delight
> to show how inexhaustible it is (*CP* 709)

The same inexhaustibility is evident in 'Mana of the Sea', where it is shown to be both more wonderful and more paradoxical. It is expressed interrogatively, the

---

[29]   Fr. 20 is altered in the third edition: 'This world, which is the same for all, no one of gods or men has made; but it was ever, is now, and ever shall be an ever-living Fire, with measures of it kindling, and measures going out.' (*3EGP* 134)

[30]   In the third edition this fragment reads: 'Fire in its advance will judge and convict all things.' (*3EGP* 135)

rhetoric inviting affirmation: 'Do you see the sea, breaking itself to bits against the islands / yet remaining unbroken, the level great sea?' (*CP* 705).

In 'Mana of the Sea', a metamorphic sea-change is described which enables the human being to be seen differently, and recognized for what s/he potentially is:

> And is my body ocean, ocean
> whose power runs to the shores along my arms
> and breaks in the foamy hands, whose power rolls out
> to the white-treading waves of two salt feet?
>
> I am the sea, I am the sea! (*CP* 705)

The metamorphosis depicted is explicable by reference to the pre-Socratic relationship between man and nature. In *Apocalypse* Lawrence writes very similarly: 'I am part of the sun as my eye is part of me. That I am part of the earth my feet know perfectly, and my blood is part of the sea' (*A* 149). Lawrence uses the 'elemental' nature of those who connect with the natural world as one pole in a crucial dichotomy, the other pole being the modern men 'who don't hear the sea's uneasiness!' (*CP* 643). The crucial point is the failure of modern man to be attuned to the sea, to hear its rhythms and its voice. The consequence is that, in its turn, the sea (like the rest of the planet) becomes threatening: hence, 'uneasy'.

In his challenging and fragmentary writing, Lawrence offers the perspective that men who are vivid and truly living are those who are in tune with the voice of the elements, and thus are able to embody the duality or opposition that provides the necessary contraries in life:

> Oh men, living men, vivid men, ocean and fire
> don't give any more life to the machines! (*CP* 639)

The ocean/fire dichotomy, and the potential for co-existence of these elements within a cosmic balance, is fundamental. In the poem 'Whales Weep Not!' the pagan, restless ocean is both hot and fertile:

> They say the sea is cold, but the sea contains
> the hottest blood of all, and the wildest, the most urgent ...
>
> And they rock, and they rock, through the sensual ageless ages ...
> and in the tropics tremble they with love
> and roll with massive, strong desire, like gods. (*CP* 694)

This sea simultaneously possesses the qualities of Heraclitean water and fire. It is within such an elemental balance that procreation, or the Blakean progression beyond contraries, can occur.

The actual residue of the opposition between fire and sea is 'salt', as expressed by Lawrence in the poem with this title:

> Salt is scorched water that the sun has scorched
> into substance and flaky whiteness
> in the eternal opposition
> between the two great ones, Fire, and the Wet.[31] (*CP* 705)

In 'The Boundary Stone' this crucial product of opposition is further contemplated. Salt is 'the boundary mark between Fire that burns, and the Wet', also referred to as a 'white stone of limits' and a 'landmark' (*CP* 706). Fire and the Wet become 'the two great and moving Ones', while the 'boundary' of salt situates blood and sweat within this dichotomy. Empedocles, between a reference to 'The sea with its silly tribe of fertile fish' (a conception rather different from Lawrence's, but one which Lawrence arguably engages with and alters) and to 'Sea, the sweat of the earth', sandwiches the aphorism 'Salt was solidified by the impact of the sun's beams' (*EGP* 226).[32] Empedocles proceeds then to give an account of a situation in which Strife retires to the 'extreme boundary' while Love is situated at 'the centre of the whirl' (*EGP* 226). In Lawrence's late poetry, salt begins as a boundary or 'limit' – the synthesis that keeps the antithetical Fire and the Wet in appropriate balance – but it assumes another significance in 'Spilling the Salt'. Here, salt is associated with the 'sunderers' or 'watchers, the dividers, those swift ones with dark sharp wings' who are in opposition to the benevolent 'angels of creation' (*CP* 706). Salt, then, plays the role of counteracting a superfluity of good, and preserving a necessary balance.[33]

It becomes clear that Lawrence is engaging with the pre-Socratic categories and vocabulary, but exploring and redefining their terms and concepts according to the development of his own poetry. Empedocles' elements, for instance, are not only

---

[31] In *The Rainbow*, almost contemporaneous with Lawrence's first reading of Burnet, salt is described as follows: 'The salt, bitter passion of the sea, its indifference to the earth, its swinging, definite motion, its strength, its attack, and its salt burning, seemed to provoke [Ursula] to a pitch of madness, tantalising her with vast suggestions of fulfilment', *The Rainbow*, ed. Mark Kinkead-Weekes (Cambridge: Cambridge University Press, 1989), p. 443.

[32] In the third edition fr. 74, 'Leading the songless tribe of fertile fish' (*3EGP* 216), is separated from its surrounding fragments, which are printed earlier as fr. 55 and 56 (*3EGP* 214).

[33] The association of salt with the 'sunderers'/'angels of creation' dichotomy hints at a biblical context; and it does seem that the pre-Socratics provide terms of reference for allusions to the elements that John Oman and James Pryse (as well as Lawrence) identify in Revelation. For example, Oman indicates that the 'living creatures' who pour out the vials of wrath over the earth represent the four elements, thus showing 'that these judgments are to take place by what we would call natural causes', in John Oman, *Book of Revelation* (Cambridge: Cambridge University Press, 1923; hereafter *BR*), p. 124. See also *AU* 11.

considered in such poems as 'The Four', but also provide Lawrence with a way of characterizing privileged human beings, who are seen as literally 'elemental'. The elemental few are described as 'men of the wind and rain / men of the fire and rock' (*CP* 637), while, in 'The Cross', it is necessary to 'serve that which is flamey or pure and watery or / swift wind or sound ringing rock / that which is elemental and of the substantial gods in man' (*CP* 637). It is the elements, here, that enable the Lawrentian gods of *Last Poems* momentarily to take substance.

Anaxagoras and Pythagoras; A Return of Returns

Lawrence used the pre-Socratics as source material, stimulus and provocation to think outside the categories of Roman and Christian civilizations. The diverse fragments and commentaries collected by Burnet frequently offer conflicting ideas and interpretations, and Lawrence makes no attempt to argue for one against the other, or to establish some kind of synthesis. Rather he takes 'hints' from the various philosophers, using them as textual springboards for his own imagination, sometimes accepting and sometimes rejecting them.

An example of profound disagreement with a notable pre-Socratic figure is evident in the poem 'Anaxagoras'. This poem engages with Anaxagoras' belief that 'all things will be in everything; nor is it possible for them to be apart, but all things have a portion of everything' (*EGP* 285; *3EGP* 259). For Lawrence, claiming that he is 'part of the sun' and that his 'blood is part of the sea', this fragment might have proved useful, yet he chose to dispute and reject it. Lawrence engages specifically with the following example provided by Burnet: 'Even snow, Anaxagoras affirmed, was black; that is, even the white contains a certain portion of the opposite quality' (*EGP* 288; *3EGP* 264). Lawrence's objection to this lies in the fact that the natural phenomenon – snow – has become (as he says in his 'Whitman' essay) 'Dead mentalised':[34]

> When Anaxagoras says: Even snow is black!
> he is taken by the scientists very seriously
> because he is enunciating a 'principle', a 'law'
> that all things are mixed, and therefore the purest white snow
> has in it an element of blackness. (*CP* 708)

The poem continues with Lawrence's critique of the 'scientific' conception of snow, reached by abstract theorizing rather than sensory perception:

---

[34]   D.H. Lawrence, 'Whitman' (final version: 1923) in *Studies in Classic American Literature*, ed. Ezra Greenspan, Lindeth Vasey and John Worthen (Cambridge: Cambridge University Press, 2003), p. 150. Similar terminology is used in an exchange between Ursula, Hermione and Birkin: see *WL* 40–45.

> I call it mental conceit and mystification
> and nonsense, for pure snow is white to us
> white and white and only white
> with a lovely bloom of whiteness upon white
> in which the soul delights and the senses
> have an experience of bliss. (*CP* 708)

Here, it is the response of the senses or sense-consciousness that is seen as important, as this reflects an attunement with the beauty and wonder of nature.

It is not, however, that Lawrence is formulating his own dogmatic principle, asserting against all-comers that snow is always and inevitably white, for he goes on to say:

> And in the shadow of the sun the snow is blue, so blue-aloof
> with a hint of the frozen bells of the scylla flower
> but never the ghost of a glimpse of Anaxagoras's funeral black. (*CP* 708)

The blueness of snow perceived here is again a direct result of sensory perception: this is offered as an appropriate response to the natural world for it is poetically observant rather than dogmatic or scientifically analytical. Perception indicates that snow *is* blue, in its depths, to the senses, while the elision 'blue-aloof' reflects its dignified separation from humankind. The 'funeral black' of Anaxagoras is absent entirely from this sensory response. It is described in this way not only because black is linked to funerals, but to reveal that the scientific laws or principles showing that snow is (in part) black are the death of sense-consciousness, and therefore the death of man's actual relationship with the cosmos.

Yet it would be wrong to generalize from this poem and assume that Lawrence was at this time in rebellion against 'science' and 'laws' per se. Such a generalization could easily be countered through reference to *Apocalypse* and in particular the fragment 'Apocalypsis II', in which Lawrence discusses the 'science' of Pythagorean numbering at great length, and with evident fascination. I will give a brief account of Lawrence's engagement with Pythagoras as articulated in his prose, before discussing the way in which number symbolism informs *Last Poems,* focusing on the poem 'Return of Returns'.

In the fragment 'Apocalypsis II' (written after *Last Poems*),[35] Lawrence engages with the question of whether 'laws' can be said to govern the universe. In this instance he interrogates 'laws' in relation to Pythagorean numbering: in relation, for instance, to the statement that 4 pebbles multiplied by 4 pebbles is 16.[36]

---

[35]   'Apocalypsis II' is included by Mara Kalnins in an Appendix to *Apocalypse and the Writings on Revelation* (Cambridge: Cambridge University Press, 1980).

[36]   In the poem 'Tortoise Shell', from *Birds, Beasts and Flowers*, Lawrence writes: 'It needed Pythagoras to see life playing with counters on the living back', and describes the tortoise shell as 'the eternal dome of mathematical law' (*CP* 355).

Trying to ascertain whether the reality of the conclusion lies in the mathematical 'laws' operative or in the fact of the pebbles themselves, he elicits the following generalization:

> The 'laws' don't 'govern' the universe. The 'laws' of the universe are only the more subtle properties of 'things'. (*A* 197)

Even if the laws do not govern the universe, however, Lawrence is driven to respond to the question 'Which "rules", the law, or the substantial object?' with 'The answer is, of course, that neither rules' (*A* 197). From this dialogue it becomes evident that Lawrence's quarrel with Anaxagoras might give a false impression of his views regarding the 'scientific', of which he is rarely so dismissive. Lawrence's fascination with Pythagoras reveals a very different response to a specifically mathematical conception of the universe, which he argues in *Apocalypse* is by no means at odds with an imaginative response.

Lawrence's acknowledgement of the significance of science is revealed in his assertions, in *Apocalypse*, that 'early science is a source of the purest and oldest religion' (*A* 131); and 'The first scientists … are very near to the old symbolists' (*A* 135). He argues that scientists can achieve an analogous state of 'supreme religious consciousness' to that of symbolists, but by a different route:

> Both ways end in the same place, the absolute somewhere or the absolute nowhere. But the method of approach is different. There is the method of association and unison, and the method of contrast and distinction. (*A* 193)

Mathematical investigation need not be divorced either from the senses or from that which is 'elemental', for according to Aristotle 'mathematical numbers' were 'not "separated from the objects of sense" ' (*EGP* 308).[37] Again, according to Aristotle, 'the Pythagoreans held that the elements of number were the elements of things, and, therefore, that things were numbers' (*EGP* 307).[38] Numbers were not merely abstractions for the Pythagoreans, and they held a fascination for Lawrence that compelled him to pause between discussing the first and second halves of Revelation in order to devote sections XVII, XVIII, XIX, XX and XXI of *Apocalypse* (as well as 'Apocalypsis II') to a discussion of them.[39]

Kalnins emphasizes Lawrence's attraction to 'Pythagoras' mathematical triangle of ten, the tetraktys of the dekad'. She highlights the Jungian significance of this symbol as a 'mandala' or 'emblem standing for the wholeness and integration

---

[37] In the third edition Burnet paraphrases Aristotle, replacing 'objects of sense' with 'things of sense' (*3EGP* 287).

[38] The third edition equivalent is almost identical: see *3EGP* 286.

[39] Lawrence's late interest in mathematics and numbering may be related back to the maths prize awarded to him at Nottingham High School, and to the young Tom Brangwen's aptitude for this particular subject.

of the self' (2*A* 22). Numbers, in Jung's interpretation, are seen as 'an aspect of the physically real as well as of the psychically imaginary' and are 'vehicles for psychic processes in the unconscious'.[40] In *The Philosophy of Plotinus*, read by Lawrence in 1929 (*DH* 109), W.R. Inge describes the tetractys and its significance for the Pythagoreans:

> [It was] a symbol consisting of a pyramid of ten units, tapering to its apex from a base of four. This symbol, they held, contained the 'fountain and root of ever-springing nature.' It was a picture of the processional movement ... of life, out of unity into plurality. The tetractys was a figure both of the Orphic 'cycle of birth,' ... and of the 'processional' movement just mentioned.[41]

In Inge's account, the symbol is interesting in its signification both of a cyclic and a processional movement: in this it resembles the planets conceived by Lawrence in terms of Anaximander's wheels, yet able to wander and take steps onward.

The propensity of Pythagorean numbers to remain physical rather than (or as well as) abstract/cerebral is emphasized by Burnet's references to the pebbles which were essential to the initial counting systems employed by the Pythagoreans. Burnet refers to Aristotle's description of the methodology employed by the Pythagorean Eurtyos (disciple of Philalaos):

> In order to find the number of anything he used to set pebbles side by side in the shape of the thing and then count them. This was simply a graphic way of showing how many dimensions a thing had, taking a single pebble as one dimension. (*EGP* 314)[42]

In *Apocalypse* Lawrence stresses the significance of pebble counting, which shows how 'the ancients saw number concrete' (*A* 130) – the number three (for instance) being three pebbles. The physicality of the pebbles (as opposed to the insubstantial '3') is instrumental in revealing the symbolic aspect of the number in question. The integrity of the number three, for example, can be observed in a row of three pebbles, in which 'the central stone [is] poised and in perfect balance between the two, like the body of a bird between the two wings' (*A* 130). Lawrence goes on to observe that 'even as late as the third century, this was felt as the perfect or divine condition of being' (*A* 130).

---

[40] C.G. Jung, *Civilisation in Transition, the Collected Works*, vol. 10, trans. R.F.C. Hull (London: Routledge, 1964), p. 424 (quoted in 2*A* 22).

[41] W.R. Inge, *The Philosophy of Plotinus*, third edition, vol. 1 (London: Longmans, 1929), p. 85.

[42] In the third edition Burnet says of Eurytos 'he used to give the numbers of all sorts of things, such as horses and men, and that he demonstrated these by arranging pebbles in a certain way' (3*EGP* 100).

Lawrence felt compelled to find out what number symbolism meant to the ancient mind as a result, partly, of observing that the whole scheme of the Apocalypse is 'entirely based on the numbers seven, four and three' (*A* 130). He finds that 'Three is the number of things divine, and four is the number of creation' (*A* 133); while 'The numbers four and three together make up the sacred number seven: the cosmos with its god. The Pythagoreans called it "the number of the right time" ' (*A* 136). Yet he asserts that the number seven has always, 'from the beginning', been semi-sacred 'because it is the number of the seven ancient planets, which began with sun and moon, and included the five great "wandering" stars: Jupiter, Venus, Mercury, Mars and Saturn' (*A* 136).[43] Thus the number has a resonance that pre-dates its Apocalyptic use and derives from the star-lore or star-cult that underlies much of the symbolism in Revelation.

In *Apocalypse* Lawrence emphasizes the astral significance of the number seven:

> Fate, fortune, destiny, character, everything depended on the stars, which meant, on the seven planets. The seven planets were the seven Rulers of the heavens, and they fixed the fate of man irrevocably, inevitably. (*A* 137)

The significance of the number seven is one that Burnet is keen to assert in his chapter on the Pythagoreans, although he emphasizes the capricious or superstitious nature of the process by which a particular number was supposed to acquire significance through diverse associations:

> Opportunity was identified with the number Seven on various fanciful grounds derived from the importance of that number in human life. The second teeth come at the seventh year, puberty at the fourteenth, the beard at the twenty-first. Besides, as Aristotle ironically adds, there are seven vowels, seven strings in the lyre, seven Pleiads, and Seven against Thebes! (*EGP* 316)[44]

Lawrence might have identified such associations as part of the unfortunate process – described in *Apocalypse* – by which a genuine symbol, with its powerful astronomical or astrological import, can degenerate into superstition, and thus forfeit its potency.

According to Lawrence, parts of the biblical Apocalypse are infused with the ancient meaning and significance afforded symbolically to specific numbers, while in other parts the number-symbolism has become merely superficial or superstitious. Lawrence identifies a process of degradation within Revelation, in which the number seven progressively loses its 'divine' implications:

---

[43]   Cf. 'The seven planets or "wandering" stars that were seen to circle in the Ecliptic path round the earth are, in their order of apparent distance, Saturn, the furthest, then Jupiter, Mars, the Sun, Venus, Mercury and the Moon', in Carter, *The Dragon of Revelation*, p. 22.

[44]   There appears to be no equivalent to this passage in the third edition.

the number seven ceases almost to be the 'divine' number, and becomes the magical number of the Apocalypse. As the book proceeds, the ancient divine element fades out and the 'modern', first-century taint of magic, prognostication, and occult practice takes its place. Seven is the number now of divination and conjuring, rather than of real vision. (*A* 137)

This degradation is analogous to the process by which (according to Lawrence) the Etruscan tombs he visited in 1927 had lost their profundity and pagan resonance as time passed, their designs becoming stylized with the onset of Greek artistry and the conquering of the Etruscan people by the Romans (see, for example, *SEP* 129–30).

In the poem 'Return of Returns', Lawrence (prior to writing *Apocalypse*) articulated the need to be sharply aware of an ancient astrological culture in which seven had its original divine significance:

> Come in a week
> Yes, yes, in the seven-day week!
> for how can I count in your three times three
> of the sea-blown week of nine.
>
> Come then, as I say, in a week,
> when the planets have given seven nods
> 'It shall be! It shall be!' assented seven times
> by the great seven, by Helios the brightest
> and by Artemis the whitest
> by Hermes and Aphrodite, flashing white glittering words,
> by Ares and Kronos and Zeus,
> the seven great ones, who must all say yes. (*CP* 702)[45]

Frederick Carter[46] describes the planetary 'wobble' incurred during the Procession of the Equinoxes as a 'nodding' motion (*DA* 41), while the seven major heavenly bodies known to the ancient world (the sun, moon and five planets: see *A* 98 and 136) have been linked with days of the week immemorially.[47] The poem initially

---

[45] Pryse interestingly interprets the apocalyptic 'Logos figure' who appears among lampstands holding seven stars (I.12–16) almost exactly according to the planetary scheme offered in 'Return of Returns', the only difference being his reference to Selene rather than Artemis (*AU* 89–90). Thus Pryse, with his assumption that star-lore lies behind the most crucial figures and symbols of Revelation, is one source underlying Lawrence's interpretation of Apocalyptic symbolism.

[46] For a full discussion of Lawrence's connection with Frederick Carter see Chapter 7, pp. 143–6.

[47] The English names (Sunday, Monday, and so on) belong to an astrological week which, independently of the Jewish-Christian week, assigned the successive hours to the

invokes a return to the 'sacred week' dictated by the benevolent assent of the seven great planets. Analogously, a passage from *Apocalypse* proceeds by asserting that in spite of the superstition that has cheapened the ancient potency of symbols, it is still possible to maintain contact with the 'old days' in which 'the moon was a great power in heaven, ruling men's bodies' and 'seven was one of the moon's quarters'. It is possible to establish the desired contact as the moon 'still sways the flux of the flesh, and still we have a seven-day week' (*A* 38).[48] In the poem, the moment of return is accomplished 'When the moon, from out of the darkness / has come like a thread, like a door just opening' (*CP* 702), indicating that astrological symbiosis will provide the opening.

In ancient times, the 'week' was mainly of use to astrologers, and the seven-day week, recognized in the Jewish calendar and thence adopted in the calendars of Christian, Muslim and various other peoples, was by no means the only option. Nonetheless, in *Apocalypse*, the impossibility of counting according to a 'sea-blown week of nine' results from the fact that 'The Greeks of the sea had a nine-day week. That is gone.' (*A* 138) In *Five Stages of Greek Religion*,[49] Gilbert Murray emphasizes the shift away from the week made up of 'three-times-three':

> Even the way of reckoning time changed under the influence of the Planets. Instead of the old division of the month into three periods of nine days, we find gradually establishing itself the week of seven days with each day named after its planet, Sun, Moon, Ares, Hermes, Zeus, Aphrodite, Kronos ... It was the old week of Babylon, the original home of astronomy and planet-worship.[50]

'Return of Returns', however, is ultimately paradoxical in its attitude to the nine-day and seven-day weeks. The poem implies that it is fortunate that the nine-day week cannot be re-established, for its demise allows man to exist according to the astrological system, in which the planets are animate and can give active assent to our attempt to return. Yet in the poem's last stanza, it is 'The ancient river week, the old one' that is rhetorically reclaimed, pointing to the nine-day

---

seven bodies in the order of their distance, and then named each whole 24-hour day from the body supposed to rule its first hour. The names Dies Solis, Dies Lunæ, Dies Martis, and so on, came into common use during the Roman Empire, and were adopted in translated form by the English and other Teutonic peoples. Cf. Carter's emphasis on the scheme of seven within the ordered processes of the astronomical apocalypse, for 'seven heavens made the familiar ancient astral series of spheres' in *The Dragon of Revelation,* p. 35.

[48] The phrase 'flux of the flesh' may suggest menstruation, the term 'flux' implying 'flow'.

[49] Lawrence initially read the earlier version of this book – *The Four Stages of Greek Religion*, published in 1912 – in 1916. I explore the significance of Murray's book for Lawrence at greater length in my next chapter.

[50] Gilbert Murray, *Five Stages of Greek Religion* (Oxford: Oxford University Press, 1925), pp. 175–6. Hereafter *FS*.

week associated with the Greeks of the sea, rather than the seven-day astrological scheme. In *Apocalypse*, Lawrence relates how the beginning of our era coincided with the 'dying of the old era of the true pagans' (*A* 90), a death which occurred – according to him – around 1000bc. He refers to the 'great and ancient civilisation of the older world', the 'great river civilisations of the Euphrates, the Nile and the Indus, with the lesser sea-civilisation of the Aegean':

> It is puerile to deny the age and the greatness of the three river civilisations, with their intermediary cultures in Persia or Iran, and in the Aegean, Crete or Mycene. (*A* 90)

The river-week thus implies a reaching back even before the sea-civilization of the Aegean celebrated in poems such as 'The Greeks are Coming!', while it also inevitably carries the Heraclitean implications of flux, inexhaustibility and conscious replenishment. Characteristically, 'Return of Returns' exists as an imaginative hybrid, establishing creative connections between the attributes Lawrence ascribed to ancient river civilizations and the nodding planets.

This aptly titled poem, along with those I have discussed earlier in this chapter (as well as the relevant passages from *Apocalypse*), suggest that Lawrence's re-reading of Burnet in 1929 enabled him to reinterpret and re-contextualize the philosophical fragments to which he had responded so favourably in 1915: his re-reading was therefore a conscious return yet also a movement or step onwards. It is appropriate, too, that Lawrence was employing new poetic forms – including a fragmentary 'pensée' style emulating the Heraclitean fragments as well as the seventeenth-century French intertexts mentioned previously – during the last year of his life. In Chapter 9, I will discuss in detail the way in which Lawrence explicitly employed Burnet's fragments even after *Last Poems* in devising a series of short prologues for the Cresset Press edition of *Birds*, *Beasts* and *Flowers*.

Chapter 6

All Sorts of Gods

> [T]here are two modes of reversion: by degeneration and decadence; and
> by deliberate return in order to get back to the roots again, for a new start.
> (*A* 137)

The poem 'Return of Returns'[1] is merely one example of the way in which, in 1929, Lawrence imaginatively dissolved the boundary separating past from present and future. His preoccupation with ancient cultures and civilizations – evident in his Etruscan writings – was partly fuelled by his acquisition of reading matter that would inform the writing of *Apocalypse*. One such book, read by Lawrence during that year, was Gilbert Murray's *Five Stages of Greek Religion* (see *DH* 110). This work, charting a progression from animism to the crystallization of specific Olympian deities (and far beyond) provides a useful framework within which to discuss Lawrence's anthropological and mythopoeic late poems.

Lawrence's interest in Murray, however, was not restricted to the last phase of his life. The year 1916 in particular had marked a surge of enthusiasm for anthropological texts, and the letter below was provoked by his excited discovery of Edward B. Tylor's book *Primitive Culture* during a period of profound disillusionment:

> When I think of art, and then of the British public ... then a sort of madness
> comes over me, really as if one were fastened within a mob, and in danger of
> being trampled to death ... One must forget, only forget, turn one's eyes from
> the world... having another world, a world as yet uncreated. Everything lies in
> *being*, although the whole world is one colossal madness, falsity, a stupendous
> assertion of not-being.
>
> Murry will read Tylers [*sic*] *Primitive Culture* before I return it. It is a very good
> sound substantial book, I had far rather read it than *The Golden Bough* or Gilbert
> Murray. (*L* ii 593)

The work by Murray that Lawrence read at this time was *Four Stages of Greek Religion*: an earlier version of the text he acquired in later life.[2] Although this letter

---

[1]   Discussed in detail at the end of Chapter 5, pp. 114–16.

[2]   At the time he wrote: 'I liked it. But I wish he were a little less popular and conversational in his style, and that he hadn't so many layers of flannel between him and his own nakedness. But the stuff of the book interests me *enormously* (*L* ii 558–9).

hints at a hierarchy of intertexts that establishes Tylor at the pinnacle, it is necessary to recollect that Lawrence typically responded with such enthusiasm to his initial contact with an important book. This had been evident in his letter to Bertrand Russell in December of the previous year, in which he articulated his response to Frazer's triumph in *The Golden Bough*: a book that Lawrence felt confirmed his intuitive faith in the existence of blood-consciousness (*L* ii 469–71).

Lawrence's imagination was clearly fired by *The Golden Bough* and *Totemism and Exogamy*: he subsequently appropriated Frazer's ideas for his own purposes while also asserting that what he was taking from Frazer's anthropology would be crucial in the future. It might seem odd, then, that Lawrence expresses a preference for the 'soundness' of Tylor over the more ingeniously interpretative and subjective method of Frazer, in the letter cited above. Yet it was apparently Tylor's rather dryly informative idiom that gave Lawrence the greatest scope for his own imaginative response. Frazer, feeling that he must 'grope [his] way with small help from the lamp of history'[3] tends to yoke disparate cultures and mythologies together, making the imaginative or at least conjectural leaps himself. He draws parallels across racial, cultural and ideological boundaries in a manner analogous to Lawrence's method in late poems such as 'All Sorts of Gods'. Tylor is as wide-ranging as Frazer (Murray is concerned solely with *Greek* religion), while also being 'scientific' rather than conjectural and judgmental; he elicits general principles from the 'correspondence of evidence' acquired through extensive cross-cultural research.

Tylor's book must have been provocative in expounding both the 'progression' and 'degeneration' or 'degradation' theories, which have been employed variously by commentators to account for the changes in civilization from primitive to modern times. Tylor subscribes predominantly to the progression theory, which charts a continuous, positive development throughout history from savagery to civilization, although his sense of 'progress' is made to incorporate brief lapses in which degeneration prevents the positive onward flow. Such 'degeneration and decadence' through undesired lapsing is the 'mode' of reversion or regression to past cultures which Lawrence clearly felt unhappy with, and which compelled him to offer an alternative model of 'deliberate return' to 'the roots'. His assumption that there *are* roots to which one can return productively is itself an indication that he disagreed fundamentally with all advocates of the progression theory. For this theory embodies an implicit recognition that primitivism is a state of ignorance beyond which it is necessary to progress, while Lawrence demanded instead a redefinition of such terms and concepts as primitivism and savagery, in order for the past and our 'roots' in it to be adequately understood.

Lawrence was profoundly dissatisfied with the 'progress' of his contemporary society in 1915–16 – a disgust only exacerbated by the horrors of World War I – and he devised his own model of degeneration as social slippage into a debilitating moral code:

---

[3]   James Frazer, *The Golden Bough*, vol. 4 (London: Macmillan, 1927), p. 223.

But we cannot leap away, we slip back. That is the horror. We slip back and go mad. The world is going mad, as the Italian and Spanish Renaissance went mad. But where is our Reformation, where is our new light? Where even is our anathema? They had Savonarola and Luther, but we can only slip wallowing back into our old mire of 'Love thy neighbour'. It is very frightening. (*L* ii 592)

Twelve years later, Lawrence wrote the satirical poem 'Love thy Neighbour—' into the 'Nettles' notebook. Placed alongside the above letter, it certainly reveals Lawrence's continuing preoccupation with the irony identified in the injunction of Mark 12:31:

I love my neighbour
but
are these things my neighbours?
these two-legged things that walk and talk
and eat and cachinnate, and even seem to smile
seem to smile, ye gods! ...

All I can say then is Nay! nay! nay! nay! nay! (*CP* 644)

Time has elapsed between 1916 and 1929, yet the poem reveals an analogous preoccupation with a society that has not regained (and perhaps cannot regain) its footing after a catastrophic slippage: it is still perceived as being in the degeneration-phase that inhibits development in the right direction.

There are other instances of shared preoccupation and imagery within the 1929 poems and the 1916 letter in which Tylor is first mentioned. While in the letter 'One must forget, only forget, turn one's eyes from the world' to evade society's ills, in the late poem 'Forget' it is alleged that 'To be able to forget is to be able to yield / to God who dwells in deep oblivion' (*CP* 725). These separated but related formulations indicate that in 1915–16 and 1929, Lawrence was intent on expressing alternative modes of being within a degraded modern world. His many alternatives to degeneracy are explored in the 'Nettles' poems in which 'living', achievable through vital connection with the cosmos, is pitted against the robotic nonexistence associated with the triumph of the machine. This conception of 'living' is then articulated in *Apocalypse:*

For man, as for flower and beast and bird, the supreme triumph is to be most vividly, most perfectly alive ... We ought to dance with rapture that we should be alive and in the flesh, and part of the living, incarnate cosmos. (*A* 149)

Such life and vividness, associated with the cosmos and more specifically with birds, beasts and flowers, derive in part from (and are illuminated by) the notion of the 'blood-being' of all living things, which Lawrence formulated in his first enthusiastic response to Frazer's *The Golden Bough.* It is blood-being or (to adopt a different kind of language employed by Lawrence) 'floweriness' that is established in the 'Nettles' notebook poems as an ideal associated both with life and death. Flowers 'achieve their own floweriness and it is a miracle' (*CP* 683), while robotic men 'don't achieve their own manhood, alas, oh alas! alas!' (*CP* 683). This lament may be related back to the poem 'Lizard' in *Pansies*, and more specifically to the lines 'If men were as much men as lizards are lizards / they'd be worth looking at' (*CP* 524). The Frazerian lizard, capable of impregnating a woman with its blood-being, is perhaps suggested here (*L* ii 470).

It seems logical to suppose that, by a process of association, the notions of primitive culture and animism assimilated by reading Tylor, Frazer and Murray in 1915–16 would still resonate in Lawrence's last years as possible alternatives to degeneracy: as past worlds that can be imaginatively created afresh. Late texts such as *Sketches of Etruscan Places*, *The Escaped Cock*, '[Autobiographical Fragment]', *Apocalypse* and *Last Poems* advocate a deliberate return to humanity's 'roots': a return that would undermine Tylor's model indicating an inevitable progression and improvement of society through time.[4]

The resulting struggle to identify and reach these roots underlies key anthropological and animist elements within the 1929 poems, and drives their shifting, deferring, fluctuating, conceptualizing of 'god' or 'God'.

Murray's First Stage: The Unnamed Gods

In *Five Stages of Greek Religion*, Gilbert Murray characterizes his 'first stage' as one of namelessness, before the titles of the Olympian gods were attached to aspects of the cosmos so as to personify them, making them man-centred. He distinguishes 'anthropophuism' from other kinds of anthropomorphism in order to define the era:

> This kind of anthropomorphism—or as Mr. Gladstone used to call it, 'anthropophuism'— 'humanity of *nature*'—is primitive and inevitable: the sharp-cut statue type of god is different, and is due in Greece directly to the work of the artists. (*FS* 26)

He stresses that the cosmic force, creature or totem is the original: that 'Allowing for some isolated exceptions, the safest rule in all these cases is that the attribute is original and the god is added' (*FS* 35). Lawrence's late poetry and other writings

---

[4]   For a discussion of Lawrence, Darwin and Spengler's 'stress on rootedness and Destiny', exemplified in the Aztec myth (posited by Lawrence as an alternative to Darwinism) see Anne Fernihough, *D.H. Lawrence: Aesthetics and Ideology* (Oxford: Clarendon Press, 1993), pp. 25; 70; 173–80. Also see the passage excised from *The Rainbow*, printed in the Textual Apparatus to the novel, ed. Mark Kinkead-Weekes (Cambridge: Cambridge University Press, 1989), pp. 655–6.

often inhabit this primitive, pre-Homeric 'first stage' of divine anonymity: the gods in the 'Nettles' notebook are often simply 'the gods', or become amalgamated into a 'God' that fights free from specificity of association.

Consequently, in these poems, 'God' seldom represents the Christian figure, but remains much closer to the animist 'God of Life' conceived elsewhere by Lawrence as intimately related to the cosmos and the seasons:

> Only in the country, among peasants, where the old ritual of the seasons lives on in its beauty, is there still some living, instinctive 'faith' in the God of Life. (*IR* 358)

In 'God is Born' (an implicit retort to the Christian God to match the explicit 'Retort to Jesus'), a poem with an ostensibly monotheistic title in fact focuses on multiple god-ly manifestations. These combine to engender wonder and awe in all living things capable of an appropriate response. 'God' is born seven times in the relatively short poem: when the 'dim flux of unformed life' splits into light and dark; when water drips and vapour rises; when sapphires cool out of molten chaos; when the 'little eggy amoeba' emerges out of foam and nowhere; when the narcissus lifts 'a tuft of five-point stars'; when the lizard swirls its tail, the peacock turns to the sun and the leopard smites the calf with a spangled paw; and when 'at last man stood on two legs and wondered' (*CP* 682–3). The poem embodies a radical reinterpretation of the Creation myth: there is no omniscient creator-god who pre-dates the cosmos, for 'God is not / until he is born'. Instead, he is born and reborn as each manifestation of wonder and beauty comes to life: 'And also we see / there is no end to the birth of God' (*CP* 683). As in Murray's first stage, the cosmic wonders are seen as both primeval and pre-eminent; the name 'God', or the names of individual gods, might be attached to them subsequently, as a means by which the jubilantly receptive can articulate some kind of response.

Often, in the 'Nettles' notebook, Lawrence alludes simply to 'the gods', their virtue being that they are divested of specificity: they remain mysterious and can enter into free interplay with mankind. They can be insubstantial essences rather than palpable beings, operating metaphorically and metaphysically. As I have mentioned in relation to Heraclitus, Lawrence refers to 'The Gods, who are life, and the fluidity of living change' and to 'undeniable new gods [who] share their lives with us, when we cease to see' (*CP* 662). He also categorizes mankind according to those who look into the eyes of the gods; those who can merely perceive the transmitted gleam from the faces of vivider men; and those who fail to recognize that there *is* any gleam (*CP* 662).

These 'gods', glimpsed sporadically by a privileged human minority, seem to exist externally, as entities beyond humankind. However, Lawrence also suggests that the gods may appear as manifestations of the inner flame, the flickering of pure life, *within* rather than beyond an individual:

> The gods are all things, and so are we.
> The gods are only ourselves, as we are in our moments of pure manifestation. (*CP* 673)

Similarly, in a poem called 'Glimpses', Lawrence writes:

> What's the good of a man
> unless there's the glimpse of a god in him?
>
> And what's the good of a woman
> unless she's a glimpse of a goddess of some sort? (*CP* 671)

Conscious aspiration, however, leads merely to arrogance and self-satisfaction: 'When men think they are like gods / they are usually much less than men / being conceited fools' (*CP* 673). Forgetfulness – the absence of strained and self-conscious thought – again seems to be the key:

> When men and women, when lads and girls are not thinking,
> when they are pure, which means when they are quite clean from self-consciousness
> either in anger or tenderness, or desire or sadness or wonder or mere stillness
> you may see glimpses of the gods in them. (*CP* 672)

Lawrence erodes the distinction between gods and men: they are merely aspects or manifestations of one another.[5]

The concept of pluralistic gods who are unnamed but can be brought into human contact or touch informs the following lines, in which Lawrence evokes a visitation from 'the gods' which is at once physical and psychological:

> Who is it smooths the bed-sheets like the cool
> smooth ocean where the fishes rest on edge
> in their own dream? …
>
> I tell you, it is no woman, it is no man, for I am alone.
> And I fall asleep with the gods, the gods
> that are not, or that are
> according to the soul's desire,
> like a pool into which we plunge, or do not plunge. (*CP* 652)

Given that the gods exist 'according to the soul's desire', the implication is that they must be mind-engendered and therefore bodiless. Yet once made actual through belief – once the faith-plunge is made – they become so 'real' as to acquire a corporeality that allows them to touch and be touched. Through becoming palpable, however, they do not forfeit the mysterious anonymity ascribed to them

---

[5]   In *Lady Chatterley's Lover* Lawrence alludes to H.G. Wells's utopian romance *Men Like Gods* (1923): a text described by Michael Squires as 'a fictional disquisition on the happy, inevitable ascent of technology' (*LCL* 346, note on 39:17). See Tommy Dukes's exclamation 'We think we're gods—men like gods!' (*LCL* 39).

in the poem 'Cold Blood', in which the narrator whose 'blood is kindled' is able to feel (without specifying) 'goddesses trafficking mysteriously through the air' (*CP* 655).

'The gods' are malleable and unlabelled, unreliant on a 'Word' or name for their being. The poem 'Name the Gods!' begins with a spirited refusal to reduce the gods through identification to any kind of order:

> I refuse to name the gods, because they have no name.
> I refuse to describe the gods, because they have no form nor shape nor substance.
>
> Ah, but the simple ask for images!
> Then for a time at least, they must do without. (*CP* 651)

The poem launches a revolt against the demand to name the nameless, also refusing to pander to those who require images (like the versions of Olympian gods provided by Greek sculptors and artists). Its ending, in which it provides (and combines) both images and names, might be seen as an odd contradiction of the initial rhetoric:

> But all the time I see the gods:
> the man who is mowing the tall white corn,
> suddenly, as it curves, as it yields, the white wheat
> and sinks down with a swift rustle, and a strange, falling flatness,
> ah! the gods, the swaying body of god!
> ah the fallen stillness of god, autumnus, and it is only July
> the pale-gold flesh of Priapus dropping asleep. (*CP* 651)

'Images', in motion rather than fixed and statuesque, here convey a sense of the gods as embodied within humans, in their pure moments. Yet interestingly, Lawrence does introduce the name of a specific pagan god – Priapus – in order to create a precise impression.[6] In later poems within the notebook, too, he veers from his refusal to name gods to the opposite extreme, naming gods in abundance.

All Sorts of Named Gods

The mysterious visitation of unnamed gods touching the poet's breast, heart and feet might be contrasted with the poem 'For a Moment', in which a tram-conductor is identified specifically as Hyacinthus, a running girl as 'Io, Io, who fled from Zeus, or the Danaë', Frieda as Isis (with Lawrence as her Osiris) and Pino Orioli as 'the

---

6 Priapus was a Greek and Roman god of fertility whose images were set to guard vineyards and gardens. These statues – often red and wooden – displayed the erect phallus and were sometimes armed with club and sickle.

wise yet horse-hoofed Centaur' (*CP* 672).[7] This subjective association of a person, known or unknown, with a particular god may be distinguished from the poems in which several gods are invoked, and brought (often incongruously) into proximity. In the poem 'Be it So' the flickering of a flame within a human results not merely in a glimpse of 'the gods' but more specifically 'one of the gods, Jesus or Fafnir or Priapus or Siva' (*CP* 674).[8] The notebook starts to seethe with a proliferation of all sorts of gods – named, given identities and even characteristics:

> I saw an angry Italian seize an irritating little official by the throat
> and all but squeeze the life out of him:
> and Jesus himself could not have denied that at that moment the angry man
> was a god, in godliness pure as a Christ, beautiful
> but perhaps Ashtaroth, perhaps Siva, perhaps Huitzilopochtli
> with the dark and gleaming beauty of the messageless gods. (*CP* 674)[9]

Like Frazer, Lawrence is taking diverse gods and juxtaposing, even categorizing them – this time as 'messageless' gods who are, by implication, free from the Word belonging to such dogmatic religions as Christianity. He is avoiding providing the

---

[7] In Greek mythology, Hyacinthus was a young and beautiful Spartan prince beloved of Apollo and Zephyrus. Io and Danaë were both pursued by Zeus; Io was the daughter of Inachus, the river god of Argos and the first priestess of Hera, the wife of Zeus. Zeus fell in love with her and, to protect her from the wrath of Hera, changed her into a white heifer. She fled to Egypt, and became associated with the goddess Isis. Danaë was a princess of Argos, and became mother of Perseus by Zeus, who visited her as a golden shower during her imprisonment. Lawrence's use of the collective noun – '*the* Danaë' – might, however, suggest a confusion with the 'Danai' (the Argives descended from Danaüs). Isis was a multiform Egyptian goddess whose most important service to her husband and brother, the vegetation god Osiris, was to look for his scattered remains and restore him to life and wholeness after he had been torn asunder by Set. For Lawrence's fictional use of the Isis myth see *The Escaped Cock* Part II (*VG* 141–63). Some Centaurs, notably Chiron, were associated with men and gods as friends, teachers and fellow warriors.

[8] In Norse mythology, Fafnir was a dragon who guarded the Nibelungs' gold hoard until slain by Sigurd. Siva (also Siwa or Shiva) was the 'Auspicious One': one of the main and most complex deities of Hinduism. He embodies seemingly contradictory qualities, being both the destroyer and the restorer; the great ascetic and the symbol of sensuality; the benevolent herdsman of souls and the wrathful avenger. Cf. 'The Man Who Was Through with the World' (*VG* 237).

[9] The Hebrew name Ashtaroth (plural form of Ashtoreth) conflates the Greek Astarte (goddess of war and sexual love) with the Hebrew word *boshet* (shame), indicating the Hebrews' contempt for her cult. Ashtaroth became a general term denoting goddesses and paganism. Huitzilopochtli was an Aztec sun and war god ('resuscitated warrior of the south'), usually represented either as a hummingbird or a warrior with armour and helmet made of hummingbird feathers; see too *The Plumed Serpent*, ed. L.D. Clark (Cambridge: Cambridge University Press, 1987), p. 62 and note on l. 10.

image merely of a single god (which would place restriction on the imaginations of those responding); he is using multiplicity and plurality to suggest anger, beauty and danger as made manifest in many cultures, not to make a moral point about 'message' and meaning.

Perhaps, too, he is trying to emphasize the complexity of mind and motive that has made the creative effort of attention in order to engender such multifarious deities. People can be many gods, just as gods can be many people. In the poem 'Two Ways of Living and Dying' man is described as 'an iridescent fountain, rising up to flower / for a moment godly, like Baal or Krishna, or Adonis or Balder, or Lucifer' (*CP* 675).[10] Each deity preserves distinct characteristics, even while co-existing or conforming to a general category (such as 'messageless') for it is a manifestation of the tribe, chief or individual that created it: it embodies the 'dark and gleaming beauty' (*CP* 674) of a specific creative urge. Yet even if each god retains specific characteristics it seems that, in Lawrence, as in Tylor and Frazer, one god leads to another: none can be freed from the inevitable process of association. If you name one god you end up by naming a good many, in order to avoid narrow image making. This happens, comically, to Henry the Hermit, the protagonist of the short story 'The Man Who Was Through with the World', written probably in May 1927:

> before he was through with everything, he had read quite a lot about Brahma and Krishna and Shiva, and Buddha and Confucius and Mithras, not to mention Zeus and Aphrodite and that bunch, nor the Wotan family. So when he began to think: The Lord is my Shepherd, somehow Shiva would start dancing a Charleston in the back of his mind, and Mithras would take the bull by the horns, and Mohammed would start patting the buttery flanks of Ayesha, and Abraham would be sitting down to a good meal off a fat ram, till the grease ran down his beard. So that it was very difficult to concentrate on God with a large 'g', and the hermit had a natural reluctance to go into refinements of the great I Am, or of thatness. (*VG* 237)

One image cannot be brought to mind without generating other related images: having read about multiple deities, it is impossible to return to one conception of 'God' with a large 'g', or to any single representation of this entity.

---

[10] Baal is a fertility deity worshipped in many ancient Middle Eastern communities, especially among the Canaanites, as one of the most important gods of the pantheon ('Prince, Lord of the Earth'). Krisha is one of the most widely revered and popular of all Indian divinities, worshipped as the eighth incarnation of the Hindu god Vishnu and also as a supreme god in his own right. In Greek mythology, Adonis is a youth of remarkable beauty, the favourite of the goddess Aphrodite (and Persephone), while in Norse mythology, Balder is the beautiful and just son of Odin and his wife Frigg, favourite of the gods, killed as a result of Loki's trickery. Lucifer, brightest of angels (associated with Venus and the Morning Star), was evicted from Heaven as a result of his pride.

An acceptance of deistic pluralism is advocated in the poem 'All Sorts of Gods', which provides the antithesis of the refusal to name gods in other poems within the 'Nettles' notebook:

There's all sorts of gods, all sorts and every sort,
and every god that humanity has ever known is still a god today
the African queer ones and Scandinavian queer ones,
the Greek beautiful ones, the Phoenician ugly ones, the Aztec hideous ones,
goddesses of love, goddesses of dirt, excrement-eaters or lily virgins,
Jesus, Buddha, Jehovah and Ra, Egypt and Babylon,
all the gods, and you see them all if you look, alive and moving today,
and alive and moving tomorrow, many tomorrows, as yesterdays. (*CP* 671)

In the displacement of time in which the future is envisaged in terms of the past ('many tomorrows, as yesterdays') and a combination of both constitutes the present ('alive and moving today') these lines are reminiscent of Eliot's 'Time past and time future / What might have been and what has been / Point to one end, which is always present'.[11] The term 'today' is the touchstone. Lawrence's mythological defining of 'today' in terms of past and future (also evident in 'Poetry of the Present') leads to this profusion – this proliferation – of gods. The deities yoked together in 'All Sorts of Gods' (as well as the other poems I have discussed) give some indication of the knowledge that Lawrence acquired throughout his life through his extensive reading of mythological texts; as well as through his first-hand experience of the many diverse tribes and peoples with whom he became familiar on his travels. Such accumulated experience, provoking a broadening in resonance and scope, testify to one aspect of these poems' late style.

The poem 'All Sorts of Gods' may also be taken as a paradigm for the intertextual process by which ideas and associations are constantly generated and acquired. Each god has particularity and specificity, yet all intermingle into the mythological web: they are 'alive and moving', not only inhabiting tomorrow, but 'many tomorrows, as yesterdays'. They are 'moving' in the sense of travelling through time; they simultaneously have the power to 'move' responsive individuals, because they command the imagination rather than the logical or reasoning mind. Lawrence claims that 'every god that humanity has ever known is still a god today', as the belief has arisen from the hearts and minds of the tribe or culture that created the particular images, and has then passed into the continuum of tradition and human history.

---

[11]   T.S. Eliot, 'Four Quartets', in *T.S. Eliot: Collected Poems 1909–1962* (London: Faber, 1963), p. 190.

Return of the Olympians

The 'Nettles' notebook is full of all sorts of gods: gods belonging to diverse mythologies and named accordingly. In the succeeding 'Last Poems' notebook, however, Lawrence stages a specifically Olympian return, as the naming of these gods unequivocally reveals. In *The Golden Bough*, describing the Alexandrian ceremony for the death and resurrection of Adonis, Frazer quotes Theocritus' observation of the lamenting people: 'Yet they sorrowed not without hope, for they sang that the lost one would come back again'.[12] In the 'Last Poems' notebook, Lawrence evokes the 'slim naked men from Cnossos, smiling the archaic smile / of those that will without fail come back again' (*CP* 688) and kindling little fires on the beaches. In this poem, 'Middle of the World', as in 'The Greeks are Coming!', 'The Argonauts' and 'For the Heroes are Dipped in Scarlet', Lawrence embarks upon a kind of 'return' that adds new complexity and new poignancy to his conception of God and the gods. The return of the deities who cannot fail to return might be seen to extend his depiction of the native creatures of a man's soul which 'cannot die' in poems such as 'The Triumph of the Machine' (*CP* 624 and 958). The 'return' of the Olympians, seen consequently as inevitable, is presented as neither surprising nor ostentatious: the gods are 'softly laughing and chatting, as ever' (*CP* 688), crouching rather as Il Duro does in *Twilight in Italy*,[13] or like the Eastwood miners of Lawrence's youth squatting on their heels as they talk and laugh after work.

In the soft laughter, the naturalness and the manner of their coming, these gods relate to the Etruscan culture, experienced by Lawrence during his trip to Italy in April 1927. In Chapter 3 I explored the extent and significance of this encounter, illustrating (through reference to the earlier poem 'Cypresses') ways in which the mythological protagonists of 'Last Poems' acquire distinctively Etruscan features and characteristics. However, it is also necessary to emphasize that they are specifically referred to as 'Greeks', and they arrive in Aegean ships from Cnossos:

> it is ships of Cnossos coming out of the morning end of the sea,
> it is Aegean ships, and men with archaic pointed beards... (*CP* 687)

This reference to the 'morning end of the sea', as well as the specific mention of Odysseus in the following poem 'The Argonauts', links directly with the letter written by Lawrence after arriving in Bandol (France) on 4 October 1929: 'I still love the Mediterranean, it still seems young as Odysseus, in the morning' (*L* vii 509).

---

[12]   Frazer, p. 225.

[13]   *Twilight in Italy and Other Essays*, ed. Paul Eggert (Cambridge: Cambridge University Press, 1994), p. 177.

The association made here of the journeying hero Odysseus with the 'morning-glamorous' Mediterranean is one that Lawrence had established in the earlier travel-book *Sea and Sardinia* (1921):

> How wonderful it must have been to Ulysses to venture into this Mediterranean and open his eyes on all the loveliness of the loveliness of the tall coasts ... There is something eternally morning-glamorous about these lands as they rise from the sea. And it is always the Odyssey which comes back to one as one looks at them. All the lovely morning-wonder of this world, in Homer's day![14]

It seems inevitable that Lawrence's vision of the returning gods in his writing of 1929 would encompass associations derived from earlier imaginative responses specifically to the Mediterranean region. In a letter written at Taormina, on 1 June 1920, Lawrence asserted that:

> The South is so different from the north. I believe morality is a purely climatic thing ... Here the past is so much stronger than the present, that one seems remote like the immortals, looking back at the world from their otherworld. A great indifference comes over me – I feel the present isn't real. (*L* iii 538)

By implication, this passage attributes a preoccupation with the past to the experience of inhabiting a particular location, so that Lawrence's physical arrival at Bandol may be identified as the provocation for his specific allusions to Greek deities at the opening of 'Last Poems'. He was enabled by his new locality (frequently in bed overlooking the sea) to perceive visions of epic grandeur, as Keats had done in Italy before him, though in very different circumstances:

> I feel more and more every day, as my imagination strengthens, that I do not live in this world alone but in a thousand worlds—No sooner am I alone than shapes of epic greatness are stationed around me, and serve my Spirit the office which is equivalent to a king's body guard—then 'Tragedy, with scepter'd pall, comes sweeping by.' According to my state of mind I am with Achilles shouting in the Trenches or with Theocritus in the Vales of Sicily. Or I throw my whole being into Triolus and repeating those lines, 'I wander, like a lost soul upon the stygian Banks staying for waftage,' I melt into the air with a voluptuousness so delicate that I am content to be alone ...[15]

---

[14]   D.H. Lawrence, *Sea and Sardinia*, ed. Mara Kalnins (Cambridge: Cambridge University Press, 1997), p. 184.

[15]   John Keats, letter written in October 1818 (less than three years before his death), in *The Letters of John Keats: A Selected Edition*, ed. R. Gittings (Oxford: Oxford University Press, 1990), p. 170. I have adopted the editor's emendations here.

In Lawrence's case, the sea-faring Olympians loomed tantalizingly in the distance, before beaching on the shores and infiltrating the society they newly discovered on arrival.

The 'Olympian' vision provokes a contrast that again finds a parallel in Keats, this time in a poem included within a letter to his brother Tom. Here, Keats refers to the contamination of the pure, magical sea (surrounding Fingal's Cave[16]) by modern vessels:

> So for ever will I leave
> Such a taint and soon unweave
> All the magic of the place—
> 'T is now free to stupid face
> To cutters and to fashion boats
> To cravats and to Petticoats.[17]

Analogously, Lawrence's poem 'Middle of the World' contrasts modern pollution with the endurance of the (magically) primitive:

> What do I care if the smoking ships
> of the P. & O. and the Orient Line and all the other stinkers
> cross like clock-work the Minoan distance!
> They only cross, the distance never changes. (*CP* 688)

The modern world, it seems, is inevitably intrusive; and although the Minoan distance itself cannot be altered, the steamships pollute the middle of the world just as (in 'The Triumph of the Machine') debris of the machine pollutes the middle earth (*CP* 625).[18]

It is possible to suggest an alternative or complementary approach, foregrounding intertextual derivation rather than biography, which may illuminate Lawrence's use of the Minoan or Olympian gods in 'Last Poems'. This approach is based on the phases described in Gilbert Murray's *Five Stages of Greek Religion*. I have already discussed the way in which the 'Nettles' notebook poems, depicting numerous unnamed gods, may be related to Murray's first, or primal, stage. Murray describes the transition from the primal to the Olympian (second) stage, conceiving the former as an 'Age of Ignorance' or 'Primal Stupidity', before Zeus came to trouble men's minds, a stage to which our anthropologists and explorers have found parallels in every part of the world:

---

[16] A sea cave situated on the uninhabited island of Staffa, in the Scottish Inner Hebrides.

[17] *The Letters of John Keats*, ed. Gittings, p. 144.

[18] Cf. Chapter 4, pp. 77–8.

> Secondly there is the Olympian or classical stage, a stage in which, for good
> or ill, blunderingly or successfully, this primitive vagueness was reduced to a
> kind of order. This is the stage of the great Olympian gods, who dominated art
> and poetry, ruled the imagination of Rome, and extended a kind of romantic
> dominion even over the Middle Ages. It is the stage that we learn, or mis-learn,
> from the statues and the handbooks of mythology. Critics have said that this
> Olympian stage has value only as art and not as religion. (*FS* 16–17)

Lawrence's attitude towards primitivism stands, of course, in absolute opposition
to the 'Primal Stupidity' approach. Yet in his poems dealing with the 'God of Life'
– and especially in those which proliferate multiple gods – he might be said to
be deliberately employing a 'primitive vagueness'. His 'Nettles' notebook poems
seem to oscillate between two different 'primitive' conceptions of the gods. The
first is the primal (pre-Christian, pre-Socratic) condition in which the seasons and
workings of nature are seen to dictate human life, so that man exists in harmony
with the cosmos and there is no need for the creation of intermediary gods to
compensate for humanity's dislocation. The second stems from the progression
beyond this in which man assumes, for instance, that the wind blows because a
greater being of some sort is blowing with his/her cheeks. This personification
of the elements led man to conceive of gods – divine powers named or unnamed
– who represented and embodied various aspects of the cosmic forces.

Lawrence's progression beyond cosmic connection and all sorts of gods to the
Olympian deities of 'The Greeks are Coming!', 'The Argonauts' and 'Middle of
the World' might usefully be explored as a deliberate echo of the psychological and
ideological progression between the first two stages of Greek religion as described
by Murray. New *order* is established: a specific mythology is invoked which is
successful in providing a contrast with the spiritually impoverished modern world.
The gods are no longer unidentifiable, but may be recognized or understood as
Odysseus, Dionysos, and later Hermes. One advantage of actualizing the gods in
this way is that they may (within a poem) be visualized, approached and conversed
with. When unnamed and mysterious 'the gods' can merely knead human feet
silently and disappear unseen; even when named, the 'Nettles' gods are offered
in profusion in order to avoid narrow image-making. Yet if the god has a specific
identity – if he is life-sized and palpable, rather than merely a gleam emanating
sporadically from a passer-by – he can come into human touch or contact: the soft
flow of touch which is so crucial in the relationships between Etruscans, which is
so significant in *Lady Chatterley's Lover*, and which is essential to the preservation
of life in '[Autobiographical Fragment]'.

A 'Last Poems' Olympian can appear as a visitor and be identified intuitively
as a deity:

> But a naked man, a stranger, leaned on the gate
> with his cloak over his arm, waiting to be asked in.
> So I called him: Come in, if you will!—

He came in slowly, and sat down by the hearth.
I said to him: And what is your name?—
He looked at me without answer, but such a loveliness
entered me, I smiled to myself, saying: He is God!
So he said: *Hermes*! (*CP* 692)

The appearance of the Olympians as palpable beings gives Lawrence a chance to enact dramatically the situation in which a vivid man recognizes, responds to and looks into the eyes of a god. The narrator is infused with the loveliness emanating from Hermes: a god who can be touched and known, rather than remaining an abstraction.

Spanning Stages: The Mythologization of 'Bavarian Gentians'

The progression from animism to the evocation of Olympian deities evident in the opening poems of the 'Last Poems' notebook may shed light on Lawrence's mythologization of the poem 'Bavarian Gentians', drafted at least four times in the 'Nettles' notebook and then twice (in extended form) within 'Last Poems' (each of these drafts having been extensively revised). The gentian flowers begin as manifestations of beauty, wonder and nobility (by implication associated with the unnamed creator-god who strives among the mud and mastodons to engender beauty, *CP* 691), causing the responsive protagonist to journey downwards into mysterious depths of fulfilment and happiness:

They have added blueness to blueness, until
it is darkness; Oh you, beauty of darkness
blue joy of my soul
Bavarian gentians
your dark blue gloom is so noble!

How deep I have gone
dark gentians
since I embarked on your dark blue fringes
how deep, how deep, how happy! (*CP* 959)[19]

The flowers embody a cosmic beauty that might be pitted against simplistic and erroneous conceptions of savagery and primitivism: 'Tell me, is the gentian savage, at the top of its coarse stem? ... is there in you a beauty to compare / to the honeysuckle at evening ...' (*CP* 684).

---

[19]   The poem cited has been slightly emended to follow Christopher Pollnitz's transcription of the 'Nettles' and 'Last Poems' notebooks and reflects the text as it will appear in the Cambridge University Press edition of Lawrence's *Complete Poems*.

Yet in the 'Nettles' notebook a pencil version exists alongside the initial draft: it may have been written soon after the first draft had been completed, or possibly when Lawrence was writing a new version of the poem into the 'Last Poems' notebook, and returned to alter and revise the original. It is impossible to tell exactly when the 'mythologization' of this poem took place, although interestingly it is possible to define a particular point in the pencil draft at which the Persephone idea first suggested itself. In the second short stanza, the first-draft line 'How deep I have gone' has unsurprisingly provoked an association with the underworld:

> It is so blue, it is so dark
> in the dark doorway
> and the way is open
> to Hades. (*CP* 959)

It is at this point that Persephone intervenes, almost as though she has taken the poet by surprise:

> Oh, I know —
> Persephone has just gone back
> down the thickening thickening gloom
> of dark blue gentians
> to Pluto
> to her bridegroom
> in the dark
>
> And all the dead
> and all the dark great ones of the underworld...
> are gathering to a wedding in the winter dark
> down the dark-blue path (*CP* 959)[20]

The flower becomes linked with a mythological return and descent into the underworld, Persephone being the goddess who emblematizes the cycle of the seasons, as she inhabits the lower and upper worlds in turn.

Lawrence's evident fascination with the myth of Persephone and Demeter is clearly indicated by a number of his late works, but (like his assimilation of Fraser and Tylor) has its origin in a much earlier period. In 1913 he read Jane Harrison's *Art and Ritual* (published in the same year): a book which he thought was 'stupidly put, but it lets one in for an idea that helps one immensely' (*L* ii 119). He was particularly struck by her account of the Eleusinian Mysteries: namely, the annual initiation ceremonies undertaken by the cult of Persephone and Demeter, held at Eleusis in Ancient Greece, probably originating in the Mycenaean period (around 1600bc) and lasting for almost 2,000 years.

---

[20] Ibid.

In her book *Persephone Rises, 1860–1927: Mythography, Gender, and the Creation of a New Spirituality*, Margot Louis discusses Lawrence's appropriation and reinvigoration of the Persephone myth in relation to the works of a number of key modernists. She highlights the prominence of this myth in a range of texts including *The Lost Girl*, 'Purple Anemones', 'The Ladybird', *Lady Chatterley's Lover* (the first and third versions), 'The Woman Who Rode Away' and 'Bavarian Gentians'.[21] In Lawrence's last novel, Louis argues that the explicit or more subtle allusions to the Persephone myth generate a 'double Hades' – one repressive and destructive (in the form of Clifford); the other vital and regenerative (Parkin/ Mellors).[22] It is also worth noting that in 'A Propos of *Lady Chatterley's Lover*', Lawrence uses a rhetorical question to indicate the desire to 'get back' a number of pagan deities and locations, including 'Demeter, Persephone, and the halls of Dis' (*LCL* 331; see Chapter 4, p. 89). Prior to the late poem 'Bavarian Gentians', this myth had strikingly underpinned the poem 'Purple Anemones' (in *Birds, Beasts and Flowers*): a poem that enacts the delights and perils of the chase in which Dis lets go of his prey only for the fun of tracking her down again (*CP* 308–309). As in 'Bavarian Gentians', flowers are inevitably associated with the fleeing Persephone, though in the earlier poem they are hostile to her ('hell-hounds on her heels', *CP* 308), while in the later poem the gentian functions as a literal torch-flower, shedding blue light as the narrator descends to attend a wedding feast.

Tylor describes the way in which the seasonal cycle has been dramatized in the myth of Persephone, and draws attention to the way in which the naming of the gods concretizes the myth's significance:

> The explanation of the rape of Persephone, as a nature-myth of the seasons and the fruits of the earth, does not depend alone on analogy of incident, but has the very names to prove its reality, Zeus, Helios, Demeter—Heaven, and Sun, and Mother Earth.[23]

Lawrence, through dramatizing this nature-myth in 'Bavarian Gentians', is able to create a vivid evocation of the descent from Demeter's white day into the Etruscan-tomb-like Hades. The Etruscan association (see Chapter 3, p. 62 gives insight into the nature of the imagined journey: it becomes (in both 'Last Poems' versions) a directed, purposeful descent rather than the tentative, wistful departure of a vulnerable soul in 'The Ship of Death' or 'Butterfly'. In 'Bavarian Gentians' the traveller descending Orpheus-wise into Hades is 'in touch' with other shadowy beings, moving from the upper world to a marriage ritual in the world below, guiding himself with the aid of a gentian rather than an acetylene lamp:

---

[21]   Margot K., Louis, *Persephone Rises, 1860–1927: Mythography, Gender, and the Creation of a New Spirituality* (Aldershot: Ashgate, 2009), p. 110. For a list of other works on this subject see p. 117 n. 11.

[22]   Ibid., p. 119.

[23]   Edward B. Tylor, *Primitive Culture*, vol. I (London: John Murray, 1903), p. 321.

> Reach me a gentian, give me a torch!
> let me guide myself with the blue, forked torch of this flower
> down the darker and darker stairs, where blue is darkened on blueness
> even where Persephone goes, just now, from the frosted September
> to the sightless realm where darkness is awake upon the dark
> and Persephone herself is but a voice
> or a darkness invisible enfolded in the deeper dark
> of the arms Plutonic, and pierced with the passion of dense gloom,
> among the splendour of torches of darkness, shedding darkness on the lost bride and
>   her groom. (*CP* 697)

The scene is vivid, yet the Persephone–Pluto relationship is conceived metaphorically, as though the gods are operating in their emblematic capacity rather than as palpable, physical beings, who interact as humans do. Persephone is 'enfolded in the deeper dark / of the arms Plutonic' and is pierced not by Pluto himself but by the 'passion of dense gloom'.

By contrast, in the draft of 'Bavarian Gentians' that appears on the following page of the 'Last Poems' notebook, the poem is much more literal. This draft contains the lines:

> and Persephone herself is but a voice, as a bride,
> a gloom invisible enfolded in the deeper dark
> of the arms of Pluto as he ravishes her once again
> and pierces her once more with his passion of the utter dark.
> among the splendour of black-blue torches, shedding fathomless darkness on the
>   nuptials. (*CP* 960)

The language is more explicitly sexual, as is anticipated earlier in the poem by the description of the flowers as 'ribbed hellish flowers erect, with their blaze of darkness spread blue'; it is also less metaphorical. Persephone is enfolded not in the 'arms Plutonic' but in the 'arms of Pluto' who 'ravishes' and 'pierces' her. The nuptials now may be envisaged clearly in terms of sexual interaction between the two pagan deities, and the narrator himself is more actively 'present' as is evident in the last three added lines in which he describes himself as a 'wedding-guest'. He has presumably received an invitation, so does not stumble arbitrarily upon the scene, and does not impose. He is part of the 'living dark': the rich fecundity of the marriage/sex ritual possessed of the quality of life identified on the descent into an Etruscan tomb, in which it is possible to feel like a participant in the incessant banqueting and revelry. The fecundity too is one whose implications extend beyond the single union to the whole of life: to the propagation of all plant and animal growth; to the oscillation of day and night; to the progression of the seasons.

Behind the Olympians: The Half-lit Regions

The poem, then, reaches back behind the Olympian gods to the raw material underlying their initial conception: to the fertility and regenerative potency of the cosmos as envisaged by primitive tribes. Murray refers to this hidden realm lurking behind the dazzling Olympian divinities:

> But we have other evidence too which shows abundantly that these Olympian gods are not primary, but are imposed upon a background strangely unlike themselves. For a long time the luminous figures dazzled our eyes; we were not able to see the half-lit regions behind them, the dark primeval tangle of desires and fears and dreams from which they drew their vitality. (*FS* 28)

The primeval potency and fertility (particularly in relation to the sexual) underlying the Olympians is suggested elsewhere in 'Last Poems', notably in the representations of Aphrodite in 'The Man of Tyre', 'They Say the Sea is Loveless' and 'Whales Weep Not!'. 'The Man of Tyre' dramatizes an encounter between its narrator and a woman emerging from the sea who possesses a 'godly and lovely' mien that immediately causes the watcher to identify her as Aphrodite:

> Oh lovely, lovely with the dark hair piled up, as she went deeper, deeper down the
>   channel, then
> rose shallower, shallower,
> with the full thighs slowly lifting of the wader wading shorewards
> and the shoulders pallid with light from the silent sky behind
> both breasts dim and mysterious, with the glamorous kindness of twilight between
>   them
> and the dim blotch of black maidenhair like an indicator,
> giving a message to the man —
>
>   ... here in the twilight
> godly and lovely comes Aphrodite out of the sea
> towards me! (*CP* 693)

I have argued that, in the 'Nettles' notebook, 'the gods' are often identified in the bodies or faces of people as they appear in sporadic manifestations. Here, the bodily beauty of the woman gives her a specific identity as a particular Olympian goddess.[24]

Yet in the poem 'Whales Weep Not!' Aphrodite inhabits the form of another manifestation of cosmic energy:

---

[24] This Aphrodite emerges from the foam yet remains crucially distinct from Lawrence's earlier Aphrodite of the foam, associated with an aggressive, masturbatory sexuality. See, for example, *WL* 172.

> And bull-whales gather their women and whale-calves in a ring
> when danger threatens, on the surface of the ceaseless flood
> and range themselves like great fierce Seraphim facing the threat
> encircling their huddled monsters of love.
> And all this happens in the sea, in the salt
> where God is also love, but without words:
> and Aphrodite is the wife of whales
> most happy, happy she! (*CP* 695)

Lawrence is evidently allowing Aphrodite (and by extension the other Olympian deities) to remain fluid, retaining their Greek labels but metamorphosing into different shapes and forms, thus retaining their dark, primeval, nameless implications. By so doing he attempts to avoid a situation in which a signifier-image is presented that instantly attaches itself to a particular definition.

'The simple ask for images' but Lawrence refuses to provide crystallized or even hard-edged versions of the Olympian gods which might equate to the gem-like poetry of the past and future he described in 'Poetry of the Present'. Murray recognizes the propensity of the Greek gods to become rigid and static:

> They crystallize hard. They will no longer melt or blend, at least not at an ordinary temperature. In the fourth and third centuries we hear a great deal about the gods all being one, 'Zeus the same as Hades, Hades as Helios, Helios the same as Dionysus', but the amalgamation only takes place in the white heat of ecstatic philosophy or the rites of religious mysticism. (*FS* 86)

According to Murray, it was at the time of Homer (the beginning of his second stage of Greek religion) that the Olympians were both crystallized and (perhaps in Hermes' case) bowdlerized:

> the contrast between the Homeric gods and the gods found outside Homer is well compared by Mr. Chadwick to the difference between the gods of the Edda and the historical traces of religion outside the Edda. The gods who feast with Odin in Asgard, forming an organized community or *comitatus*, seem to be the gods of the kings, distinct from the gods of the peasants, cleaner and more war-like and lordlier, though in actual religious quality much less vital. (*FS* 80–81)

According to this argument, Homer divested the gods of their old primitive associations which he found rather distasteful, and he has been made subject to this accusation as a consequence: 'There is not much faith in these gods, as they appear to us in the Homeric Poems, and not much respect, except perhaps for Apollo and Athena and Poseidon' (*FS* 79). The poem 'Middle of the World', in which Dionysos leans on the gate 'in all respect', suggests that Lawrence identified mutual respect and tolerance as a distinguishing mark of the Olympians portrayed in 'Last Poems'.

Hermes provides a good example of a god who actually changed radically in his Homeric incarnation. Murray describes his origin as follows:

> Originally, outside Homer, Hermes was simply an old upright stone, a pillar furnished with the regular Pelasgian sex-symbol of procreation. Set up over a tomb he is the power that generates new lives, or, in the ancient conception, brings the souls back to be born again. He is the Guide of the Dead, the Psychopompos, the divine Herald between the two worlds. If you have a message for the dead, you speak it to the Herm at the grave. This notion of Hermes as herald may have been helped by his use as a boundary-stone—the Latin *Terminus*. Your boundary-stone is your representative, the deliverer of your message, to the hostile neighbour or alien. If you wish to parley with him, you advance up to your boundary-stone. If you go, as a Herald, peacefully, into his territory, you place yourself under the protection of the same sacred stone, the last sign that remains of your own safe country. If you are killed or wronged, it is he, the immovable Watcher, who will avenge you. (*FS* 76)

Murray comments that 'this phallic stone post was quite unsuitable to Homer. It was not decent; it was not quite human; and every personage in Homer has to be both', while he also quotes Pausanias's assertion that 'thanks to Homer [Hermes] is purified of his old phallicism' (*FS* 77). This unacceptable phallicism led to Hermes being removed from the *Iliad*, while, in the *Odyssey*, he is 'so changed and castigated that no one would recognize the old Herm in the beautiful and gracious youth who performs the gods' messages.' (*FS* 77) In his Etruscan trip of April 1927, Lawrence was struck 'in the very first five minutes' by the numerous phallic symbols – 'in stone, unmistakeable, and everywhere' (*SEP* 19) around the tombs. It is certain that he would have wanted the Hermes of 'Maximus', who fills the narrator with loveliness as he leans naked on the gatepost, to retain the attributes of the pre-Homeric Hermes, though it is also appropriate for Lawrence's dramatic purposes that he is not presented in this poem merely as a stone.

It seems that Lawrence, in his poetically evoked return of the Olympians, creates a state of pre-Homeric consciousness *between* Murray's first two stages: a time when man was beginning to attach names to the cosmic 'raw material', but without personifying it to the extent that gods become named, fixed and statuesque as they did later, in Homer's time. He wants to return imaginatively to the Minoan and Etruscan ages in which the Olympian gods are emerging for the first time: Dionysos is 'young and a stranger', listening quietly and attentively to the gods who have come before him and already inhabit the land to which he has journeyed.

'Last Poems': A Superimposition of Gods

The return of the Olympians distinguishes the early verse of 'Last Poems' from the previous 'Nettles' material: consequently the progression from one notebook to the other might be seen as following Murray's linear development, even if this process stops mid-stage, before the Olympians are divested of their primeval implications. Yet the complexity of 'Last Poems' would thereby be falsified, for the previous 'God' and 'gods' are not simply rejected and superseded. The increased complexity arises from the inevitable nature of development through association: the old is not replaced by the new, the two are simply superimposed. Or, to explain the complexity in a rather different way, Lawrence does not reach any conclusion, establishing a set hierarchy of gods/images or ascertaining the most satisfactory kind of pagan return. Rather, he explores and combines images, gods and myths, overriding the improbability and incongruity latent in his approach.

So, for example, as well as the Olympian deities, Lawrence retains references to Christianity, reinterpreting aspects of the Bible by drawing on rites and rituals of primitive, pre-Christian cultures. The poem 'The Old Way of Sacrifice' in the 'Nettles' notebook juxtaposes and contrasts ancient rites with modern Christian misconceptions regarding self-sacrifice. Similarly, the poem 'Lord's Prayer' in 'Last Poems' offers a pagan alternative to a crucial text of the Christian tradition. The 'kingdom, power and glory' claimed in the poem is neither that of mercy and submission nor of unspecified grandeur, but rather 'the kingdom of the fox in the dark / yapping in his power and his glory / which is death to the goose' (*CP* 704). The narrator calls for his 'mana', a term which must be understood in its pagan rather than Christian definition:

> The bull was the chief of magic or sacred animals in Greece, chief because of his enormous strength, his size, his rage, in fine, as anthropologists call it, his *mana*; that primitive word which comprises force, vitality, prestige, holiness, and power of magic, and which may belong equally to a lion, a chief, a medicine-man, or a battle-axe. (*FS* 34)

Murray describes how in pagan ceremonies 'You devoured the holy animal to get its *mana*, its swiftness, its strength, its great endurance, just as the savage now will eat his enemy's brain or heart or hands to get some particular quality residing there' (*FS* 37).

'Mana of the Sea' (also discussed in Chapter 5, pp. 106–7) reveals 'mana' to exist in Lawrence's vocabulary as a synonym for blood-being or blood-knowledge. The poet's aspiration is expressed in the following rhetoric:

> Have I caught from it
> the tide in my arms
> that runs down to the shallows of my wrists, and breaks
> abroad in my hands, like waves among the rocks of substance? (*CP* 705)

The poem ends with the assertion 'I am the sea, I am the sea!' The poet has 'become' the sea through catching from it its mana, just as the tribes described by Lawrence in his letter about first reading Frazer (*L* ii 470) actually 'become' Kangaroos through an equivalent acquisition of blood-knowledge.

This 'mana' poem seems to suggest the primacy of the living, vital cosmos in which the most significant realization is that of the 'aliveness' of the natural world, and the wonder inherent in the creative urge. Consequently Lawrence is unwilling to lose sight of the unnamed, mysterious creator-god that sighs with tremendous creative yearning (in 'Red Geranium and Godly Mignonette') and eludes identification. In the poem 'Maximus' this god is brought into curious conjunction with a visiting Olympian:

> God is older than the sun and moon
> and the eye cannot behold him
> nor the voice describe him:
> and still, this is the god Hermes, sitting by my hearth. (*CP* 692)

The conjunction invites a series of paradoxes: God is nameless yet can be given a name or names; he is both unseen and visible; he is both insubstantial and a palpable presence. Then the two consecutive poems 'Bodiless God' and 'The Body of God' offer antithetical attitudes to the question of god's corporeality. The former, after asserting that everything beautiful has being in the flesh, and that dreams are only 'drawn from bodies that are' reads:

> And God?
> Unless God has a body, how can he have a voice
> and emotions, and desires, and strength, glory or honour?
> For God, even the rarest God, is supposed to love us
> and wish us to be this that and the other.
> And he is supposed to be mighty and glorious. (*CP* 691)

By contrast, the following poem begins 'God is the great urge that has not yet found a body / but urges towards incarnation with the great creative urge' (*CP* 691). The poems wrestle with the problem of a god who must have a body in order to be truly living yet who is also the god of becoming, eluding fixed identity; or one who is simultaneously indescribable and 'sitting by my hearth'. This is not a paradox that is, or can be, readily resolved.

Similarly, god in 'Last Poems' exists sometimes as a single creator yet has multiple or infinitely plural manifestations, as is recognized by the Man of Tyre who is 'pondering, for he was Greek, that God is one and all alone and ever more shall be so':

> So in the cane-brake he clasped his hands in delight
> that could only be god-given, and murmured:

> Lo! God is one god! But here in the twilight
> godly and lovely comes Aphrodite out of the sea
> towards me! (*CP* 692–3)[25]

Manifestations of god's plurality and capacity to metamorphose are allowed to co-exist with monotheism. Yet it is possible to discern within the phrase 'God is one god!' another implication. God with a capital 'G' is *merely* one god – that of the Christians – and there are many more: the gods of other peoples, other religions and other creeds. They are all, we must remember, alive and moving today; they will inhabit many tomorrows, as yesterdays. A pluralistic conception of gods enables different beliefs and ideologies to co-exist, thus allowing all the differences to be acknowledged and given expression. This has been made evident in the 'Nettles' notebook poem 'Bells', in which divergent faiths are linked through the numerous ways of calling, gathering or gaining the attention of others which bells demonstrate. While 'bells call the Christians to God', other tribes and creeds are called by

> … the sound of a blast through the sea-curved core of a shell
> when a black priest blows on a conch,
> and the dawn-cry from a minaret, God is great,
> and the calling of the old Red Indian high on the pueblo roof
> whose voice flies on and on, calling like a swan
> singing between the sun and the marsh,
> on and on, like a dark-faced bird singing alone
> singing to the men below, the fellow-tribesmen
> who go by without pausing, soft-foot, without listening yet who hear:
> there are other ways of summons, crying: Listen! Listen! Come near! (*CP* 623)

It is significant that the various methods are 'other ways of summons': *other*, not better or worse. Birkin's social ideal, in which people are recognized as intrinsically other and there are no terms of comparison, offers a correlative to the poem's attitude to cultural diversity and difference (*WL* 103–104).

Religions are intrinsically 'other' because they emanate from belief which itself eludes definition and rigidity, though being

> Forever nameless
> Forever unknown
> Forever unconceived
> Forever unrepresented
> Yet forever felt in the soul. (*CP* 622)

---

25   See the lines 'One and one is all alone, / and ever more shall be so' in the song 'Green Grow the Rushes, Oh!': a song involving pagan symbolism, *English County Songs*, ed. L.E. Broadwood and J.A.F. Maitland (London: Leadenhall Press, 1893), pp. 158–9.

God may be given as many names as the toy horse in 'The Rocking-Horse Winner',[26] yet he will remain, in the last resort, unknown and unknowable. The earlier poem 'Fish' contains the realization that 'I didn't know his God': the frightening but also liberating awareness of 'Other Gods / Beyond my range ... gods beyond my God' (*CP* 338). It is analogously difficult to come to terms with the multiple gods of the primitive men who 'slimly went like fishes, and didn't care' (*CP* 688). It is a consequence of this realization that forgetting or ceasing through yielding are seen as ways to come into touch with God: 'To be able to forget is to be able to yield / to God who dwells in deep oblivion' (*CP* 725).

For his last 'God' described in the 'Last Poems' notebook – the God of 'Shadows' – Lawrence returns to an unnamed and unknown deity whose presence, interestingly, is definable only in terms of the natural world, the cosmos in its seasonal oscillations:

> And if tonight my soul may find her peace
> in sleep, and sink in good oblivion,
> and in the morning wake like a new-opened flower
> then I have been dipped again in God, and new-created. (*CP* 726)

The poem seems to return to and develop the curiously premature 'Nettles' notebook poem 'Gladness of Death', revealing the fluid nature of Lawrence's poetry writing. 'Shadows' is appropriately cyclic and 'primitive' as it engages primarily with Lawrence's sense of the 'changing phases of a man's life' (*CP* 727), which seem to follow nature's pattern in which the moon waxes and wanes, and flowers blossom and fade. This birth/death oscillation provokes the knowledge that even in the most critical illness 'I shall know that my life is moving still / with the dark earth, and drenched / with the deep oblivion of earth's lapse and renewal' (*CP* 727). Lawrence's longed-for renewal in *life* was envisaged as a breaking out beyond the mid-life crisis of maladjustment and conflict, as expressed in a letter of 5 September 1929:

> How tired I am of my ill-health. – But my ill-health is the same as your loss of energy – it's a sort of masculine change of life. It's a change of the whole psychic rhythm, and of most of the psychic values. It means, not only a maladjustment to the present system, but a whole conflict and finally a break with the present system. And we have to accept the ill-health and the loss of energy. Because all the energy that ran concurrent with the present system now leaves us, drains away, like an up-rooted tree, and will not come back till we make new roots in a new emotion. (*L* vii 464–5)

Recovery, in the poem, is envisaged in terms of facilitated 'snatches of renewal':

---

[26] The horse acquires the name of each Derby winner prior to a race, allowing Paul to predict the outcome.

then I must know that still
I am in the hands [of] the unknown God,
he is breaking me down to his own oblivion
to send me forth on a new morning, a new man. (*CP* 727)

Rebirth is conceived in seasonal terms, yet the desire for intimacy must be satisfied by a Being with whom you may walk 'close together', and who takes you gently between his hands in an act of tenderness. The God who dictates the changing phases of the cosmos must not only supervise the changing phases of a man's life, but must fulfil the need for physical touch. So the God of 'Shadows' remains paradoxical, embodying aspects of many of the diverse gods who occupy the 'Nettles' and 'Last Poems' notebooks.

A critical response must refrain from attempting to 'solve' or 'resolve' the paradoxes and incongruities arising from Lawrence's struggle with 'all sorts of gods'. Rather, it should recognize that the mythology embodied and explored in these poems 'is only to the full intelligible and admirable if we realize it as a superb and baffled endeavour, not a *telos* or completion but a movement and effort of life' (*FS* 83). It is unsurprising that Lawrence made such an 'effort' in his *Last Poems,* and that such authors as Tylor, Frazer and Murray seem to have provided crucial intertexts for his late understanding of ancient civilizations. Lawrence may, as a consequence of this preoccupation, be located in an early twentieth-century tradition that attempted, via anthropology, to recover beliefs and languages that had once been important in human culture, and which in modern times may be seen as necessary again. As in his writings on the Etruscans, Lawrence's creative response to primitive cultures, myths and beliefs assumed a more pressing and vital significance during his last years, becoming a defining attribute of his late poetry.

Chapter 7
Apocalyptic Symbols

Accidental Lateness: The role of Frederick Carter

It is impossible to consider, analyse and explore Lawrence's *Last Poems* without reference to his last major prose work, *Apocalypse*, as my frequent allusions to this text throughout preceding chapters have indicated. It was Richard Aldington who gave the collective title *Last Poems* to the verse notebooks that Lawrence was compiling prior to his death (see Chapter 2, p. 23). Yet Lawrence himself chose the title *Apocalypse* for his subsequent book, indicating a direct correlation with its biblical counterpart, the last book of the New Testament. Mara Kalnins has suggested that:

> Ranging over his entire system of thought on God and man, on psychology, science, politics and art, *Apocalypse* is Lawrence's last testament, his final attempt to convey his vision of man and of the cosmos to posterity. (*2A* 11)

Apocalypse was the only large-scale work Lawrence wrote after *Last Poems*, and Kalnins attempts to convey its significance as that of a book that is a summation of crucial areas in Lawrence's thinking. This argument points to a deliberate, willed and cultivated lastness: a consciously devised 'harmonium' in Lipking's sense (see Chapter 1, n. 6), in which Lawrence is recapitulating and rounding off a literary life. It is necessary to emphasize that *Apocalypse* is radical stylistically and semantically; it strives for innovation, challenging convention and remaining incomplete (see Chapter 1, pp. 16–17). It was also the product of an important collaborative dialogue, with its roots in a much earlier phase of Lawrence's life.

Directly, *Apocalypse* dates back to December 1922 (*L* iv 365) when Lawrence, while staying in Taos, New Mexico, first entered into correspondence with the English painter and mystic Frederick Carter, who asked him to look at his manuscript and drawings on the symbolism of Revelation (see *2A* 12 and *L* iv 459–61). In *Apocalypse* Lawrence describes the feelings of liberation provoked by this initial contact with Carter's work:

> I also remember very vividly my first experience of the astrological heavens, reading Frederick Carter's *Dragon*: the sense of being the macrocosm, the great sky with its meaningful stars and its profoundly meaningful motions, its wonderful bodily vastness, not empty, but all alive and doing ... And since I am not afraid to feel my own nothingness in front of the vast void of astronomical

space, neither am I afraid to feel my own splendidness in the zodiacal heavens.
(*A* 46–7)

Lawrence was struck by the liberating nature of Carter's prose text, as well as the series of Blakean designs reflecting various aspects of the astrological heavens. Carter's work was itself going through a complex intertextual process of revision and alteration throughout the 1920s. The initial chapters of the manuscript that Lawrence saw in 1923 (along with the drawings) were published as *The Dragon of the Alchemists* in 1926; the book subsequently became *The Dragon of the Apocalypse, The Dragon of Revelation* (published in 1931), then *Symbols of Revelation* (published in 1934).

In spite of his initial enthusiasm for Carter's work, Lawrence's book would never have existed if Carter had not contacted him again during his stay in Bandol in 1929 with the request that Lawrence should write a foreword to a new version of the *Dragon*. The significance of Carter's role in Lawrence's writing on Revelation is emphasized in the rather aggrieved publisher's note that appears in the 1931 edition of *The Dragon of Revelation*, in which the publisher tries to re-establish Carter's text as the driving force behind Lawrence's book (which had been published earlier in the same year). He quotes a long letter printed in *The Times Literary Supplement* on 2 July 1931, responding to a recent review of the 1931 Florence edition of *Apocalypse*. This reviewer had complained that the edition of *Apocalypse* gave no indication of the date or origin of Lawrence's text, and the *TLS* letter set out to explain the consequences of such ignorance:

> This circumstance leads your reviewer to ascribe to Lawrence a knowledge of very many things that he derived from Mr. Carter rather than from his own 'wide reading.' Lawrence's opinions were, of course, though based on facts supplied by Mr. Carter, undeniably his own, and, indeed, though in the main coincident, yet in certain instances opposed to those of his friend. Yet it cannot be denied that Lawrence's *Apocalypse* would never have been written had Lawrence not had access to Mr. Carter's work.[1]

Undeniably it was in response to the overtures of Carter who 'sent Lawrence some rewritten material for a new book, suggesting a collaboration' (*2A* 15) that Lawrence returned enthusiastically to his study of Revelation and apocalyptic literature during his last year.

Carter visited Lawrence in mid-November 1929 and stayed until the end of the month, indicating that at this time Lawrence may well have abandoned his poetry-writing and devoted all his time to his last major work in prose. In her 'Introduction' to the Penguin edition of *Apocalypse*, Kalnins describes the development of Lawrence's writing during this period:

---

[1]   Quoted in 'A Note by the Publisher', in Frederick Carter, *The Dragon of Revelation* (London: Harmsworth, 1931), p. 8.

> By the time [Carter] left, Lawrence had written 20,000 words on Revelation and in mid-December he wrote to Carter: 'I have roughly finished my introduction, and am going over it, working it a bit into shape.' (*2A* 17)

Lawrence continued to revise the manuscript before Christmas, but shortly after this his plans changed. In January he wrote a new short introduction, which Carter chose not to include in the book now called *The Dragon of the Apocalypse*.[2] Lawrence's long first introduction (consisting of around 25,000 words with another 20,000 of deleted material) was developed into his last book, *Apocalypse*.

Thus Lawrence's writing on *Apocalypse* began as an introduction to the work of another author, but then assumed an existence and identity of its own. Interestingly, he retrospectively favoured the version of the *Dragon* that he read first in 1923:

> The *Dragon* as it exists now is no longer the *Dragon* which I read in Mexico. It has been made more—more argumentative, shall we say. Give me the old manuscript and let me write an introduction to that! I urge. But: No, says Carter. It isn't *sound*.

> Sound what? He means his old astrological theory of the Apocalypse was not sound, as it was exposed in the old manuscript. But who cares? We do not care, vitally, about theories of the Apocalypse: what the Apocalypse means. What we care about is the release of the imagination. A real release of the imagination renews our strength and our vitality, makes us feel stronger and happier. (*A* 47)

Lawrence valued the book as one that could provoke a liberating imaginative or visionary response. To derive an image from the essay entitled 'Chaos in Poetry', he believed that the book slashed through the old patched parasol protecting man from the implications of visionary insight, and created (quite literally in the case of this astrological work) 'a window to the sun' (*IR* 109). The effect of the initial *Dragon* on Lawrence was like that of Harry Crosby's poetry collection *Chariot of the Sun*, which, despite being at times nonsensical, creates insight through its symbolism that may be apprehended by sense-consciousness rather than a more limited cerebral response. Lawrence described Carter's book using terms similar to those he employed in 'Chaos in Poetry':

> It was confused: it was, in a sense, a chaos. And it hadn't very much to do with St. John's Revelation. But that didn't matter to me. I was very often smothered in words. And then would come a page, or a chapter, that would release my imagination and give me a whole great sky to move in. (*A* 45)

---

[2] The introduction was finally published posthumously as a separate essay in *The London Mercury*, July 1930 (see *A* 17).

Through taking an imaginative line, Carter (along with other key authors discussed below) liberated Lawrence from the dogmatically expounded Revelation of his youth and allowed him to glimpse a plethora of new possibilities.

Lifelong Revelations

During Lawrence's early Nonconformist childhood in Eastwood he was dosed, or overdosed, with the apocalyptic language of the King James Bible. He was exposed to the language and images of Revelation in the same way that he was exposed in early life to the 'banal' Nonconformist hymns that he felt influenced him so profoundly, and to the poems that were woven deep into his consciousness:

> I was brought up on the Bible, and seem to have it in my bones. From early childhood I have been familiar with Apocalyptic language and Apocalyptic image... I did not even listen attentively. But language has a power of echoing and re-echoing in my unconscious mind... [T]he sound of Revelation had registered in me very early, and I was as used to: 'I was in the Spirit on the Lord's day, and heard behind me a great voice, as of a trumpet, saying: I am the Alpha and the Omega' — as I was to a nursery rhyme like Little Bo-Peep! I didn't know the meaning, but then children so often prefer sound to sense. (*A* 54–5)

This passage suggests a process of interiorization that is subconscious, unwilled and irrational. The profundity and duration of such early experiences can be identified in retrospect as fundamental, so that it becomes possible to refer to 'the phrases that have haunted us all our life' (*A* 47).

A consideration of childhood influence of this sort is the focus of the very opening of Lawrence's *Apocalypse*, in which the interiorization process is identified as an extremely harmful indoctrination resulting in resentment, repudiation and constrained response. Lawrence describes the way in which he 'had the Bible poured every day into my helpless consciousness, till there came almost a saturation point' from 'earliest years right into manhood', so that it 'soaked in' and became an 'influence which affected all the processes of emotion and thought' (*A* 59). After such saturation, any fleeting contact would provoke an awareness of deep-rooted familiarity, and the triggered reaction would be one of dislike and resentment (*A* 59). Lawrence elaborates on the fixity of response occasioned by his early, brutally persistent experience of Revelation:

> Not only was the Bible verbally trodden into the consciousness, like innumerable foot-prints treading a surface hard, but the foot-prints were always mechanically alike, the interpretation was fixed, so that all real interest was lost. (*A* 59)

Lawrence's exposure to numerous, often conflicting, perspectives at various stages in his life thereafter functioned as a valuable corrective to this early process of mechanical indoctrination. He read James Pryse's *The Apocalyse Unsealed* in or before 1917;[3] much later, in 1924, he reviewed John Oman's *Book of Revelation* (having recently established initial contact with Carter).[4] Although Carter's impact was most profound, Pryse and Oman offered fascinating perspectives on Revelation in their attempts to 'explain' or disentangle its intricate message.

Pryse emphasizes the indecipherable nature of Revelation, suggesting that the text has the status of an unresolved enigma that paradoxically 'reveals nothing' to the 'ablest scholars in the ranks of orthodoxy' (*AU* 2). Reacting, like Lawrence, against the 'system of dogmatic theology formulated from the literal interpretation, the dead letter, of the books of the *Old* and *New Testaments*' (*AU* 2), Pryse attempts an 'unsealing' of the apocalyptic language and symbolism. He identifies in the text 'very clear intimations of a secret traditional lore, an arcane science, handed down from times immemorial' (*AU* 1).

In other words, Pryse assumes that Revelation contains a carefully encoded message, and that a series of 'ingenious puzzles which have baffled the profane for so many centuries' were necessary to prevent the book from an otherwise inevitable censorship by the esoteric Church (*AU* 3–4). Revelation dissimulates, masks and conceals, as its 'meaning' is 'impregnably intrenched behind symbolism, allegory, anagram, number-words, and other puzzling devices' (*AU* 80). Yet Pryse assumes that this 'meaning' is recoverable, for 'the *Apocalypse* contains its own key, and is complete in itself, coherent, and scrupulously accurate in every detail' (*AU* 219). The intention, he alleges, is not to mislead; rather, the book will 'verify the correct interpretation of the allegory', for it 'is not sealed to any one who has the developed intuitive faculty' (*AU* 219).

Like Pryse, Oman felt himself 'baffled by a problem' when faced with the text of Revelation, but one stemming from his recognition that 'no method of interpretation—historical, allegorical, mythological, astrological—gives it any connected or reasonable meaning' (*BR* vii). While Pryse credits Revelation with ingenuity and coherence, Oman proceeds from the assumption that the text itself is corrupt and disordered, thus requiring reorganization of a radical kind, rather than simply insightful interpretation:

---

[3]   See letter to David Eder (*L* iii 150). The extent to which Lawrence was affected by this book is evident in his psychoanalytic works, in which he adopts many of Pryse's key terms and concepts regarding the 'biological psyche', discussing and reinterpreting these in the light of his own thinking. See, for instance, *Psychoanalysis and the Unconscious and Fantasia of the Unconscious*, ed. Bruce Steele (Cambridge: Cambridge University Press, 2004), p. 23 and notes.

[4]   Lawrence's initial interest in Oman's book was probably a result of his early correspondence with Carter involving Apocalyptic themes (see *L* iv 583). Lawrence offered to review Oman's book and sent the finished piece to John Middleton Murry.

> That there is some disorder in the text of the Apocalypse is as near a certainty as
> a literary question can well be.
>
> The evidence is plainest towards the end of the book. Nations need healing
> (xxii. 2) after pain and sorrow have passed for ever (xxi. 4); the unclean and
> idolaters and hypocrites must be kept out of the Holy City (xxi. 27) after they
> have all perished in the lake of fire (xxi. 8); this holy city comes (xxi. 9), but the
> saints already sit in it on thrones (xx. 4), and its 1000 years end with the loosing
> of Satan (xx. 7); the Last Judgement and the Eternal State must close the book.
> (*BR* 1)

Oman offers various explanations of the way in which (for example) sections
conform or fail to conform to a certain structure or pattern, ranging from the
supposition that the manuscript sheets have at some stage 'suffered disarrangement'
to the theory that 'the sections originally were not equal, but have been made so by
the editor' (*BR* 8). He alleges that the editor found the text in utter confusion and
therefore rearranged it subjectively, and that this new structure 'did not depend
upon arguments, but upon a general impression of the sequence of the book' (*BR*
17). Oman's own reordering of the book is in part an attempt to eradicate what he
sees as the harmful intervention of this hypothetically wilful editor so as to restore
the author's original text (*BR* 15).

In his review of Oman's book, Lawrence recognizes the subjectivity of Oman's
reordering and assigns a motive to it: namely, 'the idea that the theme is the conflict
between true and false religion, false religion being established upon the Beast
of world empire' (*A* 41). Lawrence responds positively to Oman's book as an
interpretation that sees Revelation as a product of 'John's passionate and mystic
hatred of the civilization of his day, a hatred so intense only because he knew that
the living realities of men's being were displaced by it' (*A* 41). Lawrence, also
possessed by a 'mystic hatred of the civilization of his day' would undoubtedly
have found Oman's account of John's motivation congenial. However, Lawrence
goes on to assert that the interpretation, however satisfying, is not and cannot
be exhaustive, for to afford it definitive status would be to diminish the nature
of the apocalyptic text, and the symbolic method through which its insights are
conveyed:

> we cannot agree that Dr. Oman's explanation of the Apocalypse is exhaustive.
> No explanation of symbols is final. Symbols are not intellectual quantities, they
> are not to be exhausted by the intellect.
>
> And an Apocalypse has, must have, is intended to have various levels or
> layers or strata of meaning ...
>
> As a matter of fact, old symbols have many meanings, and we only define
> one meaning in order to leave another undefined. So with the meaning of the
> Book of Revelation. Hence the inexhaustibility of its attraction. (*A* 41–2)

Lawrence's attitude to his scholarly sources is evident in his assertion that 'The Apocalypse is a strange and mysterious book. One therefore welcomes any serious work upon it' (*A* 41). The value of each critical text responding to it is that each offers a single but invaluable perspective, thus expounding or illuminating one meaning, or one stratum of meaning.

When writing his book in 1929, then, Lawrence (as in his preparation for writing *Sketches of Etruscan Places*) felt that he needed to acquire a thorough familiarity with the available scholarly literature, including

> editions of the Bible, R.H. Charles's scholarly *A Critical and Exegetical Commentary on the Revelation of St. John*, *L'Apocalypse de Jean* by A. Loisy, Hesiod, Plutarch and Dean Inge's lectures on Plotinus, which he read for their accounts of ancient cosmology and cosmogony. (*2A* 15)

His wide reading, and his increasing familiarity with the biblical text in its various manifestations, confirmed that Revelation was a visionary work possessed of interpretative possibilities, a text with meanings lurking behind meanings and with the infinite appeal of the undiscovered or undiscoverable:

> When all is explained and expounded and commented upon, still there remains a curious fitful, half-spurious and half-splendid wonder in the work ... Sometimes the figures have a life of their own, inexplicable, which cannot be explained away or exhausted ... Gradually we realize the book has no one meaning. It has meanings. Not meaning *within* meaning: but rather, meaning against meaning. (*A* 48)

Even when the biblical language has been forced into an interpretative straitjacket, and its visionary potential has become suppressed or submerged, it still has the capacity to be vivid, startling and tantalizingly contradictory.

Symbolism and the Psyche

Lawrence's prolonged discussion of symbols throughout all his apocalyptic writings is in part provoked directly by his response to the biblical text of Revelation, and in part a dialogic response to Frederick Carter. Lawrence may have been led to consider the symbolic nature of the Apocalypse initially when reading Carter's passages on symbolism in the manuscript given to him in 1923, which then became a chapter entitled 'Symbol' in *The Dragon of the Alchemists*. Carter, like Lawrence, reflects on the paucity of genuine, deep-rooted symbols: 'of symbols, deeply established in the mind and consciousness, [there are] but few' (*DA* 22). He attributes a 'peculiar force in the "unconscious" mind' to the symbol, referring also to its 'power to set free emotion, to induce a mood or mode of thinking' (*DA* 11). Like Lawrence again, Carter considers the necessary receptivity with which an individual must engage with a symbol. For those 'of narrow, overmaterial mind, and habit of thought' any attempt at response will be futile,

> But to the mind capable of apprehending association and analogies of an extensive order, it is a guide and director to paths of advancement in such knowledge. Thus the symbol in its religious or mystical aspect is the medium between the exterior physical universe and the interior world of thought: it is a symbol in that it gives a true relation. (*DA* 27–8)

Through symbols (Carter asserts), it is possible to achieve a 'true balance or equilibrium of the physical world relative to the psychical' (*DA* 28). Lawrence was struggling, particularly between 1928 and 1930, to find a way in which his writing might articulate a living connection between man and the cosmos, thus achieving balance or equilibrium. In *Last Poems* Lawrence attempts to do what Carter here suggests is possible: he uses mystical or religious images and symbols as a medium in his exploration of possible relations between man's interior world of thought and the exterior physical universe.

In *The Dragon of the Alchemists*, those who use and respond appropriately to images and symbols are visionaries, perceiving the external world through 'their marvellous and resplendent web of metaphor and symbol' (*DA* 28), as well as artists and, more specifically, poets. Carter describes the early nineteenth century as a 'mystical-minded age of great poets and great adventurers, in life as in thought' (*DA* 14),[5] referring to the 'ebbing enchantment' of the 'realms of dream' which 'laid close hold on a few—on Shelley, on Coleridge, on Wordsworth, as a little earlier on Blake' (*DA* 13). Carter's approach to mysticism and symbolism often becomes psychological or psychoanalytical in keeping with his expressed aim in the book: 'the resolution of the psychological meaning of the Dragon with its kindred and associated symbols' (*DA* 22). He is concerned, as is Lawrence, with the way in which symbols provoke responses at different levels of consciousness, or subconsciousness.

According to Carter 'The poet was a stargazer, and found in his heaven the images of perfection' (*DA* 19). He asserts that both literature and religion can be best understood and explained in astrological terms, so his approach is that of conscious return to an ancient mode of apprehending and relating to the heavens. His conception of return is strikingly similar to that of Lawrence, though Lawrence does not always have such an astrological bias. Carter is also in revolt against the conceited modern assumption that ancient people living in close connection with the cosmos were less intelligent and more ignorantly superstitious than in his own time. He intimates that, for the appreciation of the possible correspondence between the older speculation on the mystical meaning of the heavenly signs and

---

[5] Cf. Lawrence's line 'Man is a thought-adventurer', in 'Books', *Reflections on the Death of a Porcupine and Other Essays*, ed. Michael Herbert (Cambridge: Cambridge University Press, 1988), p. 197 and note on l. 9.

an examination of astrology from a psychological standpoint, 'it is necessary to assume … that the thinkers of ancient times were of a mentality equal to ours and not appreciably more superstitious than we are to-day.' (*DA* 22)

The ancient thinkers whom Carter invokes postulated a conception of humanity that was quite literally bound up with and reliant on the heavenly bodies in all respects:

> In their opinion, a human being's birth had a relation to the whole universe conditioned by the moment of time at which it took place. Its tendencies, mental and physical, came into being and were even to be read in the position and relation of the signs and planets of the heavens. (*DA* 20)

Carter takes this to the extreme of arguing that 'the whole mind's book of symbols is given compactly in the stars' (*DA* 21). It is thus through a conscious return or reversion to the ancient conception of the heavenly bodies that the mythopoeic or imaginative workings of man's mind will be liberated, resulting in visionary illumination. Carter recognizes that to most modern readers 'these absurd superstitions in things alchemical and astrological are of little consequence, and far out of their habit of mind' (*DA* 18); but he feels that these belief-systems are no less valuable as a consequence. His 'return' is one that Lawrence advocates and follows in his own reaching back to the astronomical and astrological cosmology and symbolism so prevalent in his late works. Such a conceptual return, in Lawrence's view, might be capable of providing modern man with a new habit of mind and vision. It is with this aim in mind that Lawrence – in *Last Poems* and also in *Apocalypse* – imaginatively inhabits a version of Carter's ancient world of astrological symbolism, and writes about the ways to establish a new, meaningful connection. What Lawrence acquired was not, of course, what Carter would have desired, but what he incidentally provided.

The significance of symbols in Lawrence's thinking about the power of Revelation is evident throughout his principal apocalyptic writings. His ideas are found in embryonic form in the early Oman review, written in February 1924, but are most prominent in the 'Introduction to *The Dragon of the Apocalypse*' finished as late as January 1930. Perhaps as a result of Pryse's reference to the Apocalypse as 'one of the most stupendous allegories ever penned by the hand of man' (*AU* 66), Lawrence is here determined to differentiate between allegory and symbolism, and to assign Revelation to the latter category. He considers allegory to be limited in using images to express definite qualities, and affording each image a fixed place in a moral or didactic argument. Symbols, by contrast, allow for interpretative flexibility and liberation of response. They are, in Lawrence's conception of them, alive:

> You can't give a great symbol a 'meaning', any more than you can give a cat a 'meaning'. Symbols are organic units of consciousness with a life of their own, and you can never explain them away, because their value is dynamic,

emotional, belonging to the sense-consciousness of the body and soul, and not simply mental. (*A* 48)

Symbols (described by Lawrence as the images of myth) 'stand for units of human *feeling*, human experience', with the power to 'arouse the deep emotional self, and the dynamic self, beyond comprehension' (*A* 49). The power of symbols is a result of their antiquity and the cumulative process by which they become increasingly rich and resonant:

> Many ages of accumulated experience still throb within a symbol. And we throb in response. It takes centuries to create a really significant symbol … No man can invent symbols. He can invent an emblem, made up of images: or metaphors: or images: but not symbols. Some images, in the course of many generations of men, become symbols, embedded in the soul and ready to start alive when touched, carried on in the human consciousness for centuries. And again, when men become unresponsive and half dead, symbols die. (*A* 49)

The appeal of the Apocalypse for Lawrence is that it contains 'many splendid old symbols, to make us throb' (*A* 49).

It is appropriate to consider *Apocalypse* as an expression of ideas that have been reached partly through the modulation of images and symbols in the preceding poetry. Lawrence formulates a theory that is particularly appropriate to his own late work, involving an adherence to 'sense-awareness' rather than more modern methods of analysis. In the 'sense-awareness' or 'sense-knowledge' of the ancients (as Lawrence sees it), reason could be arrived at 'direct', via instinct and intuition rather than through cerebral effort. The access to this kind of awareness would not be through words but through images, and there would be no necessity for logic, for the connection would be 'emotional':

> Images or symbols succeeded one another in a procession of instinctive and arbitrary physical connection—some of the Psalms give us examples–and they 'get nowhere' because there was nowhere to get to, the desire was to achieve a consummation of a certain state of consciousness, to fulfill [*sic*] a certain state of feeling-awareness. (*A* 91)

Lawrence aims to be a writer who 'starts with an image, sets the image in motion, allows it to achieve a certain course or circuit of its own, and then takes up another image' (*A* 96), enabling 'the mind to move in cycles, or to flit here and there over a cluster of images' (*A* 97). This conception of cyclic and modulatory images seems more appropriate in describing the methodology employed in *Last Poems* than the subsequent prose text, as poetry can operate according to the 'rotary-image thought' (*A* 95) that Lawrence associated with the workings of the pagan consciousness. A poem can explore an image or impression through modulation and repetition, achieving insight without recourse to the logical constraints of argument.

Using the Symbols of Revelation: Pryse, Oman, Inge and Carter

The symbols of Revelation are interpreted variously by the writers who influenced Lawrence between 1915 and 1930. I will begin by discussing some of these interpretations (relating to the key symbols of sun, moon and dragon) before considering Lawrence's use of these particular symbols both in *Last Poems* and in his subsequent prose writings on the Apocalypse.

According to Pryse, the sun is a crucial symbol in Revelation, and his interpretation of its multiple applications exemplifies the potential of a symbol to assume and modulate through a plethora of meanings. In deciphering the Apocalypse, Pryse is always searching for meanings within meanings, and at the core he usually finds the sun, in one manifestation or another. He sees it as primordial and all-encompassing: the seven sacred planets 'only represent seven aspects of the Sun' (*AU* 67), while 'In the benediction [in VII. 9–12] the attributes of all the seven planets are ascribed to the Sun-God' (*AU* 132). The sun seems to provide a useful 'core' for Pryse as a puzzle-solving critic, for in his interpretation it is made to represent or signify almost everything.

The flexibility of the sun symbol in Pryse's account of Revelation might be attributed to its appearance in different symbolic 'aspects'. It can both adopt and be adopted by these diverse 'aspects': in X. 1–4 the Divinity described is 'the intellectual Sun, in its aspect as Kronos, the God of Time' (*AU* 143); while in II. 18–29 'the Logos has the aspect of Helios (the Sun)', thus becoming a hybrid Sun-Logos (*AU* 105). The biblical figure which appears among lampstands, holding seven stars, and with a two-edged sword emanating from his mouth is 'a fanciful picture of the Sun as the *Panaugeia*, or fount of all-radiating light' (*AU* 89), a 'figure of the Sun as the ruler of the planets' and simultaneously 'a symbol of the incarnated Self, the Second Logos' (*AU* 91). In IX. 13–15, Pryse interprets the 'golden altar' in terms of its solar significance: 'Gold is the metal of the sun, and the four-horned altar is but a different symbol for the sun and the regents of the four quarters' (*AU* 141).

The sun is crucial to Pryse's argument regarding the biological psyche, as is evident when he expounds his interpretation of the 'seventh seal' or 'conarium', 'its zodiacal correspondence being Leo, which is the house of the Sun' (*AU* 46):

> As the sun enters each sign of the zodiac it is said, astrologically, to 'conquer' the sign and to assimilate its particular quality; and the same is said of the *kundalini* as it passes through the *chakras*. Hence the hero of the *Apocalypse*, who is the Nous, or microcosmic Sun, is called 'the Conqueror.' (*AU* 97)

Thus, Pryse uses the relation of the sun to the zodiacal signs as an analogy for the way in which a vital flow of energy passes through the human form. Perhaps the largest claim he makes regarding the sun's significance in this regard is that the Apocalypse has as its 'sole theme' the rebirth into an 'imperishable solar body' (*AU* 24). Finally, Pryse often emphasizes the leonine aspect of the sun, both when referring directly to the zodiacal signs in such statements as 'The Sun is the Lion when domiciled in Leo' (*AU* 169), and when assigning characteristics to biblical figures, such as the horsemen of IX. 16–21, whose 'solar character' is indicated by 'the lion-heads of the horses' (*AU* 142).

In *The Book of Revelation*, Oman has argued for such links between astrology and primitive cults or rituals in an attempt to articulate his theory regarding the astrological symbolism of Revelation. He discerns pagan ritual behind the ostensible Christian dogma, in a way that prefigures what Lawrence was to do, and which probably influenced it: 'Pouring the vial on the sun at least suggests sun-worship and the turning of the god into the destroyer.' (*BR* 126) Lawrence does not usually relate the sun to specific deities or mythologies as he wishes to get back to a Chaldean conception of the cosmos which predates named, specific deities in fixed relation to astrological phenomena.[6] Yet it may be that the depiction of such deities as Dionysos and Osiris in his late writings was influenced by their association with astrological or cosmic symbols. In *The Philosophy of Plotinus* (one of the major texts on Lawrence's Apocalyptic book-list) W.R. Inge refers to Dionysus and Orpheus as 'two nearly connected forms of the Sun-god', and goes on to say of the Egyptian Osiris that 'his resemblance to Dionysus was close enough to tempt many to identify them'.[7] Inge relates these 'forms of the Sun-god' to the ceremonies of death and rebirth, involving 'the rending in pieces of the god or hero, the lament for him, his resurrection, and the communion of his flesh and blood as a "medicine of immortality"'.[8] Part II of *The Escaped Cock* engages directly with the mystery-cult of Osiris as a dying and reviving god, and when the Christ-figure experiences new birth through sexual arousal Lawrence writes 'A new sun was coming up in him, in the perfect inner darkness of himself' and 'his own sun dawned, and sent its fire running along his limbs, so that his face shone unconsciously' (*VG* 159). Osiris does not feature prominently in *Last Poems*, yet Dionysos is a returning or resurrected god who reappears in his ship during the poems concerned with a mythopoeic crossing of the 'Minoan distance'. Poems such as 'Shadows' articulate the 'hope of mystical death and renewal ... based on

---

[6]   Chaldea was a land in southern Babylonia (now southern Iraq), to which frequent allusions are made in the Old Testament. Many ancient writers also used the term 'Chaldean' in relation to the priests and other people educated in classical Babylonian literature, especially in traditions of astronomy and astrology.

[7]   W.R. Inge, *The Philosophy of Plotinus*, third edition, vol. 1 (London: Longmans, 1929), p. 57.

[8]   Ibid.

the analogy of nature's processes of death and rebirth'.[9] Such passages in Inge's book may have provoked Lawrence to consider the possible interrelations between his previous thinking on primitive cultures in response to the anthropological texts by Tylor and Frazer, and his new preoccupation with astrology and cosmology derived from Apocalyptic intertexts.

Carter assigns prominence to the sun and moon, which (along with the earth), 'are bound up in an intimate relationship that enters very deeply into the lost lore of the Astrologers' (*DA* 40). While sun and moon are seen as jointly responsible for 'sway[ing] the solid world' (*DA* 40), the moon's proximity to the earth results in its greater 'force' when dictating planetary motion. In fact, Carter goes so far as to assert that the moon's 'varying position' disturbs the movement of the earth's axis and causes the 'nod' entailed in the Procession of the Equinoxes. Yet the symbol that so fascinated Carter that it became the focus of every version of his book was the dragon, which (among its multiple resonances and associations) adopts the attributes of both sun and moon. In *The Dragon of the Alchemists* Carter asserts that 'in the opinion of the alchemical writers, the Dragon was significant of the Sun and the Moon in a state of change' (*DA* 14). The dragon both signifies and embodies change, and its mystery and fascination stem directly from this attribute:

> He who can hold and examine the history of this baleful changing monster, still hidden in the strange deep of the universal psyche, may find, so the stories promise, by its mastery, strange and marvellous treasure, and knowledge beyond that of the magicians of the market place. (*DA* 15)

The 'baleful changing monster' suggests a symbol that modulates constantly through different forms and aspects, and which is therefore subject to infinite interpretations.

The richness and complexity of the dragon symbol becomes evident on consideration of some of its diverse aspects. Carter emphasizes this diversity by referring to the dragon's multiple appearances in wide-ranging mythological settings:

> The Dragon held the same mysterious importance in [the alchemical writers'] philosophical system as it held in all myths, as it holds in the story of the 'fall of man' in the history of Hercules, Siegfried, St. George, and Perseus. As the serpent in the dream life of to-day, it maintains the same fascination of terror and formidable knowledge. (*DA* 14–15)[10]

---

[9] Ibid.

[10] In 'Dominant Woman', Lawrence satirically describes the way in which young women, revolting against their dominant elders, turn again to men – or 'Perseus, St. George' – to save them 'from the Dragon of the modern female' (*CP* 619).

The Apocalyptic dragon is not only a figurative 'serpent' in our dreams; it also correlates directly with Satan, the serpent responsible for the fall of mankind. Carter refers to the dragon as the 'serpent' in Paradise: the embodiment of the 'dark power that lay in wait, and brought about the primary separation, and accounted for the fallen state of man' (*DA* 23). This interpretation derives from the explicit biblical description of 'that old serpent called the Devil, and Satan' as 'the huge dragon'.[11] Pryse also makes this association, when he describes the fall of Satan as follows: 'Hurled down was the great Dragon, the archaic Snake, who is called the "Accuser" and the "Adversary," the deluder of the whole inhabited earth' (*AU* 157). (The fall of Satan as portrayed in Lawrence's late poems is discussed at length in Chapter 8, pp. 179–84.)

Yet in Pryse's conception too the dragon symbol is multifaceted, and thus not purely evil or destructive. Hence the proliferation of dragons, enabling the symbol to incorporate the antitheses of good and evil, light and dark:

> The creative Logos is the Dragon of Light, or Day-Sun; and Satan, the Adversary, is the Dragon of Darkness, or Night-Sun. (*AU* 159)

As in the case of the sun and moon symbols, the dragon assumes a specific significance in relation to Pryse's theory of the biological psyche. The dragon represents 'the glamour of sensuous life', while the 'seven heads' that at one point he is said to possess are related to the 'seven cardinal desires' which 'energize through the seven *chakras* of the physical body during incarnation' (*AU* 58).

The symbol is further complicated by Pryse's reference to the dragon later in the same paragraph as 'the eighth, a sort of by-product of the seven' and also as 'the phantom which forms after the final purification', whose 'fate is to disintegrate in the nether-world' (*AU* 58–9). Such divergent and seemingly contradictory interpretations of this principal symbol again adhere to Lawrence's sense of the symbol as flexible in the way that allegory cannot be. We encounter 'meaning against meaning', and must accept the resulting clash of images and associations as profitable and thought provoking, rather than merely confused and chaotic.

In *Apocalypse* Lawrence, following the Bible, Carter and Pryse in emphasizing the correlation between dragon and serpent, asserts that this composite symbol goes 'so deep in every human consciousness, that a rustle in the grass can startle the toughest "modern" to depths he has no control over' (*A* 123). He makes the dragon 'the symbol of the fluid, rapid, startling movement of life within us. That startled life which runs through us like a serpent, or coils within us potent and waiting, like a serpent.' (*A* 123) Here, the association is positive: it is the image derived from yoga of the serpent or dragon coiled at the base of the spine that Lawrence describes in *Fantasia of the Unconscious*, and, even more significantly,

---

[11]   James Moffatt, *A New Translation of the Bible* (London: Hodder and Stoughton, 1926), XII. 9, p. 330 (quoted in *A* 119 as 'the great dragon').

in *Women in Love,* parts of which were revised after reading Pryse in 1917.[12] Like Pryse, Lawrence evokes the dragon in different symbolic aspects, and as a result ends up with multiple dragons, identifiable this time by colour. The red dragon is 'the kakodaimon, the dragon in his evil or inimical aspect' (*A* 125), while 'The long green dragon with which we are so familiar on Chinese things is the dragon in his good aspect of life-bringer, life-giver, life-maker, vivifier' (*A* 124).

The dragon is seen as 'personal' in the sense of existing as a potentiality coiled within each of us. Yet Lawrence emphasizes that the dragon symbol more often has macrocosmic than microcosmic significance:

> The usual vision of the dragon is, however, not personal but cosmic. It is in the vast cosmos of the stars that the dragon writhes and lashes. We see him in his maleficent aspect, red. But don't let us forget that when he stirs green and flashing on a pure dark night of stars it is he who makes the wonder of the night, it is the full rich coiling of his folds which makes the heavens sumptuously serene, as he glides around and guards the immunity, the precious strength of the planets, and gives lustre and new strength to the fixed stars ... . (*A* 124)

The 'cosmic' aspect of the dragon in which the symbol is associated with the zodiacal signs and constellations is also considered by Pryse and Oman, in particular in their interpretations of the woman who is clothed with the sun, standing on the moon and crowned with twelve stars, and the dragon figure that sweeps down a third of the stars in heaven with his tail (*BR* 116). Oman refers to an astrological interpretation in which 'the sign of the woman and the dragon' are 'the constellations of Virgo and Draco' (*BR* 116), while Pryse writes that 'This constellatory symbol is Draco, the pole Dragon, which has seven distinguishing stars, and which, as depicted in the ancient star-maps, extends over seven of the zodiacal signs' (*AU* 156). So the biblical dragon seems – like the sun symbol – to derive much of its potency from the Chaldean star-lore underlying the ostensible Christian 'meaning' of Revelation.

Apocalyptic Symbolism and 'Last Poems'

Many of the ideas, interpretations and images outlined above found their way into Lawrence's thinking and writing. In *Last Poems*, he had established the sun as a crucial and dominant symbol, as if in an attempt to regain it or restore it to its true status. The poem 'Forte dei Marmi' contains the exhortation: 'Let me tell you that the sun is alive, and can be angry' (*CP* 625). The sun is animate and benevolent:

> And life is for delight, and bliss
> like now when the white sun kisses the sea
> and plays with the wavelets like a panther playing with its cubs (*CP* 709)

---

[12]   See *WL* 313 and note to l. 15.

The sun is also inevitably bound up with all sensuous experience, such as the eating of an apple described in the poem 'Mystic'. In this poem the 'insistence of the sun' can be tasted in a 'good apple', while 'some apples taste preponderantly of water, wet and sour / and some of too much sun, brackish sweet / like lagoon-water, that has been too much sunned' (*CP* 707–708). This poem emphasizes that the sun can be experienced or felt directly through sensory perception: a method of responding that is the antithesis of the abstract thought-form making described subsequently in *Apocalypse* (discussed later in this section).

In the poem 'Bells' which describes a tribal summons, the sun is associated specifically with the non-verbal, non-mental communication of ancient peoples: 'The soft thudding of drums / of fingers or fists or soft-skinned sticks upon the stretched membrane of sound / sends summons in the old hollows of the sun' (*CP* 623). The sun's 'old hollows' may be filled not only with sounds but also with numerous although often unspecified gods. In 'Sunset', for instance, 'some god of evening' leans out of the 'band of dull gold in the west' 'again and again', and 'shares being' with the receptive observer (*CP* 656). The sun can imply god or gods as well as containing them: in the poem 'The Body of God' the manifestations of god include 'women brushing their hair in the sun' (*CP* 691).

Perhaps following Pryse, Lawrence describes the sun as the house of Leo, so that it is defined according to its leonine appearance and attributes. In 'The Argonauts', 'the sun, like a lion, licks his paws / and goes slowly down the hill' (*CP* 687), while 'Invocation to the Moon' refers to the 'golden house of the sun' that the narrator has left behind, after receiving 'one warm kind kiss of the lion with golden paws' (*CP* 695). In 'Prayer' the sun's hostile aspect is conveyed through its leonine appearance: 'For the sun is hostile, now / his face is like the red lion' (*CP* 684). It is the potential hostility of the leonine sun that surfaces in reaction against modern man's inability to establish vital contact with the stars, for 'The sun can rot as well as ripen' (*A* 52), and 'many neurotic people become more and more neurotic, the browner and "healthier" they become by sun-baking' (*A* 51–2). The poems 'Forte dei Marmi' and 'Sea-Bathers' pick up on this notion of the sun's potential harmfulness, its capacity to rot. The former describes how 'the reddening sun / reddens still more on the blatant bodies of these all-but-naked, sea-bathing city people' (*CP* 625), while the latter refers to this sunburnt state as 'nullity', the antithesis of 'health' (*CP* 625). Similarly in the poem 'What are the wild waves saying—?' the question raised in the title is given the following answer:

> It seems to me they are saying:
> How disgusting, how infinitely sordid this humanity is
> that dabbles its body in me
> and daubs the sand with its flesh
> in myriads, under the hot and hostile sun! (*CP* 628)

In 'Oh Wonderful Machine!' the robotic people for whom the machine has become a symbol or emblem are people 'to whom the sun is merely something that makes the thermometer rise!' (*CP* 643): people, in other words, to whom the sun has become merely a thought-form. In 'Stoic', the opening lament is occasioned by the death of the sun through loss of contact:

> Groan then, groan.
> For the sun is dead, and all that is in heaven
> is the pyre of blazing gas. (*CP* 702)

These are the lines that bear closest resemblance to Lawrence's prose in *Apocalypse,* when he writes 'our experience of the sun is dead', and refers to the sun (in its debased thought-form state) as a 'ball of blazing gas' (*A* 51–2).

It is not only the sun that modern man, according to Lawrence, has lost or killed. He refers to the masses as 'You who have no feeling of the moon as she changes her quarters!' (*CP* 643), describing the consequences of this lack of feeling as follows:

> And the moon that went
> so queenly, shaking her glistening beams
> is dead too, a dead orb wheeled once a month round the park. (*CP* 702)

In *Last Poems* we do not see the hostile, vitriolic aspect of the moon described later in *Apocalypse*, although its freedom and beauty are employed in contrast with the trapped condition of humankind. In the poem 'Listen to the Band!' the living, animate, free moon is contrasted with the constricted 'music' of dead humanity:

> A little moon, quite still, leans and sings to herself
> throughout the night
> and the music of men is like a mouse gnawing,
> gnawing in a wooden trap, trapped in. (*CP* 656)

Modern man is 'trapped in', yet in *Last Poems* as in *Apocalypse* Lawrence finds a way in which the possibility of re-establishing contact, of making a connection, may be imaginatively conveyed. In the poem 'If you are a man—' the future is envisaged as a new kind of knowledge or connectivity; we must aim

> To know the moon as we have never known
> yet she is knowable.
> To know a man as we have never known
> a man, as never yet a man was knowable, yet still shall be. (*CP* 666)

The moon is 'knowable', but this kind of knowledge does not entail the analytical, scientific probing that results in the 'pock-marked face of the moon' (*A* 52) of which Lawrence is so scornful in *Apocalypse*. The knowledge Lawrence advocates involves the establishing of a meaningful contact, rather than an objective, mental response.

The strange, white, magical quality of the moon is similarly expressed in the following lines, from 'Return of Returns':

> When the moon from out of the darkness
> has come like a thread, like a door just opening
> opening, till the round white doorway of delight
> is half open. (*CP* 702)

Here, the description of the wafer-thin crescent moon as 'thread' and as an opening door is both visually precise and symbolic. The moon does not only have the appearance of a thin crack created when a door is nudged slightly ajar; it also provides the first hint or suggestion of a doorway opening to new worlds and different kinds of knowledge and perception.

The moon's 'enormous potency' when perceived as 'living' in the Chaldean sense is conveyed in other *Last Poems*. In 'Delight of being alone' Lawrence writes:

> I know no greater delight than the sheer delight of being alone.
> It makes me realise the delicious pleasure of the moon
> that she has in travelling by herself (*CP* 610)

Later, in *Apocalypse*, Lawrence describes the moon as 'so rounded, so velvety, moving so serene' (*A* 52). The 'poised' moon is, in the poem, a symbol for aloneness, solitude and self-sufficiency; it is integral and cannot be shattered, as is evident in Birkin's futile attempt to stone and break up the moon in *Women in Love* (*WL* 246–8). In *Last Poems* the moon's coldness or coolness suggests this ability to remain aloof and whole, rather than suggesting the potentially contemptuous and abrasive aspect described in Lawrence's 'Introduction to *The Dragon of the Apocalypse*' (*A* 53).

In 'Invocation to the Moon' the moon, personified as a 'great glorious lady' and a 'glistening garmentless beauty', is seen not only as a white doorway of delight but as a 'heavenly mansion', reached through a necessary progression beyond the glowing house of the sun. The moon is the 'garmentless lady of the last great gift', capable of bestowing upon the narrator his 'lost limbs' and 'lost white fearless breast', then setting him again 'on moon-remembering feet / a healed, whole man' (*CP* 696). The moon is also the 'last [astronomical] house' to be inhabited prior to death, for it is sympathetic to the 'personality' rather than the 'ego', and its coolness is more desirable than the intense heat of the sun. The moon is also an image of change through cyclicity, and is thus an appropriate emblem for death and rebirth conceived either in terms of reincarnation or the constantly regenerative processes of nature.

The poem 'Prayer', the last poem in the 'Nettles' notebook – also an 'invocation' to the moon – makes an explicit distinction between the sympathetic moon and hostile sun:

> Give me the moon at my feet
> Put my feet upon the crescent, like a Lord! [13]
> O let my ankles be bathed in moonlight, that I may go
> sure and moon-shod, cool and bright-footed
> towards my goal.
>
> For the sun is hostile, now
> his face is like the red lion. (*CP* 684)

In this poem the moon is the heavenly body that provides literal support in the 'autumn' of life, while the sun in its ferocious or leonine aspect is inappropriate in its brightness and vigour. Lawrence here adheres to the distinction made by Empedocles between the 'sharp-darting sun and the gentle moon' (*EGP* 225). There is a time when it is appropriate for the sun to yield its place to the moon, as is described in 'The Argonauts':

> now that the moon, who remembers, and only cares
> that we should be lovely in the flesh, with bright, crescent feet,
> pauses near the crest of the hill, climbing slowly, like a queen
> looking down on the lion as he retreats– (*CP* 687)

It is the ascendancy of the moon in this poem that enables the Argonauts, figures of ancient myth and another kind of consciousness, to return: it is the moon that can provoke change of this magnitude, and provide the link with the older, more 'connected' civilization. 'Middle of the world' describes the supremacy of the moon in her 'exaltation', risen above the hostile sun to a position of dominance:

> And now that the moon who gives men glistening bodies
> is in her exaltation, and can look down on the sun ... (*CP* 688)

---

[13]   The image of the lord standing on the crescent moon may derive directly from Revelation. Pryse refers to this figure as the 'lunar goddess' or 'Diana, the "many-breasted mother," who appears in the *Apocalypse* as the "Woman clothed with the Sun, the moon underneath her feet" ' (*AU* 37). As in the case of the sun symbol, the moon adopts various aspects in Pryse's book. For instance, Pryse refers to 'The Light of the Logos, Arche, the DIVINE SUBSTANCE, primordial matter', saying that this is 'symbolized by the Sky-Virgin, the Moon' (*AU* 66).

The moon's exaltation is thus used by Lawrence to correspond with the autumn of life ('Now it is autumn and the falling fruit', *CP* 716), and simultaneously with the rebirth into contact with mythology and the 'Minoan distance'.

The poem 'The Hostile Sun' elaborates on the distinction between sun and moon, associating the sun with 'daytime consciousness', fixity and hardness or dogmatism:

> Sometimes the sun turns hostile to men
> when the daytime consciousness has got overweening
> when thoughts are stiff, like old leaves
> and ideas are hard, like acorns ready to fall.
>
> Then the sun turns hostile to us
> and bites at our throats and chests
> as he bites at the stems of leaves in autumn, to make them fall. (*CP* 608–609)

Suffering is inflicted and destruction occurs 'though the sun bronzes us', for the solar power is 'hostile to all the old leafy foliage of our thoughts / and the old upward flowing of our sap, the pressure of our upward flow of feeling / is against him' (*CP* 609). While the sun is revealed as inimical to the parts of man's consciousness associated with his primitive anthropological roots, the moon is described as 'cool and unconcerned', 'calm with the calm of scimitars and brilliant reaping hooks / sweeping the curve of space and mowing the silence' (*CP* 609). The coolness of the moon here enables one to 'have peace'.

It seems that in his prose discussion of symbols in *Apocalypse* and his 'Introduction to *The Dragon of the Apocalypse*', Lawrence is certainly incorporating and developing ideas and images prevalent in his astronomical and astrological poems: ideas which themselves may have been provoked by his familiarity with texts like *The Apocalypse Unsealed*, and by his close contact with Carter and Carter's writing at the time of composing *Last Poems* (Lawrence renewed correspondence with Carter in August 1929 and began work on Revelation in October: see *L* vii 444 and *A* xii). In the 'Introduction', for example, Lawrence states explicitly his desire to establish contact with the heavenly bodies, a contact that existed in the days of the Chaldeans, but which has been lost by modern man:

> I would like to know the stars again as the Chaldeans knew them, two thousand years before Christ. I would like to be able to put my ego into the sun, and my personality into the moon, and my character into the planets, and live the life of the heavens, as the early Chaldeans did ... I long for the sun again, and the moon and stars, for the Chaldean sun and the Chaldean stars. Because *our* sun and *our* moon are only thought-forms to us, balls of gas, dead globes of extinct volcanoes, things we *know* but never feel by experience. (*A* 51)

In articulating this aspiration (it has not yet been achieved: 'I *would like* to know'), Lawrence emphasizes 'experience' as opposed to thought, and physical, sensory perception as opposed to mental or intellectual response. Lawrence sets up a further antithesis between 'experience' of this nature and the creation of 'thought-forms' which are abstractions from real contact. He elaborates on this notion of the 'thought-form', which he relates to the impoverished condition of the 'poor things' crawling between the heaven and earth of our modern world:

> By *experience*, we should feel the sun as the savages feel him, we should 'know' him as the Chaldeans knew him, in a terrific embrace. But our experience of the sun is dead, we are cut off. All we have now is the thought-form of the sun. He is a blazing ball of gas, he has spots occasionally, from some sort of indigestion, and he makes you brown and healthy if you let him ... We have lost the sun, and we have found a few miserable thought-forms. (*A* 51–2)[14]

The moon, like the sun, is dead, because it has become merely a thought-form. This is a result in part of the 'scientific' methods of perceiving and responding to the heavenly bodies: 'think of the pock-marked horror of the scientific photographs of the moon!' (*A* 52).

Yet Lawrence goes on to say that 'the moon is not therefore a dead nothing'; that although the scientific image is 'a great blow', 'the imagination can recover from it' (*A* 52). For it is not in fact that the moon itself has become merely a 'dead lump'; rather, modern man is projecting onto the moon a reflected image of his own nullity:

> She is not dead. But maybe we are dead, half-dead little modern worms stuffing our damp carcasses with thought-forms that have no sensual reality. When we describe the moon as dead, we are describing the deadness in ourselves. (*A* 53)

The deadness of humanity's response can provoke a violent reaction from the moon, which, like the sun, is shown in *Apocalypse* to adopt at times a hostile aspect:

> the moon is Artemis still, and a dangerous goddess she is, as she always was. She throws her cold contempt on you as she passes over the sky, poor, mean little worm of a man who thinks she is nothing but a dead lump. She throws back the

---

[14]   The language used here echoes that of 'The Woman Who Rode Away' (1924) at the point where the young Native American converses with the captured protagonist, explaining his tribe's (misguided) beliefs regarding the sun and moon. He states, for instance, that 'The sun he is alive', but 'the Indian got weak, and lost his power with the sun', in *The Woman Who Rode Away and Other* Stories, ed. Dieter Mehl and Christa Janssohn (Cambridge: Cambridge University Press, 1995), pp. 61–2.

cold white vitriol of her angry contempt on to your mean, tense nerves, nervous
man, and she is corroding you away. (*A* 53)

This passage, like so many in *Apocalypse,* derives its vehemence from the 'mystic
hatred' that Lawrence has conceived for his contemporary world, which has lost
its 'rooted connection' and established the machine as its god. Yet Lawrence's
critique of modern man in *Apocalypse* is not an embittered refutation: it is rather
an attempt to shock his fellow-men into an awareness of their own deadness, and
to provoke a response. It is a book that offers alternative modes of living and
feeling, rather than dealing in abstractions. By invoking the hostility of the sun and
moon in the context of modern man's deadness, Lawrence is trying to reveal the
extent of the dislocation that has occurred between man and the cosmos, as well as
its catastrophic implications.

A Modern Cataclysm

It is the clash of 'impulses' between 'living men' and the 'greedy classes and
masses' that has enabled Lawrence to imagine and portray in his *Last Poems* a
modern-day cataclysm or apocalypse. Modern man has adopted the machine as
his master, so it is the machine that has the power to turn in anger when it is
repudiated:

> And then, when the soul of living men repudiates them
> then at once the impulse of the greedy classes and masses breaks down
> and a chaos of impulses supervenes
> in which is heard the crashing splinter of machines
> and the dull breaking of bones. (*CP* 640)

Similarly, in 'The Triumph of the Machine', a cataclysm is occasioned by an
inward revolt of the native creatures of the soul' (symbolizing natural impulses)
when faced with the horrifically destructive, relentless power of mechanized man
and his machines:

> So mechanical man in triumph seated upon the seat of his machine
> will be driven mad from within himself, and sightless, and on that day
> the machines will turn to run into one another
> traffic will tangle up in a long-drawn-out crash of collision
> and engines will rush at the solid houses, the edifice of our life
> will rock in the shock of the mad machine, and the house will come down. (*CP* 624)

This apocalypse, resulting from a necessary revolt, ironically pushes the
indiscriminately destructive nature of the machine to its logical conclusion: that

is, self-destruction. Modern man is driven mad 'from within himself' and suffers the consequences of allowing the machine to rule him.

Both poems – 'Impulses' and 'The Triumph of the Machine' – seem to suggest a cataclysm that is a consequence of man's actions, as it entails a revolt against the god of the machine. In the poem 'Vengeance is Mine', however, the vengeance described is specifically 'vengeance of the Lord', so that the cataclysm is more genuinely identifiable as Apocalyptic. This is evident from the poem's opening: 'Vengeance is mine, saith the Lord, I will repay'. The victims of this vengeance are those who are 'stiff-necked', 'self-willed', 'self-important' 'self-righteous' and 'self-absorbed':

> all of them who wind their energy round the idea of themselves
> and so strangle off their connection with the ceaseless tree of life,
> and fall into sharp, self-centred self-assertion, sharp or soft (*CP* 616)

These fall victim to the 'unforgiving god' and experience an awful kind of conflagration, similar to the torture predicted for the 'unsealed' souls in Revelation, before they are flung into hell:

> their nerves are stretched till they twangle and snap
> and irritation seethes secretly through their guts, as their tissue disintegrates
> and flames of katabolistic energy alternate
> with ashes of utter boredom, ennui, and disgust. (*CP* 616)

This punishment is described as 'long and unremitting', and lasts until the soul of the 'stiff-necked' is 'ground to dust'.

Yet as in Lawrence's aphoristic 'mill-stone' poems (*CP* 614–16), the disintegrated corpse experiences a kind of recycling, becoming 'fertilising meal' which is subsequently used 'to manure afresh the roots of the tree of life' (*CP* 616). So new life is generated at the heart of the cosmos, the roots perhaps also implying the four pre-Socratic 'roots' or elements from which all things derive. The Lord of this poem is, therefore, different from the biblical Lord of Vengeance, for he is a cosmic rather than a Christian god who re-establishes the balance at the core of the natural cycle by repaying death and self-centred evil with life and universal growth:

> And so the Lord of Vengeance pays back, repays life
> for the defection of the self-centred ones. (*CP* 616)

Lawrence, in his late poetry and last book, is trying to offer a way in which modern man might break out of his self-centred, machine-dominated condition and 're-establish the living organic connections, with the cosmos, the sun and earth, with mankind and nation and family' (*A* 149). The poem 'Vengeance is Mine' shows that the cataclysm may have to be of great magnitude in order to succeed: destruction must precede creation, thus adhering to a crucial universal duality. He expresses the belief that John of Patmos's mystic hatred for his fellow-men was so intense only because 'he knew that the living realities of men's being were displaced' (*A* 41) and – in his poems and last book – explores numerous possibilities of 'return' that might rectify this displacement. Recognizing that 'the long light of Christianity is guttering to go out, and we have to get at new resources in ourselves',[15] Lawrence's predominant aim in *Apocalypse* is didactic and altruistic: to find new ways of living and being.

It is probable that Lawrence began writing *Apocalypse* in mid-November 1929, and I suggest that he broke off his poetry writing at that time, when applying himself to the longer prose work. If so, the last book directly succeeded the poems, and might usefully be seen in part as a 'writing up' of certain crucial ideas formulated in the course of his poetry writing. Arguably then, *Apocalypse* stands in relation to *Last Poems* as *Sons and Lovers* does to *Love Poems*, *The Rainbow* does to *Look! We Have Come Through!* and *Fantasia of the Unconscious* does to *Women in Love*. Both *Apocalypse* and *Fantasia* are examples of prose exegesis which engage with and interpret ideas formulated and explored imaginatively through other kinds of writing. Nonetheless, it is impossible to determine an exact chronology: to ascertain, for instance, particular phases of poetry writing that correspond with particular stages in Lawrence's preparation for *Apocalypse*. It is undeniable, though, that a common language and field of reference inform the poetry notebooks and the prose work. Along with *Sketches of Etruscan Places*, then, *Apocalypse* exists as one of the most crucial intratexts that can be considered in relation to *Last Poems*, illuminating the creative processes entailed in Lawrence's late style.

---

[15]   'On Human Destiny' in *Reflections on the Death of a Porcupine and Other Essays*, ed. Herbert, p. 208.

Chapter 8
Ascension and Carpentry

In previous chapters I have considered a number of full-scale prose works that exemplify aspects of Lawrence's late style and have a significant bearing on his late poetry. This process has culminated in a discussion of *Apocalypse*, the major non-fictional work of 1929, the writing of which drew on and largely post-dated *Last Poems*. Yet during 1929 Lawrence also composed a number of shorter pieces of non-fiction: articles, essays and reviews often written in response to a specific request and motivated by financial necessity. Conducive in their brevity to a writer whose health was failing, these pieces did not always inspire great enthusiasm in their author at the outset, but often provoked a highly satisfying result. One notable article of this period was 'The Risen Lord', enclosed with a letter to Nancy Pearn on 2 August 1929, which Lawrence referred to as a 'nice article, much too good for [Everyman]' (*L* vii 401): a piece articulating Lawrence's 'idea of a religion for the young' (*L* vii 401), to be placed by Everyman within a series on this theme. The title immediately suggests a connection with the two-part story *The Escaped Cock*, composed between April 1927 and July 1928: a connection emphasized by the fact that on the same day Lawrence sent 'The Risen Lord' to Nancy Pearn, he also wrote to Harry and Caresse Crosby – 'American publishers of *de luxe* editions in Paris' (*LEA* 265) – to find out how their Black Sun edition of *The Escaped Cock* was progressing (*L* vii 398–9). James T. Boulton cites Lawrence's observation in 1929 that the novella and the article shared the 'same idea' (*L* vii 516), highlighting also how keen Lawrence was about the publication of them both. Precisely at the time the late poems were being entered into the two notebooks, then, Lawrence was preoccupied with his fictional and non-fictional prose works on the subject of resurrection. (He had previously written a short article entitled 'Resurrection' in January 1925 and painted a picture with the same title in May 1927.[1])

It is notable, too, that within a few days of sending off his Everyman piece, Lawrence posted another article to Nancy Pearn (on 5 August). This essay had been solicited by the editor of *Star Review* – Lady Emily Lutyens – who had invited him to contribute an article on the subject of 'Men and Women' (also the initial title of Lawrence's piece) for a series about living conditions in the modern world (*LEA* 274). In December, while preparing the article for re-publication in the book that would become *Assorted Articles* (1930), Lawrence altered the title to 'Men Must Work and Women as Well'. Developing a central idea articulated in previous 'pansy' poems (discussed below), Lawrence here vilifies the modern

---

[1] See *Reflections on the Death of a Porcupine and Other Essays*, ed. Michael Herbert (Cambridge: Cambridge University Press, 1988), pp. 233–5 and *L* vi 56.

tendency towards spiritualism and obsessive cleanliness: a harmful, regressive process that makes wholesome physical labour increasingly distasteful – even shameful. His social critique typically extends to the materialism of the greedy consumer, associated with the machine and therefore the antithesis of life.

At first glance, there may appear to be little correlation between an article concerning a new religion for the young, and one which offers a critique of the working lives and relationships of adults. Yet on closer investigation it becomes evident that religion and work are profoundly allied in some of Lawrence's late works. In 'The Risen Lord', Lawrence writes:

> If Jesus rose as a full man in the flesh he rose to do his share in the world's work, something he really liked doing. And if he remembered his first life, it would neither be teaching nor preaching, but probably carpentering again, with joy, among the shavings. (*LEA* 271)

The resurrected man of one article reflects the life-principle expressed in the other. He is reborn from abstract spiritualism and acquires an earthy physical presence: one that allows him to do a job that he enjoys, working with his hands rather than his brain. In 'The Risen Lord', as in a number of the late works, there is also a dissolving of the distinction between God and man's life-experiences. Like the figures that are 'not outlined' but have 'flowing contour[s]', that Lawrence identified on the Etruscan tomb-walls (*SEP* 123), it is often difficult to see where God ends and man begins. Lawrence's religion for the young rejects any aspect of Christian teaching that does not tally with lived human experience: he cannot accept an event (such as the Ascension) with which people fail to empathize. The concept of a resurrected life on earth as a bodied man who can work and perform sexually bridges the empathic impasse, forming the basis of a religion that is not always at one remove.

This chapter, then, will consider the late poetry notebooks in relation to the 'religion and work' articles of 1929, also indicating connections with fictional resurrection narrative such as *The Escaped Cock* and '[Autobiographical Fragment]', the latter dating back to October 1927. It will also incorporate a discussion of the way in which the late poems employ and subvert Christian terms and symbols, exploring the connection between such images and human relations within the modern world. The final section of this chapter will focus on the very last work Lawrence wrote, composed during the last days of his life at the Ad Astra Sanatorium in Vence (February–March 1930): a review of Eric Gill's *Art-Nonsense and Other Essays*. In this fragment, Lawrence wilfully redefines Gill's Catholic representation of the man-God relationship through particular reference to work. To the last, Lawrence reveals his capacity to improvise and misinterpret in the interests of his own didactic purpose or imaginative vision.

Absorbing Work

> For God's sake, let us be men
> not monkeys minding machines
> or sitting with our tails curled
> while the machine amuses us, the radio or film or gramophone.
>
> Monkeys with a bland grin on our faces. (*CP* 450)

Work, according to a little cluster of *Pansies* poems (*CP* 448–53), has to be 'like an absorbing game' (*CP* 450): if not, there is no point in doing it. Direct, forthright and unremitting, these poems advocate a kind of work that is individual and attentive, resulting in the creation of unique items that retain the warmth of the hands that have made them. In two poems – 'Whatever Man Makes' and 'Work' – this mode of creativity is typified by the absorbed weaving undertaken by Navajo women and Hindus, generating a rich web of organic, natural imagery that serves as a correlative to their committed endeavours. The women are like 'slender trees putting forth leaves' (*CP* 451) and their white robes are wrapped around them like foliage. The creative process entailed in making cloth is extended to the building of houses and then cities: edifices that by implication have the Etruscan attribute of impermanence, and which are described in terms of a snail putting forth its shell; a bird leaning its breast against its nest to shape it; or a beaver nibbling its 'mansion' (*CP* 451). While bird, snail and beaver emblematize nature's laws of nascent creativity, the monkeys of 'Let us be Men' are their antithesis: they are the static automata who operate machines blankly, without absorption. Operating machines, they are also soothed and nullified by machines, which are seen as the transmitters of merely passive entertainment (ironically Lawrence labels one of his 'work' poems 'We are Transmitters', using this phrase in a positive sense to designate the way in which life can pass from a human creator to the thing made). In 'Men Must Work and Women As Well', Lawrence observes that 'The film, the radio, the gramophone were all invented because physical effort and physical contact have become repulsive to man and woman alike' (*LEA* 277).

In the article, Lawrence defines the apparent aim of scientific and cultural 'progress' as the reduction of essential yet onerous tasks to a minimum, freeing up leisure time so that there might be 'More films, more motor-cars, more dances, more golf, more tennis and more getting completely away from yourself' (*LEA* 276). In Chapter 2 I indicated ways in which frenzied motion represents meaningless, wheel-like fixity, and this sense is similarly conveyed in the rhetoric of this article. Within the late poem 'There are no gods—', the need for such frivolous leisure pursuits as tennis and the motor-car result not merely in the evasion of self but also in the evasion of the creative unknown:

> There are no gods, and you can please yourself
> have a game of tennis, go out in the car, do some shopping, sit and talk, talk, talk
> with a cigarette browning your fingers. (*CP* 651)

Interestingly, the epizeuxis employed here is a recurrent rhetorical device in the article, though with a slightly different purpose. The repetition of 'talk' invokes the monotony of meaningless conversation, while in the article the equivalent device emulates the banging of a fist on a table. 'Resentment, resentment, resentment—' hammers home modern humanity's attitude to physical effort and contact. Later in the article we encounter a variation on this theme:

> Recoil, recoil, recoil. Revulsion, revulsion, revulsion. Repulsion, repulsion, repulsion. This is the rhythm that underlies our social activity, everywhere, with regard to physical existence. (*LEA* 283–4)

Characteristically, the prose of this article operates through rhythmic force and repetition: here it is heavy, bludgeoning and stubborn in order to convey powerfully a mass resistance to life.

Education is seen as a corrupting force, particularly among the working classes, such as those inhabiting a mining district. It is the contention of the article that board schools[2] are pernicious in this context, given that ninety per cent of children will not be able to 'get on' and will end up as malcontents, resistant to the physical labouring jobs they are then forced to undertake (*LEA* 279). An analogous progression, this time from board school to robot, is expressed in the poem 'But I say unto you: Love one another':

> Oh I have loved the working class
> where I was born,
> and lived to see them spawn into machine-robots
> in the hot-beds of the board-schools and the film.
>
> Oh how have I loved the thought of thoughtful people
> gentle and refined,
> and lived to find out
> that their last thought was money
> and their last refinement bluff, a hate disguised,
> and one trapped one's fingers in their brassy, polished works! (*CP* 644)

While the working classes are associated straightforwardly with the machine, the transformation of the 'gentle and refined' is more sinister. The kind of mechanization that they espouse is more insidiously destructive: it is 'polished' and pristine rather than oily and black. Implicit in this poem is the article's distaste

---

[2] Board schools were established in the wake of the 1870 Education Act to provide elementary education, eventually both compulsory and free. After the Education Act of 1902, independently elected school boards ceased to exist, but elementary education for the vast majority of children continued under the auspices of the local education authorities.

for the fastidious cleanliness of which Mr Ford's 'super-factories' provide the most 'shining' example in modern industry. Lawrence attributes genius to Ford for recognizing modern man's desire for abstraction and mechanized work that it is not necessary to enjoy. Yet he sees in the bright, clean factories that result the denial of an essential truth:

> Mr. Ford forgets that his clean and pure and harmonious super-factory, where men only pull shining levers or turn bright handles, has all had to be grossly mined and smelted, before it could come into existence. Mr. Ford is one of the various heavens of industry. But these heavens rest on various hells of labour, always did and always will. (*LEA* 280)

Science, Lawrence claims, leaves us in the lurch as it fails to remove the 'hells' from beneath the 'heavens' of exalted industry. Yet the point is made that if the colliers were not informed that they were in hell, they would not be aware of the fact and might enjoy their work (as they used to). The heaven/hell dichotomy reflects the process of indoctrination by which humankind can be made to believe that one state of being equates to fulfilment when the opposite is true.

It is interesting to note how often the late poems employ religious terminology when condemning mechanization. In 'Man and Machine', for instance, one belief system appears to have been superseded by another:

> Man invented the machine
> and now the machine has invented man.
>
> God the Father is a dynamo
> and God the Son a talking radio
> and God the Holy Ghost is gas that keeps it all going. (*CP* 641)

These stanzas elide processes of modern invention and primal creation, with ironic and subversive consequences. Man has become the slave of the machine: therefore he is seen as its creation rather than its creator. As man worships his creator, the machine is deified, acquiring the attributes of the holy Trinity. The poem 'Oh Wonderful Machine!' analogously employs terminology from a Christian context to indicate this process of reversal, in which a machine is operated by 'some knock-kneed wretch': a wage-slave earning two pounds per week. The narrator of the poem satirically demands:

> Oh great god of the machine
> what lousy archangels and angels you have to surround yourself with!
> And you can't possibly do without them! (*CP* 643)

The 'almighty machine' is paradoxically in thrall to its wage-slave, which is tantamount to the assertion in the poem 'Masses and Classes' that 'God cannot do without me!' (*CP* 641). This perverse interdependence results in a hypothetical 'machine-driven unity of lunatics' (*LEA* 284) in the article, or in the kind of blind destruction envisaged in poetic terms within 'The Triumph of the Machine'.

Ultimately, the article sees the machine as material and anti-physical, impelling humankind toward a revulsion for bodily presence and work. In offering tentative solutions, Lawrence asserts rather vaguely that labour must be made as likeable as possible (an unlikely goal, he admits, given current developments) and that a few individuals must get back their bodies. Both 'The Risen Lord' and *The Escaped Cock* (like *Lady Chatterley's Lover*) form part of a counter-trend that reverses this relentless regression towards disembodied spirituality, positing rebirth as a way of regaining physical touch.

Resurrection Narratives

'The Risen Lord' functions as an ideological corrective both to mechanization and to debased religion. It is asserted at the outset that the Church errs in throwing emphasis on the birth of Christ and on his crucifixion, neglecting the significance of Easter and the Resurrection. Examining the implications of this emphasis across three generations, Lawrence attributes to the (pre-war) elderly a belief that man is essentially the Christ-Child with woman as his saviour, while the middle-aged men, ravaged by the war and essentially womanless, accept Christ crucified as their image and 'take the great cry: *Consummatum est! – It is finished!* as their last word' (*LEA* 269). The young cannot really identify with either of these positions, and consequently find themselves at an end rather than a beginning:

> For they, the young, came into the field of life after the death-cry *Consummation est!* had rung through the world, and while the body, so to speak, was being put into the tomb. By the time the young came on to the stage, Calvary was empty, the tombs were closed, the women had lost forever the Christ-child and the virgin-saviour, and it was altogether the day after, cold, bleak, empty, blank, meaningless, almost silly... everywhere the closed grey disillusion of Christ Crucified, dead, and buried, those grey empty days between Good Friday and Easter. (*LEA* 269)

The 'closed grey disillusion of Christ Crucified, dead, and buried' is an interesting formulation, given that death and burial would normally be associated not with disillusionment but with insentience (the emptiness of death). Although this line ostensibly relates to the period *before* the Resurrection on Easter Day, it is more appropriate when applied to the psychological image of Lawrence's own 'man who had died' (in *The Escaped Cock*) after he has risen and left the tomb. Filled with an 'unspeakable disillusion', feeling that desire is dead and with a tendency to lie back down and recover oblivion (*VG* 125–6), the adventure of this Christ figure (who is 'still young' might be taken as a parable for modern youth in its struggle to find meaning in life after the post-war cry of *Consummatum est!*

While in abstract terms 'The Risen Lord' extols the virtues of carpentry (physical labour) above 'teaching and preaching', the protagonist of *The Escaped Cock* recognizes that 'The teacher and the saviour are dead in me; now I can go about my own business, into my own single life' (*VG* 132). Through figurative if not literal rebirth (he is cut down from the Cross too soon), he acquires the wisdom of hindsight, recognizing that his past life and 'mission' have been compromised by the kind of insincere feeling condemned in the late poem 'Retort to Jesus':

> And whoever forces himself to love anybody
> begets a murderer in his own body. (*CP* 653)

This brief aphorism implicitly derides a mission entailing promiscuous sympathy, or the embracing of multitudes for which Whitman was so explicitly condemned.[3] The rectified error is acknowledged in the lines: 'Yet I would embrace multitudes, I who have never truly embraced even one. But Judas and the high Priests saved me from my own salvation, and soon I can turn to my destiny like a bather in the sea at dawn, who has just come down to the shore, alone.' (*VG* 132)

In 'The Risen Lord', Lawrence gives an account of the development undergone by his own protagonist in the earlier story:

> If Jesus rose as a full man, in full flesh and soul, then he rose to take a woman to himself, to live with her, and to know the tenderness and blossoming of the two-ness with her; he who had been hitherto so limited to his oneness, or his universality, which is the same thing. If Jesus rose in the full flesh, he rose to know the tenderness of a woman, and the great pleasure of her, and to have children by her. He rose to know the responsibility and the peculiar delight of children, and also the exasperation and nuisance of them. If Jesus rose as a full man, in the flesh, he rose to have friends, to have a man friend whom he would hold sometimes to his breast, in strong affection, and who would be dearer to him than a brother, just out of the sheer mystery of sympathy. (*LEA* 271)

This aspiration for a relationship with one woman, supplemented by the love of one man, echoes Rupert Birkin's desire for 'another kind of love' (*WL* 481), while the friends surrounding them hark back to Lawrence's Rananim. Yet just as Ursula's rejection of Birkin's idea as obstinate and perverse points to its implausibility, so the dramatized experiences of the man who died belie the idealism of the article. This resurrected man indeed finds a desirable woman (the priestess of Isis)

---

[3] See, for example, 'Whitman' (1922 version), in *Studies in Classic American Literature*, ed. Ezra Greenspan, Lindeth Vasey and John Worthen (Cambridge: Cambridge University Press, 2003), pp. 424–5.

who is able to provoke his sexual arousal and resurrect him into touch; he also impregnates her. But circumstances (including the interference of the woman's mother) prevent him from remaining with her to experience the delight and the nuisance of children. Rather, he leaves secretly in a boat, without having made friends or singled out a male companion. His experience reflects the paradox expressed in the poem 'Future Religion':

> The future of religion lies in the mystery of touch.
> The mind is touchless, so is the will, so is the spirit.
> First comes the death, then the pure aloneness, which is permanent
> then the resurrection into touch. (*CP* 611)

The Escaped Cock narrative bears out the notion that (near-)death is followed by a period of isolation and disillusionment, before the protagonist learns to come into touch and be sexually resurrected. Yet here aloneness is not just touch's precursive condition: it remains permanent, and by implication, co-exists with the togetherness of human contact. By leaving at the end of the tale, the man who died indicates *his* permanent need for aloneness, but in so doing he moves out of physical touch.

So, when we consider Lawrence's question 'Christ risen in the full flesh! What for?' (*LEA* 270), we must accept that the answer (or answers) will be different according to the text under investigation. One significant difference between tale and article is that the former dramatizes the experience of an individual while the latter gropes for an image with which it can furnish the young. The Risen Lord figure of the article, rhetorically celebrated and uncomplicated in its supremacy, is established as both lynch-pin and contrary. It attempts to rectify the Church's skewed emphasis on Christ's birth and crucifixion (at the expense of his resurrection), also posing a challenge to the following image:

> Christ risen in the flesh in order to lurk obscurely for six weeks on earth, then
> be taken vaguely up into heaven in cloud? Flesh, solid flesh, feet and bowels
> and teeth and eyes of man, taken up into heaven in a cloud, and never put down
> again?' (*LEA* 270)

The ascension, in Lawrence's view, lies beyond any genuine kind of understanding. As though in defiance of the pure abstraction of this idea, he uses the analogy of an aeroplane that takes people up into the air and then brings them down again to illustrate the point that 'Flesh and blood belong to the earth, and only to the earth. We know it' (*LEA* 270). This is by no means Lawrence's first challenge to the notion of bodiless ascension: in the poem 'St. Matthew' (within the subsection 'The Evangelistic Beasts' of *Birds, Beasts and Flowers*, 1923), Matthew sees ascent as necessarily balanced by descent; the move upwards creates the desire for its antithetical downward trajectory:

So I will be lifted up, Saviour,
But put me down again in time, Master,
Before my heart stops beating, and I become what I am not. (*CP* 321)

The significance of the downward path is indicated by the vividly evoked birds, beasts and flowers that await the returning traveller: the earth is a place where 'beasts drop their unlicked young', 'the adder darts horizontal' and 'flowers sprout in the acrid humus' (*CP* 321). Later in this chapter I will discuss the way in which such a balance between ascent and descent features within a number of late poems in relation to Satan's fall.

In 'The Risen Lord' Lawrence aims to create a palatably 'human', fleshly Christ who works as a carpenter, fights the money-makers and enjoys family life. Both the article and the late poems express cynicism regarding the Protestant Church's capacity to espouse such an image: one that can be intuitively accepted by the young. Lawrence writes 'The Protestant Churches have had their day / and served their great purpose' (*CP* 609), and 'I doubt whether the Protestant Churches, which supported the war, will ever have the faith and the power of life to take the great step onwards, and preach Christ Risen. The Catholic Church might' (*LEA* 269). The view expressed in 'The Risen Lord' that the Catholic Church is more likely than the Protestant to break with tradition and move forwards is attributed to the fact that the Mediterranean countries have always celebrated Easter as the greatest of the holy days. Lawrence alludes to this preeminent religious festival using superlatives such as 'most splendid', 'finest', 'gladdest', 'holiest' and 'most joyful' (*LEA* 269), also alleging that 'this, to the old faith, is still the first day in the year' (*LEA* 269). Strikingly close is the imagery of the poem 'The Church', in which the same sense of joy and celebration at Easter is conveyed:

If I was a member of the Church of Rome
I should advocate reform:
the marriage of priests
the priests to wear rose-colour or magenta in the streets
to teach the Resurrection in the flesh
to start the year on Easter Sunday
to add the mystery of Joy-in-Resurrection to the Mass
to inculcate the new conception of the Risen Man. (*CP* 609)

In *Lady Chatterley's Lover* it is suggested that if the colliers wore scarlet trousers and short white jackets they would become 'men again' (*LCL* 219), by implication experiencing greater job-satisfaction, liberation and natural exuberance, like the dancers of the poem 'For the Heroes are Dipped in Scarlet'. The gaudy priests, dipped here in rose or magenta, are implicitly made into Etruscans painted in the vermilion that indicates insouciance and free, instinctive motion.

In keeping with this connection, the Risen Lord of the article is associated with the ritual of seasonal growth and change: the year belonging to him is 'all the full-flowering spring, all summer, and the autumn of wheat and fruit' (*LEA* 267). He is reborn in order to live the life of the flesh 'as peonies or foxes do', and the 'two-ness' he might experience with a woman is referred to as a 'blossoming' (*LEA* 271). The joyful celebrations of Easter among Mediterranean peoples again entail ritual appropriation of the seasons, through iconography associated with the natural world: 'In Sicily the women take into church the saucers of growing corn, the green blades rising tender and slim like green light, in little pools, filling round the altar. It is Adonis. It is the re-born year. It is Christ Risen (*LEA* 269–70). Adonis (according to Greek mythology) was killed while hunting then resurrected, and his resurrection was celebrated at midsummer. Christ and Adonis are elided here as dying and reviving gods, much in the manner of the late poems discussed in Chapter 6, in which all sorts of gods from diverse mythological and cultural contexts are yoked together. It is crucial that Lawrence's vision of Christian rebirth in the article can encompass the pagan, just as the resurrected protagonist of *The Escaped Cock* achieves renewal through the priestess of Isis, so that he is both Christ and Osiris.

In another 'resurrection narrative' – '[Autobiographical Fragment]' (written shortly after his Etruscan tour) – the inhabitants of Lawrence's hybridic landscape also carry dishes of simple food to and from the room in which they peacefully and naturally recline.[4] The narrator lies down in a cave within the rock to sleep – a cavity resembling the tomb of *The Escaped Cock* – and wakes to find himself reincarnated in an Etruscanized futuristic Eastwood (here called Newthorpe), in 2927. This is the year of the acorn, and the Risen Lord of this fragment is immediately struck by the 'floweriness' of the strangers who find him. These people combine the 'ease' of the Etruscans with the wholeness and completeness not of a Grecian artefact but of a fruit:

> That was the quality of all the people: an inner stillness and ease, like plants that come to flower and fruit. The individual was like a whole fruit, body and mind and spirit, without split. (*LEA* 62)

The mind/body/spirit union suggests the kind of 'wholeness' that is envisaged at the end of 'The Ship of Death' in which the body 'emerges strange and lovely' and the soul steps 'into her house again / filling the heart with peace' (*CP* 720). The reacquisition of the body at the end of this poem testifies to the emphasis on resurrection in the flesh (as distinct from bodiless spirituality) also expressed in the articles discussed above.

---

[4]   It is very likely that this circular chamber, with its 'column of rock' at the centre and a 'broad bed of rock' around the edge on which people recline (*SEP* 17), is modelled on the Inghirami tomb at Cerveteri: see Bethan Jones, 'Shaping, Intertextuality and Summation in D.H. Lawrence's *Last Poems*', unpublished PhD thesis (Nottingham University, 1998), p. 295.

The women of '[Autobiographical Fragment]' are described as comely as 'rose-berries on a bush', while by contrast the reclining blond-haired man to whom the narrator is taken has 'the beauty of a flower rather than of a berry' (*LEA* 62–3). A man of the green guard has the 'same quiet, fruit-like glow of the men who had found me, a quality of beauty that came from inside, in some queer physical way' (*LEA* 65). When the people dance, the men are 'stamping softly, like bulls', while the women are 'softly swaying, and softly clapping their hands, with a strange noise, like leaves' (*LEA* 64).

These extraordinary beings are frightening to the uninitiated observer:

> I was afraid: afraid for myself. These people, it seemed to me, were not people, not human beings in my sense of the word. They had the stillness and the completeness of plants. And see how they could melt into one amazing instinctive thing, a human flock of motion. (*LEA* 65)

The juxtaposition of 'completeness' and 'melt' is striking: paradoxically these people appear to have a wholeness that is in no way fixed or rigid, but enables them to remain fluid. It seems that Lawrence has to perceive the inhabitants of a new world, achieved after resurrection, in non-human or super-human terms. In *The Escaped Cock* Part II the slaves on the shore (one of whom rapes the other) represent the 'common' people while the Priestess of Isis, with her still trance of pagan ritual, exists at one remove: an aristocratic being.

The narrator of '[Autobiographical Fragment]' suffers through feeling less anthropologically 'whole' than the native inhabitants, yet the envy is juxtaposed with an onrush of transferred energy:

> It made me feel a curious, sad sort of envy, because I was not so whole, and at the same time, I was wildly elated, my rushing sort of energy seemed to come upon me again. I felt as if I were just going to plunge into the deeps of life, for the first time: belated, and yet a pioneer of pioneers. (*LEA* 62–3)

The concept of transferred vitality anticipates the later poem 'We are Transmitters', in which people who transmit life into their work find that still more life 'rushes into [them] to compensate' (*CP* 449).[5] In the above quotation, the protagonist is able to experience vicariously the kind of strength and elation that characterizes the life of the plant- or flower-like Newthorpe residents, showing that this contact is one reliant on touch and warmth. It is as if the narrator has been precipitated into a world in which the 'life-loving' Etruscans are able to provide a soft flow of touch:

---

5   Similarly, in 'Whatever Man Makes', the Navajo woman weaving a rug must 'run the pattern out in a little break at the end / so that her soul can come out, back to her' (*CP* 448).

> They lifted me, and I leaned on one, standing, while the other washed me. The
> other I leaned on was warm, and his life softly warmed me. The other one rubbed
> me gently. I was alive. I saw my white feet like two curious flowers, and I lifted
> them one after another, remembering walking. (*LEA* 59)[6]

The description of the feet as 'curious flowers' relates to 'Shadows' in which the
poet, who has been 'walking still / with God' so that they are 'close together'
conceives renewal as 'odd wintry flowers upon the withered stem, yet new,
strange flowers' (*CP* 726–7). The contact is not one that relies on words, although
it suggests the 'music of lost languages' spoken by the returning gods in 'Middle
of the World':

> I turned to look at the man I was resting on, and met the blue, quiet shimmer
> of his eyes. He said something to me, in the quiet, full voice, and I nearly
> understood, because it was like the dialect. He said it again, softly and calmly,
> speaking to the inside of me, so that I understood as a dog understands, from the
> voice, not from the words. (*LEA* 60)

The sense of simultaneous intimacy and command, rather than the meaning of
the words, is what matters, and there is no forced effort of communication which
would contradict the ease of exchange.

As in *The Escaped Cock*, the narrator of '[Autobiographical Fragment]' is
resurrected into touch. Rather than the hands of the woman of Isis, who rubs oil
into the Christ-figure's wounds, the warmth of the Newthorpe inhabitants has the
power to heal:

> And almost immediately the soft, warm rhythm of his life pervaded me again,
> and the memory in me which was my old self went to sleep. I was like a wound,
> and the touch of these men healed me at once. (*LEA* 62)[7]

The title of Whitman's poem 'The Wound-Dresser', the term 'pansy' (incorporating
the French term 'panser': to soothe or dress a wound) and the more obvious 'pensée'
association all serve as contexts for the necessary and almost instantaneous healing
of a wound described here.

This tale breaks off suddenly during a conversation in which the narrator
recognizes himself to be like a butterfly which 'shall only live a little while' (*LEA*
68). Its truncated ending distinguishes '[Autobiographical Fragment]' from *The*

---

6   This citation is reminiscent of the passage in *The White Peacock*, in which George
rubs Cyril's wet body, and the two experience a mutual touch that is 'superb' (*The White
Peacock*, ed. Andrew Robertson, Cambridge: Cambridge University Press, 1983, p. 222).
Lawrence never leaves such experiences completely behind but is always revisiting and
recreating them.
7   I have altered 'these man' in *LEA* 62 to 'these men'.

Escaped Cock, while these works are also markedly different in genre: one is a futuristic personal fantasy while the other fictionally dismantles and radically intertwines two fundamental myths with their roots in the far past. Yet, given the proximity of their composition (the fragment was written between the composition of Parts I and II of the tale) and the fact that they were both directly inspired by the Etruscan trip, it is unsurprising that these two pieces are linked, particularly in evoking a gradual transition through sleep and reawakening into a new state of consciousness and a new capacity to relate. One succinct extract from 'The Risen Lord' indicates its indebtedness to the two fictional resurrection narratives that originated in the Etruscan experience of 1927: 'The Lord of the rising wheat and the plum-blossoms is warm and kind upon earth again, after having been done to death by the evil and the jealous ones' (*LEA* 270). Echoing the Christ figure of *The Escaped Cock* in his cry 'They did me to death!' (*VG* 156) and attributing warmth, kindness and seasonal renewal to his return, the passage reflects a redefinition of Christian belief that lies at the heart of Lawrence's late vision.

Christ and Satan; Ascension and Decline

The protagonist of *The Escaped Cock* is a man of few words, and his manner of speech is rather biblical and archaic.[8] By contrast, when the protagonist of 'The Risen Lord' gets a chance to speak, he sounds decidedly modern. The article enacts a fascinating shift from third to first person: this occurs towards the end, but there is still plenty of scope for what is effectively a vituperative monologue. This last section articulates the Risen Lord's response to Satan (or Mammon, as he often calls him), when faced with temptation in the wilderness. Another radical reversal of the biblical story is enacted as, this time, Christ finds the temptations silly and profoundly untempting. The reason given is that he has 'died to that sort of self-importance and self-conceit' (*LEA* 271): an echo of *The Escaped Cock*'s Christ figure arising disillusioned with his mission and profoundly detached. The meeting between Christ and Satan in the wilderness is used here merely as a pretext that triggers a confrontation and reveals the Risen Lord as feisty, defiant, and extremely accomplished in the art of withering scorn. The principal rhetorical devices are evident in the following passage:

> But let me tell you something, old man! Your name's Satan, isn't it? and your name is Mammon? You are the selfish hog that's got hold of all the world, aren't you? Well look here my boy, I'm going to take it all from you, so don't worry. The world and the power and the riches thereof, I'm going to take them all from you, Satan or Mammon or whatever your name is. (*LEA* 271–2)

---

[8]   See, for example, the dialogue between the man who died and Madeleine (*VG* 132–3).

This voice is one of strident defiance: 'let me tell you' and 'look here my boy'. The opponent is undermined through cumulative rhetorical questions that ultimately serve to reveal the absurdity of his multiple names: being both Satan and Mammon is tantamount to being unnamed, as is revealed by the casual verbal shrug: 'or whatever your name is'. There is utter confidence to this voice, too: 'I'm going to take …' is reiterated and leaves little room for dissent, while Satan is given no opportunity to get a word in edgeways. Arguably, this bludgeoning, rhetorical monologue provides a conversational equivalent to the earlier part of the article: it is more obviously combative but it uses many of the same rhetorical strategies. Both first and third person voices operate through assertion rather than argument; through repetition for emphasis; through declamation and exclamation; through the forthright denunciation of perceived error.

Satan, described here unusually by means of an anti-Semitic image, becomes a 'hook-nosed, glisten-eyed, ugly, money-smelling anachronism' (*LEA* 272) – among a plethora of other insulting terms – thus equating to the 'money-smelling man in a motor-car' (*CP* 645) of the poem 'As thyself —!'. Satan as Mammon is associated with mob-mentality, machines and prostitution: he is essentially an anti-life force inimical to anything spontaneous, joyful or creative. The outpouring of all the narrator hates about Satan provokes its antithesis: a list of things natural and spontaneous, such as a peeping squirrel, a columbine flower, a man singing a bawdy song, a young girl sitting and wondering, and even a man that kicks a 'fool dog' that attacks him (*LEA* 272). The beauty of the latter is identified in 'the swift fierce turn and lunge of a kick, then the quivering pause for the next attack' (*LEA* 272). He exhibits the blend of anger and spontaneity also evident in the late poem 'Man is more than *homo sapiens*':

> I saw an angry Italian seize an irritating little official by the throat
> and all but squeeze the life out of him:
> and Jesus himself could not have denied that at that moment the angry man
> was a god, in godliness pure as a Christ, beautiful (*CP* 674)

It is interesting that while a number of the late poems associate such displays of spontaneity with godliness, it is Jesus (also called Christ here) who is evoked in this poem, playing on his association with denial.[9] The poem 'For a Moment' does not contain a specific allusion to Christ and is not concerned with manifestations of anger; nevertheless it is analogous in indicating ways in which a sudden response or action can reveal something transcendent in a person:

---

[9] Oddly, though, the 'Jesus' and 'Christ' figures here seem to be subtly different: Christ (with whom the angry man is compared) is as pure and beautiful as the article's Risen Lord. By contrast, Jesus's acknowledgement of the man's momentary godliness seems to be against his better judgement.

In the green garden darkened the shadow of coming rain
and a girl ran swiftly, laughing breathless, taking in her white washing
in rapid armfuls from the line, tossing it in the basket,
and so rapidly, and so gracefully, flashing, fleeing before the rain
for a moment she was Io, Io, who fled from Zeus, or the Danaë. (*CP* 672)[10]

In 'Be it so', however, Jesus is specified as one among a list of gods who exemplify an inner flame that 'flicker[s] forth in sheer purity' (*CP* 674) when a man or woman is freed from self-conceit. It is perhaps because the Risen Lord has been the one to voice his appreciation for such displays of spontaneity in the article that the poems frequently hark back to this association. Yet it is also the case that Satan, in the late poems, is made to serve an entirely different purpose.

Taunting Satan for never having risen from the dead, the scornful protagonist of Lawrence's article mocks: 'when did you ever rise? Never! So go you down to oblivion, and give your place to the risen men...' (*LEA* 272). Yet in the late poems, Satan's fall is seen as positive and necessary, while he is also given a chance to answer back. The most explicit poem on this subject is 'When Satan Fell', in which the fall occurs 'because the Lord Almighty rose a bit too high, / and a bit beyond himself' (*CP* 710). Satan's fall restores a crucial balance made explicit at the end of this poem in the lines 'And hell and heaven are the scales of the balance of life / which swing against each other' (*CP* 710). Ironically, Satan's retort to God employs a number of rhetorical strategies through which the Risen Lord of the article establishes his confidence and pre-eminence:

'Are you so lofty, O my God?
Are you so pure and lofty, up aloft?
Then I will fall, and plant the paths to hell
with vines and poppies and fig-trees
so that lost souls may eat grapes
and the moist fig
and put scarlet buds in their hair on the way to hell,
on the way to dark perdition.' (*CP* 710)

Like the Risen Lord, Satan's words ring with challenge, evident again within cumulative rhetorical questions. The same confident defiance is conveyed in 'Then I will fall...', as though this falling were a conscious choice, followed by a list expressing direction and purpose. While the Risen Lord of the article is associated with the growth of fruits and plants, here it is Satan who has the capacity and intent to nurture vines (also associated with Dionysos in poems such as 'Middle of the

---

[10]   The poem cited has been slightly emended to follow Christopher Pollnitz's transcription of the 'Nettles' and 'Last Poems' notebooks and reflects the text as it will appear in the Cambridge University Press edition of Lawrence's *Complete Poems*.

World'); figs (with their sexual connotations); and poppies, in order to provide sustenance for hell-bound souls.[11]

To understand this reversal, it is necessary to allude to two other poems in which Satan's fall is evoked. In both these poems Satan acquires another name, but rather than Mammon, which provokes so much derision in the article, the name Lucifer is used as an identifier. In a poem with this title, the narrator uses a single, insistent rhetorical question to challenge the orthodox interpretation of Satan's fall: 'But tell me, tell me, how do you know / that he lost any of his brightness in falling?' (*CP* 697). The retained brightness of the falling Lucifer is contrasted with the dullness of the 'orthodox angels', who are 'tarnished by centuries of conventionality' (*CP* 614). Here, the fall of Lucifer/Satan represents the equivalent of the cosmic shift from Pisces into Aquarius, seen as a footstep onwards (*CP* 616; 713). The poem 'Old Archangels' lends weight to this interpretation, alluding to 'Orthodox Michael' and 'whispering Gabriel' who have 'had their term of office', so that now

> It is Lucifer's turn, the turn of the Son of the Morning
> to sway the earth of men,
> the Morning Star. (*CP* 614)

The iconography has shifted so that Satan/Lucifer acquires his cosmic attribute and is seen as profoundly influential, according to the astrological processes described in *Apocalypse*. Curiously, this Lucifer and the Risen Lord of the article have the same capacity to reinvigorate the earth and its inhabitants. They spring from the same creative imagination that has perceived a need for profound and radical change.

To indicate a further layer of complication and contradiction in the presentation of Satan, Mammon and Lucifer within these late texts, it is necessary to observe that even the portrayal of Lucifer in the poems is not consistent. In 'The Hands of God', for instance, Lucifer is neither to be derided nor admired: rather, he is seen as a victim to be pitied. His descent is here emblematic of a more widespread and catastrophic fall that can result when a man or woman slips through God's hands into a kind of never-ending free-fall:

> Did Lucifer fall through knowledge?
> Oh then, pity him, pity him that plunge!

---

[11]   These 'lost souls' will also be furnished with scarlet, the colour of gods and heroes, on their journey to perdition. The poem 'Evil is Homeless' sets up an antithesis of lost souls in which 'Hell is the home of souls lost in darkness, / even as heaven is the home of souls lost in light' (*CP* 711), using Persephone and Attis as examples of souls who can exist within both. Unlike the Satan who plants bright flowers on the road to Hades, Dante in this poem is seen as 'colour-blind / to the scarlet and purple flowers at the doors of hell' (*CP* 711) and associated with grey uniformity.

> Save me, O God, from falling into the ungodly knowledge
> of myself as I am without God ...
>
> That awful and sickening endless sinking, sinking
> through the slow, corruptive levels of disintegrative knowledge
> when the self has fallen from the hands of God (*CP* 699)

This poem contributes a third voice: not that of the Risen Lord or of Satan, but of the potential victim of the described fall offering up a prayer. Man's potential fall is envisaged in a number of different ways within the late poems: as a fall from organic connection ('The Breath of Life'); a fall from life ('Real Democracy'); a fall or collapse into robotic egotism ('Worship'): and a 'fall from God' ('Only Man'). The poem 'Abysmal Immortality' functions as a companion piece to 'The Hands of God', making even more explicit the consequences and nature of this fall:

> man can break away, and fall from the hands of God
> into himself alone, down the godless plunge of the abyss;
> a god-lost creature turning upon himself
> in the long, long fall, revolving upon himself
> in the endless writhe of the last, the last self-knowledge
> which he can never reach till he touch the bottom of the abyss
> which he can never touch, for the abyss is bottomless. (*CP* 700)

Within a poem that twists and turns back on itself, enacting the plunge described, it becomes evident that the fall is one from connection with a fundamental and nurturing life-principle into self-obsession and egoism. This is seen to be uniquely human, as the poem 'Only Man' indicates that 'no cobra nor hyaena nor scorpion nor hideous white ant / can slip entirely through the fingers of the hands of god / into the abyss of self-knowledge' (*CP* 701). The abyss is devastating in being bottomless, and the process of falling is irreversible, as is made evident by the poem 'Fatality', in which fallen man is seen as a leaf severed from a tree which cannot be put back. In 'Vengeance is Mine', it is those who 'fall into sharp, self-centred self-assertion, sharp or soft' (*CP* 616) who incur God's wrath.

In the article, during the tirade against Satan, the notion that man has newly risen from his own self-importance (the kind of egoism condemned in the poems) is forcibly voiced. The rising of the resurrected man counters the infinite downward plunge. Yet two poems – 'There are no gods' and 'Climbing Down' – offer a new conception of descent that can be envisaged positively. In the former the reference is very brief: one's capacity to be imaginatively receptive to 'the gods' is seen as 'like a pool into which we plunge, or do not plunge' (*CP* 652). Unlike the previous 'godless plunge', this poem ends poised at a moment of choice, offering the possibility of a leap out into the creative unknown. 'Climbing Down' begins cynically, conveying the fear inherent in people who are afraid of taking such a plunge, or 'climbing down from this idiotic tin-pot heaven of ours' (*CP* 667) because they are uncertain of what they will find when they reach the bottom. The poem's initial disillusionment is evident in the conviction that 'They needn't bother, most of them will never get down at all, / they've got to stay up' (*CP* 667), while those who do descend will need to 'suffer a sense-change / into something new and strange' (*CP* 667). Yet the poem proceeds to a vision of the altered, sense-changed state of being, in a way that counters the earlier cynicism but does not quite succeed in shrugging it off:

> Become aware as leaves are aware
> and fine as flowers are fine
> and fierce as fire is fierce
> and subtle, silvery, tinkling and rippling
> as rain-water
> and still a man,
> but a man re-born from the rigidity of fixed ideas
> resurrected from the death of mechanical motion and emotion. (*CP* 667)

This descent, paradoxically, is another way of describing the article's rising. Both envisage a rebirth from egocentrism and mechanization into a condition of natural, cosmic connection.

Iconography of Human Experience

The article and poems are not principally iconoclastic: rather, they entail a radical reinterpretation of Christian ideologies and images in terms of the human. Lawrence writes in 'The Risen Lord': 'What we have to remember is that the great religious images are only images of our own experience, or of our own state of mind and soul' (*LEA* 267). The article erodes the distinction between risen lord and risen *man*, while a number of the late poems interpret the divine in terms of the human. In 'The Cross', for instance, the line 'Christ, the human consciousness' (*CP* 636) reveals the extent to which the poem slips easily into such a blurring of categories, while in 'God and the Holy Ghost' it is alleged that 'The Holy Ghost is the deepest part of our own consciousness' (*CP* 621). Lawrence is concerned here not with the spiritual abstractions characterizing orthodox religion, but with the fleshly manifestations of the divine: the way in which the icons are creatively devised by humankind, and the way in which they can be profoundly affected by these symbols. In *Apocalypse*, Lawrence defines a symbol as the product of years of accumulated experience (see Chapter 7, p. 152), and his use of the iconography and language of religion within the late poems both taps into the established field of association and frivolously discards it, replacing it with his own. 'The Cross' implicitly engages with and develops symbolically the earlier conviction expressed in 'Tortoise shell': that 'The Cross, the Cross / Goes deeper in than we know, / Deeper into life' (*CP* 354). It opens with the declamatory cry 'Behold your Cross, Christians!' – immediately establishing the language of the poem within an archaic, biblical register. Yet this symbol is made to represent two fundamental binaries, without which mankind is allegedly lost:

> With the upright division into sex
> men on this side, women on that side
> without any division into inferiority and superiority
> only difference,
> divided in the mystic, tangible and intangible difference
>
> And then, truth much more bitter to accept
> the horizontal division of mankind
> into that which is below the level, and that which is above.
> That which is truly man, and that which is robot,
> the ego-bound. (*CP* 636)

In this poem, the task of risen men is to re-establish the 'mystic barriers of sex' (distinguishing male from female) and the hierarchical division between the base and the beautiful. Here, the key religious symbol (lent weight by its age-old power and significance) functions as the paradigm for a characteristically Lawrentian social critique. The horizontal division, represented by the cross's bar, corrects the perverse hierarchy in which robotic, mechanized man subjugates those who are natural and elemental: men of the wind, rain, fire and rock. This is revealed as the poem's real premise, as it steers away from the central symbol in order to grapple more explicitly with the societal issue. Although 'risen man and risen lord' are mentioned here they are not given prominence as protagonists; they also have a more problematic role to occupy than in the article. Rather than being joyful forerunners, they are here charged with the task of ideological revolution, for the robotic hordes must be 'made to submit' (*CP* 637) to the new hierarchy that the Cross represents. Given that most of Lawrence's transcendent individuals in these poems are gentle and tentative, this could prove a difficult mission.

Like Christian symbols, rituals and commandments are made subject to wilful misinterpretation in order to expose the evils of the modern world. In 'Shedding of Blood' a biblical dictum is thrown explicitly into question then defined by means of a deceptive interrogative that establishes the premise on which the rest of the poem is founded:

> 'Without shedding of blood there is no remission of sin.'
> What does it mean?
> Does it mean that life which has gone ugly and unliving is sin
> and the blood of it must be spilt? (*CP* 678)

The biblical lines, advocating a purge, provide the neat pretext for a poem equivalent in emphasis to 'Humanity Needs Pruning'. Here, instead of a rotting tree, the 'base and squalid' are symbolized by the 'scabbed and ugly lamb' as distinct from the 'firstling lamb, without spot or blemish' (*CP* 679). Yet the poem is not principally about the purging of degenerate humankind. Rather, it concerns the preservation of 'that which is noble and generous and spontaneous in humanity' (*CP* 679), as distinct from the 'mean, cowardly, greedy, egoistic degenerate blood' (*CP* 679) which must be spilled. The purging is more abstract, but again it is clear that the biblical phrase is merely a springboard for the further development of an idea explored metaphorically elsewhere.

Analogously, the poems with ostensibly biblical titles such as 'But I say unto you: Love one another —', 'Love thy neighbour —', 'As Thyself —' and 'Commandments' are poems of rejection and repudiation. The question 'Who then, O Jesus, is my neighbour?' resonates through this cluster of poems, in which the narrator struggles to identify his fellow men among the robotic hordes. The biblical commandments are, by implication, seen as anachronistic – no longer applicable to the modern world in which people are predominantly unlovable:

> When Jesus commanded us to love our neighbour
> he forced us either to live a great lie, or to disobey:
> for we can't love anybody, neighbour or no neighbour, to order,
> and faked love has rotted our marrow. (*CP* 654)

This poem finds another way of renouncing the love of multitudes that the Christ figure of *The Escaped Cock* rejects as a false, stultifying aspect of his old ideology. By their very nature, commandments might be associated with the superseded mission of the 'saviour' who fortunately rejected such dogmatism, gave up teaching for carpentry and rose up beyond interference. Yet it is not only such extreme tools of didactic omnipotence that are 'corrected' in these poems: rather, the most fundamental principles of the creation myth are undermined. The title of the poem 'Let there be Light!' is a declamatory echo of the biblical phrase,[12] then proceeds by indicating that it was, in fact, never uttered: 'If ever there was a beginning … / there was no Verb / no Voice / no Word' (*CP* 681). God-as-creator is humanized and trivialized through becoming 'Mr God' reaching out towards a light-switch (see Chapter 2, p. 25). This image is seen as an example of *man*'s conceit: in the terms of 'The Risen Lord', this image (like that of the Ascension) is not one that can in any way be related to our own experience. Against this incomprehensible image Lawrence shores his own less definite impression of creative origins:

> All we can honestly imagine in the beginning
> is the incomprehensible plasm of life, of creation

---

[12] See Genesis 1:3.

struggling
and *becoming* light. (*CP* 681)

This sense of creative yearning into being was one that he would also develop in the poems 'Red Geranium and Godly Mignonette' and the 'God is Born' sequence (discussed in Chapter 2, pp. 33–5). Again, in 'Red Geranium and Godly Mignonette', the idea of divine creation is satirized through God being presented as a magician figure who undergoes a process of comic deliberation – 'tum-tiddly-um' – before revealing the flowers with a 'hey-presto!' and a flourish (*CP* 690). The absurdly humanized or personified God, for Lawrence, testifies to the limitations of humanity's imaginative and creative powers. He indicates that it is up to us to find something better – to reach out for new definitions that will facilitate receptivity to the unknown – and in his late works he never stopped trying to achieve this aim. Arguably, the poem 'Shadows' is the nearest he came to identifying a God who could exist as a companion – a God he could walk with:

> … I am walking still
> with God, we are close together now the moon's in shadow…
>
> then I must know that still
> I am in the hands of the unknown God,
> he is breaking me down to his own oblivion
> to send me forth on a new morning, a new man. (*CP* 726)

This (unfallen) narrator finds God to be a palpable yet mysterious presence that both accompanies and cradles him. Yet this vision did not provide Lawrence with an answer: in 1930, days before his death, he was still wrestling with this same issue of how to define God.

Last Words in Protest

> It all depends what you make of the word God. (*IR* 358)

Lawrence's unfinished review of Eric Gill's *Art-Nonsense and Other Essays*, written at the Ad Astra Sanatorium shortly before his death, was the last work he ever wrote (*IR* lxxxix). It is a forthright review, a hybrid of praise and protest, in which the condemnation of Gill centres on his Catholicism and his misconception of God. Lawrence takes issue with such phrases as 'art is collaboration with God in creating', seeing this as symptomatic of the 'modern hobnobbing with God' (*IR* 356) that he considers 'nasty' and despicable. Gill's discussion of the phrase 'God is Love' clearly rankles, not least as a result of Gill's assertion that the Essential Perfection of man is not found in his physical functions or 'material exercise of his organs', but instead in his worship of God, which is 'perfect in Charity' (*IR* 356).

This, according to Lawrence, 'means really nothing', and he proceeds to condemn Gill's tendency to underline words for emphasis.

Lawrence attributes Gill's mishandling of God (and associated absolutes) to the fact that he has been discovered to be Roman Catholic. Making an assumption that Gill is one of the 'new English Catholics', he categorizes this group as 'the last words in Protest. They are Protestants protesting against Protestantism', swallowing whole such absolutes as Chastity, Obedience and Humility (*IR* 356). In the review Lawrence has a specific agenda with regard to Gill, and his critique of Catholicism is vehement and rhetorically charged from the outset. (This might be seen as particularly ironic given Lawrence's championing of the Catholic Church against the Protestant in poems discussed earlier in the chapter, where it is suggested that the former might take the radical step of flamboyantly celebrating Easter and bodily resurrection.) Later in the review, Lawrence returns to the shortcomings of Catholicism but with a different emphasis, and a more urgently didactic tone. It is seen as having 'fallen' into the same disaster as the Protestant Church, and needs to be born again. In the poem 'Future Religion', this rebirth has been interpreted as a way of celebrating the resurrection of the flesh as distinct from the ascension of a disembodied spirit. In the Gill review the emphasis is different: the rebirth of the church entails a redefinition of God as a vital rather than a moral principle. Lawrence's quarrel with Gill and with God can be – and is – rectified by a shifting of emphasis and a process of redefinition. Through inventive reading and writing, he rescues them both.

In the case of the Etruscans, I have argued that Lawrence appropriates them for his own purposes and uses his imaginative conception of them as a life-affirming paradigm. In the case of *Apocalypse*, the biblical text is creatively manipulated to reflect cosmological vitalism. In the late review considered here, Lawrence misreads Gill so as to find in him 'more ... than in all Karl Marx or Professor Whitehead or a dozen other philosophers rolled together' (*IR* 357). The two paragraphs that prompt this accolade concern the nature of work in its relation to egoism and the service of God. They are poised, balancing their oppositional hypotheses, in the manner of a rather enigmatic Heraclitean aphorism:

> That state is a state of Slavery in which a man does what he likes to do in his spare time and in his working time that which is required of him. This state can only exist when what a man likes to do is to please himself.
>
> That state is a state of Freedom in which a man does what he likes to do in his working time and in his spare time that which is required of him. This state can only exist when what a man likes to do is to please God.[13]

Lawrence must have found in these paragraphs an echo of his own expressed conviction regarding the necessity of work that induces intense concentration

---

[13]   Eric Gill, *Art-Nonsense and Other Essays* (London: Cassell Walterson, 1929), p. 1. Quoted in *IR* 357.

on the job in hand (here he uses the example of soldering a kettle), provoking a state of happy absorption. Yet Gill's antithesis to egoism – offered in the phrase 'to please God' – poses Lawrence a real problem. In an act of interpretative dexterity, therefore, he divests the term God of its Catholic – and indeed Christian – implications, asserting instead: ' "To please God" in this sense only means happily doing one's best at the job in hand, and being livingly absorbed in an activity which makes one in touch with—with the heart of all things; call it God … It is a state of absorption into the creative spirit, which is God.' (*IR* 357) Lawrence defines one abstraction (God) through reference to two others (the heart of all things and the creative spirit), as though abstractions were interchangeable and susceptible to infinite interpretations.

Yet God does not remain merely a de-Christianized abstraction in the review: there is a tacit acknowledgement that this would not suffice. The argument hinges on the line 'It all depends what you make of the term God', which twists the review round in a new direction, so that a slightly different limitation in man's capacity to understand God catalyzes a fresh definition. The argument now is that God has become a 'fetish-word, dead, yet useful for invocation' (*IR* 358), and the answer lies in the alternative label 'Almighty God', for 'We have to square ourselves with the very words' (*IR* 358). Almighty God is definable according to a number of specific attributes, which are listed here as strength, glory, honour, might and wisdom. This God can serve more readily as inspiration for the happily absorbed worker for 'the presence of the god enters into the thing made' (*IR* 358). Interestingly, however, Almighty God metamorphoses into 'a god' and 'the god of the craftsman', shifting (in the course of four lines) from an all-powerful deity to the (implicitly pagan) embodiment of a specific creative spirit. Happy absorption is referred to as a state of 'being with God' – as though it were possible to distinguish between the omnipotent presence (God) and the localized or specific off-shoot that lodges within a human being or object lovingly made (god). Receiving from God/ god some kind of power establishes a precise analogy with the process described in the poem 'Lord's Prayer', in which the attributes associated in the Gill review with Almighty God pass through invocation to the human recipient, who is in turn established in connection with the natural world and its laws:

All things that turn to thee
have their kingdom, their power, and their glory…

Like the kingdom of the fox in the dark
yapping in his power and his glory
which is death to the goose…

And I, a naked man, calling
calling to thee for my mana,
my kingdom, my power, and my glory. (*CP* 704)

Christianity and animism meet head to head in this poem, while in the review, one manifestation of God or god slides into the next.

The review breaks off and does not end, but its last words on the 'God' issue are significant: 'Why oh why will people keep on trying to define words like Art and Beauty and God, words which represent deep emotional states in us, and are therefore incapable of definition.' (*IR* 358) One answer is that definitions, like deities, proliferate and multiply: Lawrence cannot accept Gill's version of God so he counters it with his own. Any fixed or dogmatically imposed meaning would testify to emotional stasis and indicate resignation, while creative engagement can juggle contradictions and grope for understanding. Lawrence's last written words would be those of protest, struggling himself with multiple definitions and vilifying others' obsessive need to define.

Chapter 9

How to Make an End

The Prologues to *BirdsBeasts*[1]

In the context of a broader consideration of Lawrence's late style, this study has focussed on last works within a range of genres, including his last novel, his last travel book, his last full-scale non-fictional work on cosmology, myth and religion, his last review and the collection posthumously published as *Last Poems*. Ironically, however, the two late poetry notebooks do not seem to incorporate the last work written by him in this genre. Concurrently and subsequently, Lawrence turns out to have been exploring a new style of poetry writing late in 1929 and early in 1930, which we can see in the fragments written as prefaces to the Cresset Press (1930) edition of *Birds, Beasts and Flowers*, as well as in the short piece entitled 'Fire'.

The prologues to *BirdsBeasts*, written between 1 and 12 November 1929, were probably concurrent with the last poems to have been written into the 'Last Poems' notebook. They were created to order, in response to a request made by the wood-engraver Blair Hughes-Stanton,[2] who had undertaken the designs for the Cresset Press edition of *BirdsBeasts*. The fragments may have their roots in a letter to Hughes-Stanton of 30 August 1929, in which Lawrence expressed his willingness to compose 'a new foreword, on the essential nature of poetry or something like that' (*L* vii 457). A further letter, written almost two months after, reveals that in the interim Lawrence had been requested to compose not a general foreword, but a series of short prologues that would be placed at the beginning of each sub-section of the edition. A letter to Laurence Pollinger reveals Lawrence's initial lack of enthusiasm about the idea, but also his willingness to oblige if at all possible – an approach that seems in accord with his unfailing determination to help Hughes-Stanton, who was at the time very short of money and in need of publicity:

> I haven't got a copy of *Birds Beasts and Flowers* here, but will get one, and see
> if there is any point or amusement in a hundred-word caption before each of the
> nine parts. If I see any point, and can do it, I'll do it, but at present feel perfectly
> blank before the idea. (*L* vii 535)

---

[1] '*BirdsBeasts*' or '*Birds Beasts*' are abbreviations that Lawrence adopted in correspondence when referring to his poetry collection *Birds, Beasts and Flowers*, first published in 1923.

[2] See *L* vi 411, note 3.

Lawrence was evidently waiting for a copy of his book over the next couple of weeks, as in another letter to Pollinger written on 1 November he professed: 'I haven't got a copy of *Birds Beasts,* but when my trunks come, I'll see if I can put in those bits in front of the separate sections – as Hughes-Stanton wants – though I don't in the least know how to begin' (*L* vii 549). Evidently the 'bits' were written with alacrity once the book did arrive, for by 12 November Lawrence was writing:

> Here are the nine bits – I hope they will do – if not don't use them – just put them
> in the fire – I only did them because you wanted them, so you and the publishers
> can do as you like. (*L* vii 563)

The tone here is flippant and non-committal, suggesting that Lawrence had no interest in the 'bits', which had been written only as an offer of friendship.

Nevertheless, it would be wrong to consider the fragments unworthy of comment simply because Lawrence chose to adopt a casual tone when sending them to a friend for the publishers to consider. This was a tone he often adopted when facing possible rejection, ridicule or censorship from people who had the power, though not necessarily the expertise, to judge his work. In his last years, Lawrence was frequently driven to cynicism regarding issues of publication and censorship, and may have felt compelled to guard against this by asserting the slightness of his work. The prologues are, in fact, both significant as late works and curiously experimental.

The prologues are interesting stylistically, as they create new and diverse forms that amalgamate free-verse with prose passages. They also engage with and challenge conventional notions of quotation, by interweaving fragments derived from notable pre-Socratic philosophers with Lawrence's own stylistic imitation of the embodied material, without clarifying the distinction between them. This blurring or merging of categories may be seen as merely another superficial gripe against a resented readership:

> About the Cresset Press: the 'bits' to go in front of the *Birds Beasts* sections are
> part original and sometimes quotations from the fragments of Xenophanes and
> Empedokles [*sic*] and others, but I should like it all put in inverted commas, and
> let them crack their wits (the public) to find out what is ancient quotation and
> what isn't. (It is nearly all of it me.) (*L* vii 573)

Yet this statement raises fascinating questions about the nature of textual assimilation and authorial integrity/originality: what does it mean for a piece of writing to be 'nearly all of it me'? Lawrence creates a text that must be 'solved' (like the enigmatic Revelation), establishing a kind of intertextual riddle. Yet the little prologues are more than a mere puzzle, for they imply that the new text is not only provoked by but is also inseparable from the ancient fragments that have been its source or inspiration.

The source text in question is Burnet's *Early Greek Philosophy*, which, as I have argued in Chapter 5, was of such crucial significance to Lawrence during this period. I have already quoted the letter of 10 October 1929 in which Lawrence wrote to S.S. Koteliansky requesting a copy of the book, which he felt would be relevant to his work on the Apocalyptic material (see Chapter 5, p. 94). As in 1915, Lawrence acquired a copy of Burnet – this time the third edition (1920) – intending once more to write from within the camp of the pre-Socratics, thus returning to earlier material and preoccupations in a way that Lipking might perceive as neatly cyclical. The title *Birds, Beasts and Flowers* – derived from a hymn learnt by Lawrence in early childhood (see *SP* 302) – links the poetry of 1923 right back to Lawrence's youth, the period of the Nonconformist hymns discussed in 'Hymns in a Man's Life' (written in 1928). The title may also allude to the phrase 'beasts and birds and the fishes' which appears in Burnet, as fragment 21 of Empedocles:

> For out of these have sprung all things that were and are and shall be—trees and men and women, beasts and birds and the fishes that dwell in the waters, yea, and the gods that live long lives and are exalted in honour.
>
> For there are these alone; but, running through one another, they take different shapes—so much does mixture change them. (*3EGP* 209)

It does seem appropriate that Lawrence should return to *BirdsBeasts* in order to 'complete' it late in 1929, and it is clear that the verse of *Last Poems* aptly continues and elaborates on motifs and myths with which he had been preoccupied in his earlier poetry collection, such as the Etruscan civilization. The poem 'Cypresses' embodies an anticipation of the approach to the Etruscans that Lawrence would adopt after his actual visit to the tombs in 1927 (see Chapter 3, pp. 51–4). 'Purple Anemones' connects with 'Bavarian Gentians' through its evocation of Dis, Hades and Persephone in the underworld, and its association of this myth with flowers. Images of mechanism and iron in poems such as 'Almond Blossom' and the 'bad smell' at the core of America in 'Evening Land' pre-empt such poems as 'The Triumph of the Machine' and 'We Die Together', in which iron is sunk deep into modern man and contaminates the middle-earth. The critique of Bolshevism offered in 'Hibiscus and Salvia Flowers' is one to which Lawrence would return in the 'Nettles' notebook and the published *Nettles* volume of 1930 (as well as in *Lady Chatterley's Lover*[3]), particularly in formulating a political dichotomy in poems such as 'Bourgeois and Bolshevist'. All of the 'Evangelistic Beasts' poems use imagery strikingly similar to that employed by Carter, and then Lawrence, in their apocalyptic writing, and 'St. John' is particularly striking in its close correlation with the imagery of the later poem 'Phoenix':

Phoenix, Phoenix,
The nest is in flames,

---

[3] See *LCL* 38–9.

Feathers are singeing,
Ash flutters flocculent, like down on a blue, wan fledgeling. ('St. John', *CP* 329–30)

The phoenix renews her youth
only when she is burnt, burnt alive, burnt down
to hot and flocculent ash. ('Phoenix', *CP* 728)

In both poems, flocculent ash signifies a 'change' or rebirth in which the old is burnt in order for a fresh start, or new adjustment, to ensue.

According to this argument, Lawrence might be seen to be fulfilling his poetic destiny, re-reading his previous work and finding latent in it the seeds that would enable him to revisit, re-write and complete it. The Cresset Press edition, too, with its elaborate designs and engravings would furnish Lawrence with the opportunity to create his own equivalent of the 'tablets of bronze' (like Blakean plates) on which he had vowed to 'write out Herakleitos [*sic*]' (*L* ii 364) back in the summer of 1915.

Yet I have suggested that the specific Burnet edition he was using shows that Lawrence was working with new, as well as familiar, material. This is proved irrevocably by the quotations used in the *BirdsBeasts* prologues. As Pinto and Roberts observe in their notes to *Complete Poems,* Lawrence derived his quotations from the third edition of Burnet published in 1920 rather than the texts he had used in 1915:

> [Bertrand] Russell must have given him the 1st Edition (1892) or the 2nd (1908). The quotations in *BBF*, however, seem to come from the 3rd Edition, as they refer to a passage that does not occur in the two earlier ones. (*CP* 995)

The passage to which Pinto and Roberts refer must be the prologue to 'Animals': 'Once, they say, he was passing by when a dog was being beaten, and he spoke this word: "Stop! don't beat it! For it is the soul of a friend I recognised when I heard its voice" ' (*CP* 376). Lawrence's text here is almost identical to that of the third edition (*3EGP* 118), and differs from the text of the second, which reads: 'Once, they say, he was passing by when a dog was being ill-treated. "Stop!" he said, "don't hit it! It is the soul of a friend! I knew it when I heard its voice"'.[4] I suspect, however, that Pinto and Roberts were actually unaware of the presence of this passage in the second edition: not only is it slightly altered, but it appears in a different section from its location in the third.[5]

---

[4]   John Burnet, *Early Greek Philosophy* (London: Black, 1908), p. 124.

[5]   In their notes the editors refer to page 84 of the third edition, in which a commentary on the above quotation occurs in the 'Pythagoras' section and then is listed directly among the Xenophanes' fragments, while in the second edition the quotation appears only in the commentary section on 'Xenophanes' (I will discuss the editorial referencing of this fragment later).

The question of multiple editions has complicated the task of the puzzle-solving critics attempting to crack the Lawrentian code and separate ancient quotation from Lawrentian paraphrase or pastiche. In their notes to *Complete Poems* Pinto and Roberts identify the sources for some of the pre-Socratic quotations but fail to locate others, particularly when the fragment is embedded in a longer prose passage, or when Lawrence adds to or alters parts of the text before weaving it into his own prologue.[6] It seems that Lawrence is working in two ways with Burnet: on the one hand he is quoting the fragments he knows intimately from memory, just as in his essay 'The Nightingale' (1926) he quotes Keats without needing to consult a written text. In the case of the Keats essay, this leads to error in the form of accidental or creative misrepresentation.[7] In 'Reptiles' Lawrence begins his prologue with a favourite Heraclitean insight, which he both misquotes and extends so the ending of the first 'quotation' sounds primarily Lawrentian:

> 'HOMER was wrong in saying, "Would that strife might pass away from among gods and men!" He did not see that he was praying for the destruction of the universe; for, if his prayer were heard, all things would pass away—for in the tension of opposites all things have their being—'[8]

Instead of Heraclitus' 'perish' Lawrence writes 'pass away', and he appends to the fragment the highly Lawrentian phrase 'for in the tension of opposites all things have their being—', indicating (erroneously) that this phrase is an unbroken continuation of the previous words. In fact, the appended phrase derives from fragment 45 of Heraclitus:

> Men do not know how what is at variance agrees with itself. It is an attunement of opposite tensions, like that of the bow and the lyre. (*3EGP* 136)

It is possible that Lawrence decided consciously to add the phrase, as he shows elsewhere that he feels quite at liberty to alter quotations to suit his own purposes, without acknowledging the changes. Yet the substitution for 'perish', as well as the altered punctuation, suggests that he was in fact quoting from his memory of the editions he had encountered earlier in life. By contrast, the quotations from the third edition are either transcribed from the text or derived from a much shorter-term act of memory, for the material was new and not deep-rooted in Lawrence's subconscious. These two processes thus appear to have been in progress simultaneously.

---

[6]   For their notes on the *BirdsBeasts* prologues in which Pinto and Roberts trace the origins of the allusions (with varying degrees of success) see *CP* 995–1001.

[7]   See Bethan Jones, 'Shaping, Intertextuality and Summation in D.H. Lawrence's *Last Poems*', unpublished PhD thesis (Nottingham University, 1998), pp. 60–61.

[8]   D.H. Lawrence, *Birds, Beasts and Flowers* (London: Cresset Press, 1930), p. 105. Hereafter *BBF*.

When Lawrence adds material or alters a quotation, the textual puzzle becomes more problematic. For instance, Pinto and Roberts fail to identify the line in 'Flowers': 'Oh Persephone, Persephone, bring back to me from Hades the life of a dead man', commenting 'This seems to be a quotation, but we have been unable to trace its origin' (*CP* 996). In fact, the quotation derives from the end of fragment 111 of Empedocles, which reads: 'Thou shalt bring back from Hades the life of a dead man' (*3EGP* 221). By adding the Persephone reference, Lawrence has created a link with the poem 'Purple Anemones', with all the poetic and mythological resonances that it has acquired in the intervening composition of 'Bavarian Gentians'.

Similarly, in 'Fruits', Pinto and Roberts assert that 'The last sentence of this preface seems to be a quotation, but we have been unable to trace its origin' (*CP* 996). This line reads: 'No sin it is to drink as much as a man can take and get home without a servant's help, so he be not stricken in years'. The origin is to be found in Xenophanes, the words embedded in his first fragment: presumably the reason that the *Complete Poems* editors could not find it. Xenophanes' words are: 'no sin is it to drink as much as a man can take and get home without an attendant, so he be not stricken in years' (*3EGP* 117). The editors also fail to give the correct reference for the 'Animals' quotation 'Once they say ... heard its voice' (see above). This derives from fragment 7 of Xenophanes, appearing on page 118 of the third edition. Lawrence's text is almost identical: he merely omits the noun 'Pythagoras' which appears within brackets in Burnet, inserts commas strategically and omits the word 'that' twice to reduce superfluous length. Pinto and Roberts say of the quotation 'this is a story told of Pythagoras by Xenophanes quoted by Burnet, op. cit., p. 84', referring not to the fragment itself but to Burnet's paraphrased version located earlier within his commentary on Pythagoras. Burnet's commentary reads: 'Some verses are quoted from Xenophanes, in which we are told that Pythagoras once heard a dog howling and appealed to its master not to beat it, as he recognised the voice of a departed friend' (*3EGP* 84). Although a note directs the reader to 'Xenophanes, fr. 7.' there is no page reference for this fragment, and as there is no full section on Xenophanes (he appears in a chapter entitled 'Science and Religion') Pinto and Roberts presumably did not look far enough.

The Cresset Press edition adheres to Lawrence's desires regarding the 'nine bits', using quotation marks for the entire text in each case, without attempting to identify and highlight the direct allusions. It would be problematic to attempt such a differentiation between direct citation and text which clearly derives from Burnet but which alters or extends it: ought the quotation marks to be applied to the latter as well as the former? Clearly there is a thin stylistic dividing line between the pre-Socratic words and Lawrence's own: hence the confusion of intent and practice in the use of quotation marks by Pinto and Roberts.

In the first (1964) edition of *Complete Poems* the editors express their intention of proceeding a step beyond the Cresset Press edition by separating Burnet-text from Lawrence-text and highlighting this distinction:

The Cresset Press text places every paragraph of the prefaces in inverted commas. Where Lawrence is evidently speaking in his own person, these quotation marks have been deleted in the present text, but they have been retained where it seems to be clear that the passage is a quotation.[9]

In the 1964 *Complete Poems* edition (and in the reprint of 1967 which reproduces the 1964 text exactly) the editors adhere to this decision to try to distinguish Lawrence from Burnet. Interestingly they leave quotation marks around text which they believe to be quotation but have not found, such as the passage in 'Fruits' beginning 'No sin is it ...' and 'Oh Persephone, Persephone, bring back to me ...' in 'Flowers'. By making such assumptions about textual origin they inevitably create an editorial inconsistency, for when Burnet-text has not actually been traced it is impossible to separate with any authority the original from the Lawrentian deviation. When Pinto and Roberts find the source of a quotation they take pains to differentiate even very minutely between Burnet-text and Lawrence-text through their interpolation of quotation marks, as is evident in the opening section of 'Ghosts', which reads (in the 1964 and 1967 texts):

AND as 'the dog with its nostrils tracking out the fragments of the beasts' limbs, and the breath from their feet that they leave in the soft grass', runs upon a path that is pathless to men, so does the soul follow the trail of the dead, across great spaces.[10]

Here, Lawrence's deviation from Burnet-text is clearly (and accurately) marked. In the light of this general approach, the 'Persephone' quotation in 'Flowers' should read:

Oh Persephone, Persephone, 'bring back to me from Hades the life of a dead man.'

Even this representation would not be quite adequate. Lawrence's quotation does not entirely match the Burnet text: the words 'to me' are added. Similarly, if the texts are closely scrutinized, it may be seen that the 'Ghosts' quotation also cited above is, in Lawrence's version, not an exact reproduction of Empedocles' fragment: Lawrence writes 'beasts' instead of the singular 'beast's', and makes no concession to the fact that the two words 'The dog' which begin Empedocles' fragment appear in brackets in the Burnet text. A quotation system that could indicate such changes would, however, be extremely complex, intricate, clumsy and probably superfluous.

Between the second (1967) and third (1972) editions of *Complete Poems*, Pinto and Roberts decided to reject their quotation policy in these fragments and revert to the Cresset Press presentation of the text. They do so without making any real

---

[9] *The Complete Poems of D.H. Lawrence* (London: Heinemann, 1964), 2 vols, p. 995.
[10] Ibid. p. 406.

acknowledgement of the fact; they say merely in the preface to the third edition that 'For this edition a number of errors have been corrected after comparison of the text with the most authoritative sources'.[11] The third edition of *Complete Poems* gave rise to the widely reproduced Viking/Penguin paperback text, and this paperback still erroneously prints Pinto and Roberts's explanation for the reasons why their quotation marks differ from those employed in the Cresset text, when in fact they no longer differ.[12]

It seems likely that the decision to revert to the Cresset text was provoked by the editors' attention to the letter (cited above) in which Lawrence requests quotation marks for his entire text. This letter, written long after the final dispatch to Hughes-Stanton of the manuscript, must be seen as Lawrence's final statement of intention regarding the texts in question. The Cresset Press edition thus becomes a more authoritative text even than the manuscript itself, and no doubt Pinto and Roberts came to this conclusion between 1967 and 1972. Their decision also suggests that the editors were unable to make the desired distinction between allusion and new material: it is nowhere absolutely evident that Lawrence is speaking in his own person rather than from the perspective, or through the words of, 'some character in whose soul [he] now live[s]'.[13]

Paradoxically, through textual assimilation, Lawrence seems to have forced critics and readers into a position in which they must accept that a text simultaneously derives from precursive writing and (through weaving and assimilation) belongs to the author who processes and adopts it: we must take Lawrence at face value when he writes 'It is nearly all of it me'.

The *BirdsBeasts* Prologues: Free-verse or Another Kind of Prose?

The *BirdsBeasts* prologues appeared in print first in the Cresset Press edition of 1930; they were then reproduced in *Phoenix*[14] and in *Complete Poems* by Pinto

---

[11]   *The Complete Poems of D.H. Lawrence* (London: Heinemann, 1972. third reprint of 1964 edition with minor revisions), p. 26.

[12]   The only discrepancy is a residual textual error in 'Flowers' which occurred as a result of the editorial intervention which led Pinto and Roberts to add quotation marks earlier on. A superfluous quotation mark appears after 'beans!', in order to distinguish the actual quotation from Lawrence's additional 'saith Empedokles'. The editors did not notice that this particular set of quotation marks is in fact closed later anyway, after the word 'beans-cod'. In the 1972 Heinemann text (reproduced by Penguin), then, we are made aware of the editorial imposition that has altered (then reinstated, *almost* entirely) the Cresset Press text.

[13]   *The Letters of John Keats: A Selected Edition*, ed. R. Gittings (Oxford: Oxford University Press, 1990), p. 158.

[14]   *Phoenix: The Posthumous Papers of D.H. Lawrence*, ed. Edward D. McDonald (London: Heinemann, 1936), pp. 65–8.

and Roberts. Although the publishers of these editions ostensibly published Lawrence's original texts, the discrepancies between them highlight the problems raised with regard not only to the status of quotations and allusion, but to the wider question of form. Both the *Phoenix* and *Complete Poems* texts engage in a kind of regularization of the original, resulting in the loss of certain distinctive features that are characteristic of Lawrence's unique use of form in the prologues. It is necessary, first, to describe the Cresset Press edition of the texts, before proceeding to explore the ways in which the later versions differ.

The prologues are printed in this edition on pages facing the design by Hughes-Stanton that precedes each sub-section of the book. The nine titles are 'Fruits', 'Trees', 'Flowers', 'The Evangelistic Beasts', 'Creatures', 'Reptiles', 'Birds', 'Animals' and 'Ghosts'. Each prologue is printed in italics, with the opening word appearing in capitals. The fragments convey a sense of immediacy and spontaneity in spite of their archaic diction. They do not stand on ceremony but launch into their particular subject, rather in the manner of the poems in which Lawrence begins with a direct address or exhortation: 'Oh, do not tell me the heavens as well are a wheel' ('The Wandering Cosmos', *CP* 713) and 'So guns and strong explosives / are evil, evil' ('Murderous Weapons', *CP* 715). The *BirdsBeasts* prologues begin with such lines as 'FOR fruits are all of them female …' (*CP* 277); 'OH put them back …' (*CP* 319), 'BUT fishes are very fiery …' (*CP* 331), 'YES, and if oxen or lions had hands …' (*CP* 376) and 'AND as the dog …' (*CP* 406). These prologues are unashamedly fragmentary: they seem to delight in adhering to the challenging obscurity of the Heraclitean mode, without engaging in unnecessary preamble. Like the previous *Pansies* they are characterized by brevity, giving an impression of transience, yet the language is less straightforward, weighed down as it is by its enigmatic philosophical resonances and implications. The form is dislocated in its yoking together of disparate allusions without reflecting any need to provide linking passages or explanation. Thus it often has the feel of utterance – an aspect enhanced by the italics of the text, relating to *BirdsBeasts* as a whole, in which italics designate direct speech or interior monologue. The prologues are littered with dashes indicating interrupted thought, speech or line, again emphasizing the dialogic nature of the fragments. We are clearly presented with a series of many-voiced texts rather than a unified introduction sequence embodying a single perspective, and as the identities of the many speakers remain shadowy, no strain is overtly prioritized.

The fragments are either written in continuous prose or contain passages of prose within them. 'The Evangelistic Beasts' and 'Ghosts' consist of a single paragraph without line breaks of any kind. 'Fruits' contains one long paragraph (ending with an indication that the quotation is incomplete, or a continuation implied) followed by a shorter quotation in separate quotation marks, indented so as to indicate a new paragraph. The cases of 'Trees', 'Flowers', 'Creatures', 'Reptiles', 'Birds' and 'Animals' are rather different, and much more interesting. In these, prose chunks of varying lengths – sometimes as short as a single line – follow each other in quick succession, without paragraph indentations. Instead of indenting, Lawrence simply takes a new line for each quotation or remark, in the manner of a free-verse poem. Arguably, these fragments push the free-verse form to its logical conclusion, expanding the lines to incorporate whole paragraphs and entire quotations: fragments are housed within fragments, juxtaposed so as to create a curious blend of poetry and prose.

'Flowers' provides the most striking example of this, and links most obviously to Lawrence's free-verse poetry: to *Last Poems* in particular. It begins as though it had already begun: 'AND long ago, the almond was the symbol of resurrection' (*CP* 303)[15] (this, although in quotation marks, appears to be Lawrence rather than Burnet). A line break follows, before another (unspecified) voice provides the material for potentially undermining or questioning the initial assertion: 'But tell me, tell me, why should the almond be the symbol of resurrection?' (*CP* 303). Suddenly, as readers, we are made aware of a second speaker – of a dialogue – emphasizing that the extended free-verse form is conveying utterance. The voice questions with the same insistence evident in the line 'Tell me, is the gentian savage, at the top of its coarse stem?' in the poem 'Flowers and Men' (*CP* 684). Although (in the *BirdsBeasts* fragment 'Flowers') a question is asked, it bears within itself the necessary response: it is a question that is not intended to raise doubts but to provoke interest, so that the curiosity will be satisfied by the forthcoming explanation. Lawrence follows this second exhortation with 'Have you not seen, in the wild winter sun of the southern Mediterranean, in January and in February, the re-birth of the almond tree, all standing in clouds of glory?' (*CP* 303). This is unbroken prose, or, in the terms of my analysis, a line of free-verse poetry that has extended beyond normal bounds in order to incorporate the narrative description that provides the question with its rhetorical force.

Again the question is answered by the inquisitive second voice: 'Ah Yes! ah yes! would I might see it again!' (*CP* 303). The response is appropriately effusive, and we acquire an impression of this speaker. S/he seems like the narrator of the 'God is Born' poems, or of 'Red Geranium and Godly Mignonette', showing the necessary willingness to engage with and respond to the wonder of this cosmic/godly manifestation. The first speaker, prone to scholarly exegesis wrapped in the longer complexities of prose, expands and expounds as follows:

---

[15] On 29 September 1929, Lawrence wrote to Maria Huxley, requesting 'a little brochure on *The Olive Tree* and *The Vine*' which might enable him to write 'essays on various trees ... of the Mediterranean' (*L* vii 501). She found an article on the almond tree which she had typed by Jehanne Moulaert and sent to Lawrence, who acknowledged it in a letter of 26 October: 'The typescript has just come, and thank you very much' (*L* vii 541). Later still, on 19 December, he asked 'what Jehanne paid for the typing of that almond-tree article – so nice it is' (*L* vii 602). For references to the almond trees at Bandol in January and February 1930 see *L* vii 633, 634 and 646; also Earl and Achsah Brewster, *D.H. Lawrence: Reminiscences and Correspondence* (London: Secker, 1934), pp. 228–9.

> Yet even this is not the secret of the secret. Do you know what was called the almond bone, in the body, the last bone of the spine? This was the seed of the body, and from the grave it could grow into a new body again, like almond blossom in January. (*BBF* 41)

The second voice, capable (it seems) of response but lacking in ancient wisdom, responds with '... No, no, I know nothing of that' (*CP* 303). At this point in the poem the first set of quotation marks is closed, and Lawrence (unbeknown to Pinto and Roberts) turns to Burnet for two pre-Socratic quotations. The first dialogic exchange (up to '... No, no, I know nothing of that', *CP* 303) is almost certainly all Lawrence's. It provides an appropriate context for the first poem in the section – 'Almond Blossom' – just as the opening of 'Fruits' introduces 'Pomegranates'. Lawrence's own contributions to the fragments are most often evident when the prologue bears closest resemblance to the poems that follow it, or when it is most illuminating in relation to these poems.

The apparently odd shift from the first dialogue to the altered Empedoclean fragment 'Oh Persephone, Persephone, bring back to me from Hades the life of a dead man' (*CP* 303) is similarly explicable in terms of the second poem in the sub-section: 'Purple Anemones'. This poem, treating its subject matter flippantly and ironically, unlike the fuller poem 'Bavarian Gentians', focuses on the pursuit of Persephone, the 'husband-snared hell-queen', by Dis (*CP* 309). The switch to another quotation from Empedocles is more problematic, and may be attributed, perhaps, to Lawrence's sense of amusement and his desire to include the particular quotation 'Wretches, utter wretches, keep your hands from beans! saith Empedokles [*sic*]'. Lawrence elaborates on the bean theme, adopting the scholarly voice evident in the first section of the poem:

> For according to some, the beans were the beans of votes, and votes were politics. But others say it was a food-taboo. Others also say the bean was one of the oldest symbols of the male organ, for the peas-cod is later than the beans-cod. (*BBF* 41)

It is difficult to tell how serious Lawrence is being here. Perhaps he felt the need to justify his inclusion of the 'bean' quotation, and finds a useful opportunity to discuss the male equivalent to the subject of the earlier 'Figs' poem. The prologue ends with a 'quotation' that seems to be Lawrence rather than Burnet-text. It begins as though contradicting a previous assertion, then reveals itself to be on a different tack, as though Lawrence were convincing his readers that he was quoting, and quoting without altering the original: 'But blood is red, and blood is life. Red was the colour of kings. Kings, far-off kings, painted their faces vermilion and were almost gods' (*CP* 303). This quotation neatly refers to the remaining poems in the section: namely 'Sicilian Cyclamens' and 'Hibiscus and Salvia Flowers'. Its emphasis on red or vermilion (the colour of gods and heroes in *Last Poems*) links the 'tiny rose cyclamens' (*CP* 310) growing between the toes of shaggy

Mediterranean savages with the 'Rosy, rosy scarlet' (*CP* 313) of the hibiscus and salvia flowers, saluted in preference to the 'loutish bolshevists' who presume to adopt the colour of these flowers and pin them on their breasts (*CP* 317).

Although Pinto and Roberts fail to identify many citations, they produce a text that has greater integrity than the *Phoenix* version. Their text does not conform exactly to the Cresset Press original: it alters the number of words printed in capitals at the opening of the fragments, it does not use italics to emphasize the fact that the text is dialogic, and omits almost all of the dashes which indicate fragmentation or interruption.[16] In 'Flowers', for instance, the following 'dashed' words appear in the Cresset Press edition but were omitted in *Complete Poems*: 'Resurrection.–'; 'resurrection? –'; 'glory? –'; 'that. –' and 'man–.'. In spite of these omissions, the text at least preserves the odd forms of the fragments, allowing Lawrence to retain the free-verse/prose amalgam appropriate for his new allusive style.

The *Phoenix* version, by contrast, is conspicuous, and reprehensible, in its deviation from Lawrence's form. The editor (Edward D. McDonald) attempts to regularize or normalize the text by sorting it into neat paragraphs, sometimes joining lines together so the appearance is more consistent. 'Flowers' provides a good example of this approach. To begin with, the first words are indented, placing them at the opening of a prose paragraph. Then, unlike Pinto and Roberts, McDonald does not take a new line for 'But tell me', thus failing to distinguish the second voice from the first. New paragraphs, with their first lines indented, are taken for 'Have you seen …'; 'Ah yes!' and 'Yet even', again losing the effect of a conversation or verbal exchange. There is no new line taken at all for the second speaker's final response to the first: 'No, no, I know nothing of that–', again confusing the identity of the two voices, who should be differentiated by the length of their rejoinders. Then, for the last three quotations, McDonald inserts new paragraph breaks, indenting accordingly.

These changes may appear to be insignificant. Yet they reveal a lack of understanding of the text, making assumptions regarding editorial superiority, while the formal interest of Lawrence's text is forfeit when the process of regularization occurs. An advocate of regularized text might argue that Lawrence cared very little about these fragments, while the editor has taken the trouble to make these corrections: they might cite as evidence the letter in which Lawrence tells Hughes-Stanton that he might cheerfully burn the fragments if they are unsuitable (*L* vii 563). Yet the fragments do not exist in a stylistic vacuum: they are not the only texts that explore the possibility of combining prose and free-verse in this way. The same kinds of combination are evident in the fragment 'Fire', which is arguably the last poem Lawrence ever wrote, later even than the *Last Poems*, which are usually interpreted as his final poetic statements.

---

[16] Typists and printers in the early and mid-twentieth century were reluctant to print dashes at the end of lines. This was strikingly evident in many of Lawrence's texts, none more so than his play *The Daughter-in-Law*, in which over seventy dashes were excised in all from the two typescripts and from the text of the first edition.

'Fire': Fragment, Free-verse or Prose-poetry?

It is almost certain that the fragment 'Fire' was written after the *BirdsBeasts* prologues, and very likely that it succeeded either all or almost all of the *Last Poems*. It can be located (although not with absolute certainty) in the period between Lawrence's completion of the prologues and his letter to Laurence Pollinger of 25 November 1929 in which he requests comprehensive inverted commas around each fragment over which the baffled public must 'crack their wits' (*L* vii 573). The poem can conjecturally be located between these dates as it seems to have coincided with the Brewsters' acquisition and decoration of their house Château Brun, and with Lawrence's early visits to this new home. On 14 November Lawrence informed Max and Kathe Mohr that the Brewsters were to move in at the end of the week; then on 21 November, in another letter to Max Mohr, he gives the following account of the place:

> The Brewsters have taken the Château Brun, and paid 1,200 francs for six months rent. Now the workmen are white-washing the inside, for 700 frs. – and Earl and Achsah are supposed to be painting the doors and windows, also white. The whole interior is to be snow-white, like a pure, pure lily: imaginez-vous, Monsieur, comme un tombeau! But Earl does not want to go to the house, he is afraid of being there all alone with his Achsah, so when they go to paint the doors, after an hour he has a head-ache, and must come home. I'm afraid it is going to be very difficult. – They have bought two old chairs and a set of fire-irons (for six frs) so far. I don't know how they'll ever really move in to the house: they really worry me. (*L* vii 570)

It is unclear whether or not Lawrence is writing this account having already visited the house, or whether he is merely relaying the Brewsters' description. He must have visited at around this time, however, as the Brewsters describe his presence there at the time of the initial painting:

> One morning we all went by automobile to look at the new place, taking Lawrence with us. He pottered about and watched the painting and finally squatted on his heels by the fireplace, making a fire with twigs to dry the new colour-washed walls. He sat there feeding the fire with the bits of stick I carried in. Looking like a collier, he stayed all morning perched on his toes, elbows on knees. Frieda called out: 'Look at Lorenzo sitting on his heels. He always does it—just like a miner.' She seemed almost vain of his accomplishment.[17]

The discrepancy between the reports offered by Lawrence and the Brewsters is interesting: while Lawrence emphasizes the cold, tomb-like nature of the

---

[17] Edward Nehls, *D.H. Lawrence: A Composite Biography*, vol. 3 (Madison: University of Wisconsin Press, 1959), p. 416.

whitewashed room the Brewsters refer to the literal and figurative warmth of the scene in which Lawrence crouches miner-fashion before the fire. They give another account that conveys the same impression, but this time includes a reference to the poem 'Fire', which Lawrence was allegedly writing at this time, in direct response to his experiences at the Château Brun:

> He would sit contentedly by our hearth warming his feet, and insisting that it was the first time during the winter that they had been warm. He declared that if he had the actual presence of a fire before him in his house, instead of *chauffrage centrale,* he would gain new strength: for man lived by the elements and he should not deny fire. It was at this time that he wrote a poem to fire.[18]

This reference to the 'Fire' poem is significant in two respects: it provides a specific context for the writing of the poem and also shows that the poem was public, at least to some extent, as Lawrence either read it to the Brewsters or talked about it. Significantly, too, it is referred to as a 'poem' about fire, although it is, in fact, a prose-poem – something rare in Lawrence's output – and is not included in *Complete Poems*.

The poem differs from the *BirdsBeasts* prologues in that the language is less obviously mimetic, and it does not have the same tissue of enigmatic citation. Yet it is richly allusive – more subtly, more poetically and less dogmatically so – while preserving a simplicity of language that has been evident throughout *Last Poems*. This poem bridges the gap between the late notebooks' style and the new

---

[18]   Brewster, p. 306. E.W. Tedlock gives the following information about the 'Fire' fragment: 'Like "The Elephants of Dionysos" this text evidently dates from the period of composition of *Apocalypse.* The notebook from which the manuscript has been removed was a birthday gift from Harwood Brewster, and bears an inscription' dated September 11, 1929. By late September Lawrence was in Bandol, Var, France, where *Apocalypse* was written in the next few months', in E.W. Tedlock, *The Frieda Lawrence Collection of D.H. Lawrence's Manuscripts: A Descriptive Bibliography,* (Albuquerque: University of New Mexico Press, 1948), p. 214.

In *D.H. Lawrence: A Calendar of his Works* (Manchester: Manchester University Press, 1979), Keith Sagar places the poem's composition at the end of December rather than in November, asserting that the Brewsters 'did not move into their new house at Bandol until late December' (p. 189). The fragment was initially drafted on the back of sheets of *Apocalypse* – 'A manuscript ... containing notes for *Apocalypse* also contains "The Elephants of Dionysos" and "Fire" ' – and Sagar uses his argument that Lawrence began writing *Apocalypse* in December to support his dating of the fragments. It seems likely, however, that Lawrence began writing *Apocalypse* before this – in mid-November, when Carter arrived – which means that the fragments may be a month earlier than Sagar supposes. The Brewsters were certainly paying regular visits to their new house and having the whitewashing done long before the beginning of December. Lawrence thought they would move in at the end of the week of 14 November, and on 21 November was giving vivid descriptions of the painting that was taking place.

form of the fragments, creating a hybrid that is both appropriate for its content and innovatory.

The poem seems to have been provoked by the awareness of 'real' fire by contrast with the artificial, unelemental nature of '*chauffrage centrale*'. It begins with a narrative voice reminiscent of the first speaker in 'Flowers' and of the punchy, down-to-earth style of *Pansies,* launching into an interrogative:

> Fire: did you ever warm your hands at
> the combustion of carbon and oxygen,
> or glow in the face from the formation
> of carbon dioxide by means of combustion?[19]

The question is not answered but is followed by a further series of interrogatives intermingled with images that combine and proliferate. The first is:

> What do you see there, then, as the
> twigs crackle and the gold rushes out
> and ripples flapping brilliant to
> a peak of gold within the smoke? (F 44)

These two four-line 'sentences' of the poem's opening are juxtaposed in order to create a contrast between the inappropriately 'scientific' method of generating heat and the sensory response. They reflect the assertion made by Lawrence (according to the Brewsters) that he had never really been warm in a centrally heated house, but became warm at their fire.

Stylistically, the poem has the feel of an invocation. E.W. Tedlock, in his description of the manuscript, quotes the four lines above and comments: 'The rest of the sketch is a poetic answer to this question, ending somewhat in the form of an invocation'.[20] In Lawrence Clark Powell's manuscript listings, the fragment is given the title 'Invocation to Fire',[21] and even though this is an imposed label (Lawrence's sketch was untitled, except for the word 'Fire' printed with a colon immediately following, at the beginning of the poem's first line), it seems appropriate, and emphasizes the 'poetic' status of the work. Just as in 'Invocation to the Moon', in which the goddess is addressed as 'You beauty, O you beauty' (*CP* 695), so fire here is invoked and addressed as an animate force: 'Oh lovely Fire, what / is it but you, lovely Fire, that / was not and is, to my joy'. The request to Fire – 'I only ask that / you shall be with me, bright,

---

[19]   'Fire' in T.A. Smailes, 'D.H. Lawrence: Seven Hitherto Unpublished Poems', *The D.H. Lawrence Review*, vol. 3, no. 1 (Spring 1970), p, 44. Subsequent short citations from this poem derive from pp. 44–5; longer extracts are indicated by the abbreviation F.

[20]   Tedlock, p. 214.

[21]   Lawrence Clark Powell, *The Manuscripts of D.H. Lawrence: A Descriptive Catalogue* (Los Angeles: Los Angeles Public Library, 1937), p. 55.

rustling, / fierce-fanged fire' – is also strikingly similar to the equivalent lines in the moon poem: 'Be good to me, lady, great lady of the nearest / heavenly mansion, and last!' (*CP* 695). Similarly, the next line of 'Fire' – 'I only delight in / your companionship that is nakeder / and more interpenetrating than love' – correlates with the description of the moon-goddess who is the 'greatest of ladies', 'because naked you are more wonderful than anything we can stroke —' (*CP* 695).

Like the moon invocation, 'Fire' uses repetition to achieve an incantatory, rhapsodic or mesmeric effect. The reiteration of 'Oh lovely' achieves this, as in the poem 'The Man of Tyre', in which the words 'Oh lovely, lovely' are used to express the wonder and rapture of the man who watches a woman he identifies as Aphrodite emerge from the water. Similarly, towards the end of the poem the phrase 'beautiful fire, / beautiful fire' – like 'it is warm, it is warm' in 'Butterfly' – conveys something of the comfort derived from close proximity with this elemental source of heat, which is itself seen as a wonder. A sense of urgency, the need to establish contact and provoke response, is also achieved by reiterated words, as in 'Oh pour, pour, pour into / the vessels of my heart', like the repetitions of 'O build' and 'O build it' in 'The Ship of Death'.

The imagery also links this poem to a variety of Lawrentian descriptions used previously both in poetry and prose. Fire 'lies red' in a kind of dormant potency, like the serpent coiled at the core of life in *Women in Love* (*WL* 451). It then 'writhes a little', implying motion like that of the Lawrentian snake which 'writhed like lightning and was gone' (*CP* 351). This fire does not disappear, however, but 'changes upon / itself', the quality of metamorphosis linking it with such late poems as 'Change' and particularly 'Phoenix'. The Phoenix allusion becomes more explicit through the words, 'I ask not how / you nest and crackle so red, / with pinions of swift gold, among / the moving transfigured twigs!' as well as the description of fire as 'swift, swift ruddy one feathered with / gold'. The poem's vision is one implying (if not directly asserting) a kind of rebirth or transfiguration through the change that fire can occasion, thus echoing the following lines from 'Phoenix': 'Then the small stirring of a new small bub in the nest / with strands of down like floating ash / shows that she is renewing her youth like the eagle, / immortal bird' (*CP* 728). Fire also possesses Heraclitean fluidity and power: 'All things are an exchange for Fire, and Fire for all things' and 'Fire in its advance will judge and convict all things' (*3EGP* 135).

According to the pre-Socratic insight, fire must co-exist with the wet: with ocean. Appropriately then, fire takes on liquid properties and becomes wine which will pour into the poet's chilled heart: 'Oh pour, pour, pour into / the vessels of my heart, run / in through the branched hands'. The poet craves a baptism of fire through metamorphosis or assimilation, creating a striking parallel with the poem 'Mana of the Sea' in which the poet asks:

> Have I caught from it
> the tide in my arms

that runs down to the shallows of my wrists, and breaks
abroad in my hands, like waves among the rocks of substance? ...

And is my body ocean, ocean
whose power runs to the shores along my arms
and breaks in the foamy hands, whose power rolls out
to the white-treading waves of two salt feet? (*CP* 705)

The image of wine/ocean switches to one of delicate, external contact, in which fire will 'hover / like a butterfly ruddy on the cheeks / that were chill, pulsing them with / brilliant warmth'. This butterfly reference, connecting with the invocatory 'Butterfly' poem, subsequently provokes the warmth/frost and inside/outside dichotomies at the end of the poem. This contrast is already latent in 'Fire', in the earlier reference to 'Oh / lovely fire on this chill day, as / the sun goes down', linking to 'The Argonauts' with its description of the leonine sun 'lick[ing] his paws' in readiness to sink and give way to the moon (*CP* 687). The fire takes effect 'in / this twilight, now the sun has gone / and the blue shadow is thinking of / hoar-frost, outside the house'. Again the sensation of being 'before the fire' is contrasted with the awareness of coldness and the unknown outside and beyond. The blue shadow is not only the light reflecting on snow as described in 'Anaxagoras'; it also harbours something of the threat or strangeness of the unknown conveyed in 'The Flying-Fish' in the description of 'the other sun shaking its dark blue wings'.[22] Yet the 'Fire' poem finishes positively, with affirmation, and not merely the wistful acceptance of 'Butterfly' in 'it is enough' (*CP* 696). Instead it ends 'But I / am before the fire, and my heart / is open'.

The line-break indications I have used are reflected in a text provided by T.A. Smailes, who prints 'Fire' in an article entitled 'D.H. Lawrence: Seven Hitherto Unpublished Poems' (see note 19). In his text, the fragment is lineated clearly as a poem, with lines shorter and more uniform in length than is habitual in Lawrence's free-verse. Keith Sagar prints the fragment very differently in his *Selected Poems* edition of 1972 as a block of prose, assuming that the line-divisions are merely arbitrary. He refers to two 'prose-poems', 'The Elephants of Dionysus' and 'Fire', and is contemptuous of what he sees as Smailes's versifying of the text: "Fire is also published in Smailes, but incorrectly, as verse'.[23] It is evident from Lawrence's manuscript that the line breaks are determined at least in part by the width of the page. However, it could be argued that there is integrity in Smailes's decision to reproduce the manuscript faithfully, allowing the reader to make his/her own decisions regarding Lawrence's intentions.

---

[22] D.H. Lawrence, 'The Flying-Fish', in *St. Mawr and Other Stories*, ed. Brian Finney (Cambridge: Cambridge University Press, 1983), p. 209.

[23] Keith Sagar, *D.H. Lawrence: A Calendar of his Works* (Manchester: Manchester University Press, 1979), p. 189.

If Lawrence, as Smailes implies, had specific reasons for lineating the poem as he does, it is necessary to consider possible reasons for this. He may have wished to prioritize certain words by placing them at line endings or beginnings, such as the reiterated question 'What is it ...?' or the words 'writhes', 'fierce-fanged', 'swift', 'gold', 'brilliant' and 'beautiful'. The last line of the poem is shortened to two words, and thus invested with simplicity, directness and heightened impact. The poem as a whole seems to use free-verse in a way that differs from and extends Lawrence's previous writing: the style is less restricted than ever, combining naturalistic speech-rhythms used in prose with poetic imagery. It eludes artifice of form and remains fluid, yet manages to incorporate the repetitions and modulations characteristic above all of *Last Poems*.

'Fire' cannot simply be classed with 'The Elephants of Dionysus' as a prose-poem, for the two pieces of writing are utterly different stylistically. If the *Phoenix* text is to be trusted – Tedlock says 'The text in *Phoenix* follows that of the manuscript'[24] – 'Elephants' has a conventionally paragraphed prose form and gives a chronological narrative account, rather than capturing a descriptive moment through poetic invocation. It begins as follows:

> Dionysus, returning from India a victor with his hosts, met the Amazons once more towards the Ephesian coasts. O small-breasted, brilliant Amazons, will you never leave off attacking the Bull-foot, for whom the Charites weave ivy-garlands? Garlands and flutes. Oh, listen to the flutes! Oh, draw near, there is going to be sacrifice to the god of delight![25]

This paragraph is representative of the whole text, beginning as it does with narrative account, before launching into a series of exclamations: 'Oh', 'O', 'lo', and 'Ah'. The fragment seems to differ from 'Fire' in that its principal aim is to tell a story, employing an ancient style that incorporates utterance traditionally associated with poetry. While 'Fire' is a poem that incorporates prose techniques, 'Elephants' is a piece of prose that incorporates poetry. While 'Fire' resembles an expanded free-verse poem, 'Elephants' resembles a contracted short story.

'Fire' retains a pre-Socratic flavour through its celebration of elemental fire, and through the conscious archaisms – terms such as 'pinions', 'whence' and 'whither' – that contrast refreshingly with the scientific references to 'carbon dioxide' and 'combustion'. It seems an odd hybrid stylistically: a cross between the *BirdsBeasts* prologues, the free-verse form of *Last Poems*, and even the short prose section style of *Apocalypse*. It is impossible to ascertain Lawrence's purpose for this little poem: whether or not it was just a one-off form deemed appropriate for a particular description, or whether it marked the onset of what would have been a new wave of creativity – another kind of writing. Returning to Lipking's notion of a harmonium, this fragment links oddly with a short piece by Keats (also

---

[24]   Tedlock, p. 213.

[25]   *Phoenix*, p. 59.

left untitled, but usually referred to as 'This living hand') quoted and discussed by Lipking in his final chapter:

> This living hand, now warm and capable
> Of earnest grasping, would, if it were cold
> And in the icy silence of the tomb,
> So haunt thy days and chill thy dreaming nights
> That thou would wish thine own heart dry of blood
> So in my veins red life might stream again,
> And thou be conscience-calmed – see here it is –
> I hold it towards you.[26]

Images of warmth and chill, of pulsing or streaming life in contrast with icy silence or hoar frost, suggest a possible link between the two pre-death poems. Ironically Lawrence referred to the whitewashed house of the Brewsters – the very house warmed by the fire he evokes in his poem – as a 'tombeau' in his letter to Max Mohr (although he may simply be echoing an overheard remark in describing it as such). Lawrence's words 'But for me, oh again I am a wine- / cup, and my chill heart is empty / of wine' seem to demand the same transferral of life to him from another that is requested in Keats's fragment. They may relate, also, to Keats's lines: 'O, for a draught of vintage!' and 'O for a beaker full of the warm South' from a poem in which the narrator seeks escape from a world in which 'youth grows pale, and spectre-thin, and dies'.[27]

These are not parallels I wish to emphasize, however, as they seem to fall into Lipking's trap of classifying and analyzing texts merely in terms of their biographical implication, emphasizing that these are pre-death poems and must be analyzed as such. The Lawrence and Keats texts link most interestingly in that we are entirely unaware of their function or destination. Lipking says of 'This living hand':

> No one can say exactly when or why these lines were written. Indeed, we cannot say with any certainty even that Keats meant them to be a poem. Jotted in the manuscript of his faery burlesque, *The Jealousies* (or *Cap and Bells),* and thus presumably dating from the end of 1819, they were not published until 1898; nor is there any indication that the author thought them complete or fit for the press. (*LP* 181)

Keats jotted this fragment down on an apparently unrelated literary manuscript, just as Lawrence scribbled 'Fire' onto note-sheets for *Apocalypse.* The former might have been meant as a poem in its own right; it might have been intended for

---

[26]   John Keats, 'This living hand', in *John Keats: The Complete Poems*, third edition, ed. John Barnard (London: Penguin, 1988), p. 459.

[27]   Ibid. p. 346.

a dramatic role, in which it would emerge from the mouth of a particular character; it might have been intended solely for Fanny Brawne: Lipking discusses all these possibilities. He identifies the fragment as a piece of writing that gives us as readers a 'rare feeling of intimacy; for once Keats speaks directly to us without formality or mask' (*LP* 181). Christopher Pollnitz argues that the reading and deciphering of Lawrence's draft versions of *Last Poems* give us an intimacy of this kind (see Chapter 1, p. 7).

Yet even this sense of intimacy is bound up with the critic's awareness of a chosen poet's impending death: Pollnitz emphasizes the 'cough-prints' evident on the *Last Poems* manuscript that provoke in us a poignant and vivid awareness of the illness that was to kill Lawrence shortly after. Lipking, even while identifying an incompleteness in the writing of Keats's enigmatic poetry fragment, has to formulate an alternative vision in which snug coherence can be provided by the reader of such a work:

> That is why the fragment fits so snugly at the end of Keats' poems: to emphasize that the process of his work can never be completed save by our own responsive acts of attention. (*LP* 183)

It is interesting that he chooses the Lawrentian phrase 'act[s] of attention' (*IR* 113) to formulate his sense of reader-response – or reader-responsibility. His view here rests on an acceptance of the co-authorship in which reader and writer interact in the intertextual process. Still, though, he is attempting to override his real insight: that poets do not and cannot shape their poetic careers. If Keats or Lawrence had lived a month longer there would have been still more 'last' texts, probably suggesting a new direction or a fresh start. Terms such as 'shaping' and 'summation' are never satisfactory in defining either the makings of a life or of a poem: the complexity of such processes belies and eludes definition. Lawrence – in the poem 'Fire' which could be referred to as his last poem – expresses his wish to remain free from questioning, shaping and the awareness of an end, in order to live:

> I ask not how nor whence nor
> whither, for if I ask I shall only
> answer myself with a thousand
> damp equivocations.
> … Elude, then, elude their cold
> and mean little questions, these
> pale-lipped be-spectacled men!
> … But I
> am before the fire, and my heart
> is open. (F 45)

The word 'open' works powerfully against the implications of closure (even though, paradoxically, it achieves a kind of poetic closure at the end of this piece).

It reveals an optimism that suggests beginnings rather than endings. In January 1930 Lawrence wrote to Mabel Dodge Luhan 'I wish we could start afresh with this year' (*L* vii 616): an aspiration like that of Tennyson's Ulysses, yearning to set out. If Lawrence had been given this opportunity, as he was after *Collected Poems,* the new year would no doubt have given rise to a new phase of living and writing: to a literal journey, and to another kind of poetry.

In the introduction to *On Late Style* (discussed in Chapter 1), Michael Wood cites the following passage in which Said investigates the way in which an artist's lateness impacts on style:

> 'Late style'—the term is Adorno's—can't be a direct result of aging or death, because style is not a mortal creature, and works of art have no organic life to lose. But the approaching death of the artist gets into the works all the same, and in many different ways. (Quoted in *OLS* xiii)

Directly, the awareness of impending (if not imminent) demise infiltrated the poignant death poems as well as the deepened religious and philosophical vision evident in *Sketches of Etruscan Places* and *Apocalypse*. It increased the urgency with which Lawrence confronted such issues as resurrection and the afterlife. Yet approaching death also had the effect of catalyzing works asserting that 'the vast marvel is to be alive' (*A* 149): an intensified celebration of the wonder and renewal within every aspect of the phenomenal world. His late and last works – finished and unfinished – elude Lipking's model of serenity through being fragmentary and combative, while constantly striving for newness. Adorno describes Beethoven's late work as 'catching fire between extremes' (*OLS* 10), and this seems an apposite aphorism with which to epitomize late Lawrence. The extremes or contraries may be birth and death (or death and rebirth); beginnings and endings; pre-Socratic or elemental dualisms; paganism and Christianity; the individual and the masses; or the natural and the mechanistic. No last work by Lawrence attempts definitively to settle or summarize: these texts find rest only in change, glimpsing a phoenix in every fire.

Bibliography

Works by D.H. Lawrence

Manuscripts

F   Autograph manuscript of an untitled prose poem (Roberts E132) beginning 'Fire: did you ever warm your hands at', written in early to mid-November 1929. (Text reproduced in T.A. Smailes; see below p. 218.)

L   Notebook (Roberts E192) held at the Harry Ransom Humanities Research Center, The University of Texas at Austin, containing the poems written between late September and mid-November 1929, and published as 'Last Poems' by Richard Aldington in 1932.

N   Notebook (Roberts E192) held at the Harry Ransom Humanities Research Center, The University of Texas at Austin, containing poems published in *Pansies, Nettles* and (posthumously) as 'More Pansies' by Richard Aldington in 1932. This notebook was probably filled between December 1928 and September 1929.

Published Texts and Editions

'A Review of *The Book of Revelation* by Dr John Oman', in *Apocalypse and the Writings on Revelation*, ed. Maria Kalnins (Cambridge: Cambridge University Press, 1980).

Aaron's Rod, ed. Mara Kalnins (Cambridge: Cambridge University Press, 1988).

Apocalypse, ed. Mara Kalnins (London: Penguin, 1995).

Apocalypse and the Writings on Revelation, ed. Mara Kalnins (Cambridge: Cambridge University Press, 1980).

'Apocalypsis II', in *Apocalypse and the Writings on Revelation*, ed. Mara Kalnins (Cambridge: Cambridge University Press, 1980).

'[Autobiographical Fragment]', in *Late Essays and Articles*, ed. James T. Boulton (Cambridge: Cambridge University Press, 2004).

Birds, Beasts and Flowers (London: Cresset Press, 1930).

'Chaos in Poetry' ('Introduction to Harry Crosby's *Chariot of the Sun*'), in *Introductions and Reviews*, ed. Neil Reeve and John Worthen (Cambridge: Cambridge University Press, 2005).

The Complete Poems of D.H. Lawrence, 2 vol., ed. Vivian de Sola Pinto and Warren Roberts (London: Heinemann, 1964).

The Complete Poems of D.H. Lawrence, 2 vol., ed. Vivian de Sola Pinto and Warren Roberts (London: Heinemann, 1967. 2nd reprint of 1964 edn, with minor revisions).

The Complete Poems of D.H. Lawrence, 2 vol., ed. Vivian de Sola Pinto and Warren Roberts (London: Heinemann, 1972. 3rd reprint of 1964 edn, with further minor revisions).

The Complete Poems of D.H. Lawrence, ed. Vivian de Sola Pinto and Warren Roberts (London: Penguin, 1993).

'The Crown', in *Reflections on the Death of a Porcupine and Other Essays*, ed. Michael Herbert (Cambridge: Cambridge University Press, 1988).

D.H. Lawrence: Selected Poems, ed. Keith Sagar (London: Penguin, 1972).

D.H. Lawrence: Selected Poems, ed. Mara Kalnins (London: Dent, 1992).

D.H. Lawrence's Paintings, with an introduction by Keith Sagar (London: Chaucer Press, 2003).

The Escaped Cock, in *The Virgin and the Gipsy and Other Stories*, ed. Michael Herbert, Bethan Jones and Lindeth Vasey (Cambridge: Cambridge University Press, 2005).

The First and Second Lady Chatterley Novels, ed. Dieter Mehl and Christa Jansohn (Cambridge: Cambridge University Press, 1999).

'Flowery Tuscany', in *Sketches of Etruscan Places and Other Italian Essays*, ed. Simonetta de Filippis (Cambridge: Cambridge University Press, 1992).

'The Flying-Fish', in *St Mawr and Other Stories*, ed. Brian Finney (Cambridge: Cambridge University Press, 1983).

'Foreword: An Answer to Some Critics', in *Psychoanalysis and the Unconscious and Fantasia of the Unconscious*, ed. Bruce Steele (Cambridge: Cambridge University Press, 2004).

'Foreword to *Fantasia of the Unconscious*', in *Psychoanalysis and the Unconscious and Fantasia of the Unconscious*, ed. Bruce Steele (Cambridge: Cambridge University Press, 2004).

'Foreword to *Pansies*', in *D.H. Lawrence: Selected Poems*, ed, Mara Kalnins (London: Dent, 1992).

'Hymns in a Man's Life', in *Late Essays and Articles*, ed. James T. Boulton (Cambridge: Cambridge University Press, 2004).

'Insouciance', in *Late Essays and Articles*, ed. James T. Boulton (Cambridge: Cambridge University Press, 2004).

'Introduction to *The Dragon of the Apocalypse* by Frederick Carter', in *Apocalypse and the Writings on Revelation*, ed. Mara Kalnins (Cambridge: Cambridge University Press, 1980).

Introductions and Reviews, ed. Neil Reeve and John Worthen (Cambridge: Cambridge University Press, 2005).

'John Galsworthy', in *Study of Thomas Hardy and Other Essays*, ed. Bruce Steele (Cambridge: Cambridge University Press, 1985).

Lady Chatterley's Lover, ed. Michael Squires (Cambridge: Cambridge University Press, 1993).

Lady Chatterley's Lover, ed. Michael Squires (London: Penguin, 1994).

Last Poems, ed. Richard Aldington and Giuseppe Orioli (Florence: Orioli, 1932; New York: Viking, 1933).

Late Essays and Articles, ed. James T. Boulton (Cambridge: Cambridge University Press, 2004).

The Letters of D.H. Lawrence, 7 vol., general ed. James T. Boulton (Cambridge: Cambridge University Press):

—— *Letters* I (1901–13), ed. James T. Boulton (1979).

—— *Letters* II (1913–16), ed. George J. Zytaruk and James T. Boulton (1981).

—— *Letters* III (1916–21), ed. James T. Boulton and Andrew Robertson (1984).

—— *Letters* IV (1921–24), ed. James T. Boulton, Elizabeth Mansfield and Warren Roberts (1987).

—— *Letters* V (1924–27), ed. James T. Boulton and Lindeth Vasey (1989).

—— *Letters* VI (1927–28), ed. James T. Boulton and Margaret H. Boulton with Gerald M. Lacy (1991).

—— *Letters* VII (1928–30), ed. Keith Sagar and James T. Boulton (1993).

—— *Letters* VIII (Previously Uncollected Letters; General Index), ed. James T. Boulton (2000).

'The Man Who Was Through with the World', in *The Virgin and the Gipsy and Other Stories*, ed. Michael Herbert, Bethan Jones and Lindeth Vasey (Cambridge: Cambridge University Press, 2005).

'Men Must Work and Women as Well', in *Late Essays and Articles*, ed. James T. Boulton (Cambridge: Cambridge University Press, 2004).

'The Nightingale', in *Sketches of Etruscan Places and Other Italian Essays*, ed. Simonetta de Filippis (Cambridge: Cambridge University Press, 1992).

'On Human Destiny', in *Reflections on the Death of a Porcupine and Other Essays*, ed. Michael Herbert (Cambridge: Cambridge University Press, 1988).

Phoenix: The Posthumous Papers of D.H. Lawrence, ed. Edward D. McDonald (London: Heinemann, 1936).

Phoenix II: Uncollected, Unpublished and Other Prose Works by D.H. Lawrence, ed. Warren Roberts and Harry T. Moore (London: Heinemann, 1968).

The Plumed Serpent, ed. L.D. Clark (Cambridge: Cambridge University Press, 1987).

'Poetry of the Present' ('Introduction to the American edition of *New Poems*'), in *D.H. Lawrence: Selected Poems*, ed. Mara Kalnins (London: Dent, 1992).

'The Proper Study', in *Reflections on the Death of a Porcupine and Other Essays*, ed. Michael Herbert (Cambridge: Cambridge University Press, 1988).

Psychoanalysis and the Unconscious and Fantasia of the Unconscious, ed. Bruce Steele (Cambridge: Cambridge University Press, 2004).

The Rainbow, ed. Mark Kinkead-Weekes (Cambridge: Cambridge University Press, 1989).

Reflections on the Death of a Porcupine and Other Essays, ed. Michael Herbert (Cambridge: Cambridge University Press, 1988).

'Review of Eric Gill's *Art-Nonsense and Other Essays*', in *Introductions and Reviews*, ed. Neil Reeve and John Worthen (Cambridge: Cambridge University Press, 2005).

'The Risen Lord', in *Late Essays and Articles*, ed. James T. Boulton (Cambridge: Cambridge University Press, 2004).

Sea and Sardinia, ed. Mara Kalnins (Cambridge: Cambridge University Press, 1997).

Sketches of Etruscan Places and Other Italian Essays, ed. Simonetta de Filippis (Cambridge: Cambridge University Press, 1992).

Studies in Classic American Literature, ed. Ezra Greenspan, Lindeth Vasey and John Worthen (Cambridge: Cambridge University Press, 2003).

The Symbolic Meaning, ed. Armin Arnold (Arundel: Centaur Press, 1962).

'Twilight in Italy', in *Twilight in Italy and Other Essays*, ed. Paul Eggert (Cambridge: Cambridge University Press, 1994).

The Virgin and the Gipsy and Other Stories, ed. Michael Herbert, Bethan Jones and Lindeth Vasey (Cambridge: Cambridge University Press, 2005).

The White Peacock, ed. Andrew Robertson (Cambridge: Cambridge University Press 1983).

'Whitman', in *Studies in Classic American Literature*, ed. Ezra Greenspan, Lindeth Vasey and John Worthen (Cambridge: Cambridge University Press, 2003).

'Why the Novel Matters', in *Study of Thomas Hardy and Other Essays*, ed. Bruce Steele (Cambridge: Cambridge University Press, 1985).

The Woman Who Rode Away and Other Stories, ed. Dieter Mehl and Christa Janssohn (Cambridge: Cambridge University Press, 1995). *Women in Love*, ed. David Farmer, Lindeth Vasey and John Worthen (Cambridge: Cambridge University Press, 1987).

Works on D.H. Lawrence

Aldington, Richard, 'Introduction', *Apocalypse* (London: Secker, 1932).

Aldington, Richard, 'Introduction to "Last Poems" and "More Pansies" ', in *The Complete Poems of D.H. Lawrence,* vol. 2, ed. Vivian de Sola Pinto and Warren Roberts (London: Heinemann, 1964).

Aldington, Richard, *Literary Lifelines: The Richard Aldington–Lawrence Durrell Correspondence*, ed. Ian S. MacNiven and Harry T. Moore (London: Faber, 1981).

Arnold, Armin, 'Introduction', *The Symbolic Meaning* (Arundel: Centaur Press, 1962).

Brewster and Brewster, Earl and Achsah, *D.H. Lawrence: Reminiscences and Correspondence* (London: Secker, 1934).

Bouchouchi, Fella, 'D.H. Lawrence's Cosmopoetics', in *Etudes Lawrenciennes* no. 30 (2004).

Burwell, Rose Marie, 'A Checklist of Lawrence's Reading', in *A D.H. Lawrence Handbook*, ed. Keith Sagar (Manchester: Manchester University Press: 1982).

Carter, Frederick, *D.H. Lawrence and the Body Mystical* (London: Denis Archer, 1932).

Chambers, Jessie ('E.T.'), *D. H. Lawrence: A Personal Record* (London: Jonathan Cape, 1935).

Chaudhuri, Amit, *D.H. Lawrence and Difference* (Oxford: Oxford University Press, 2003).

Clark, L.D., *The Minoan Distance: the Symbolism of Travel in D.H. Lawrence* (Tucson: University of Arizona Press, 1980).

Corke, Helen, *The Croydon Years* (Austin: University of Texas Press, 1965).

Cowan, J.C., *D.H. Lawrence's American Journey: A Study in Literature and Myth* (Cleveland, Ohio and London: Press of the Case Western Reserve University, 1970).

Ellis, David, *D.H. Lawrence: Dying Game, 1922–1930* (Cambridge: Cambridge University Press, 1998).

Ellis, David, *Death and the Author: How D.H. Lawrence Died and Was Remembered* (Oxford: Oxford University Press, 2008).

Ellis, David, 'Verse or worse: the place of "Pansies" in Lawrence's Poetry', in *D.H. Lawrence's Non-Fiction: Art, Thought and Genre*, ed. David Ellis and Howard Mills (Cambridge: Cambridge University Press, 1988).

Fernihough, Anne, *D.H. Lawrence: Aesthetics and Ideology* (Oxford: Clarendon Press, 1993).

Filippis, Simonetta de, 'Introduction', *Sketches of Etruscan Places and Other Italian Essays* (Cambridge: Cambridge University Press, 1992).

Gilbert, Sandra, *Acts of Attention: The Poetry of D.H. Lawrence* (Ithaca and New York: Cornell University Press, 1972).

Hanchant, W.L. and Clement, M., *The Times Literary Supplement* (July 2, 1931).

Jones, Bethan, 'Shaping, Intertextuality and Summation in D.H. Lawrence's *Last Poems*', unpublished PhD thesis (University of Nottingham, 1998)

Kalnins, Mara, 'Introduction', *Apocalypse* (London: Penguin, 1995).

Kalnins, Mara, 'Introduction', *Apocalypse and the Writings on Revelation* (Cambridge: Cambridge University Press, 1980).

Kalnins, Mara, 'Introduction', *D.H. Lawrence: Selected Poems* (London: Dent, 1992).

Kalnins, Mara, 'Symbolic Seeing: Lawrence and Heraclitus', in *D.H. Lawrence: Centenary Essays*, ed. Mara Kalnins (Bristol: Bristol Classical Press, 1986).

Kezich, Giovanni, 'Lawrence in Etruria: *Etruscan Places* in Context', in *D.H. Lawrence: Etruscan Places*, ed. Massimo Pallottino (London: Olive Press, 1994).

Kinkead-Weekes, Mark, *D.H. Lawrence: Triumph to Exile, 1912–1922* (Cambridge, Cambridge University Press: 1996).

Laird, Holly, *Self and Sequence: the Poetry of D.H. Lawrence* (Charlottesville: The University Press of Virginia, 1988).

Lawrence, Frieda, *Not I, But the Wind...* (London: Heinemann, 1935).

Lockwood, Michael, *A Study of the Poems of D.H. Lawrence* (Basingstoke: Palgrave Macmillan Ltd., 1987).

Marshall, Tom, *The Psychic Mariner: A Reading of the Poems of D.H. Lawrence* (London: Heinemann, 1970).

Murfin, Ross, *The Poetry of D. H. Lawrence: Texts and Contexts* (Lincoln: University of Nebraska Press, 1983).

Nehls, Edward, *D.H. Lawrence: A Composite Biography*, 3 vol. (Madison: University of Wisconsin Press, 1957; 1958; 1959).

Pallottino, Massimo, 'Introduction', *D.H Lawrence: Etruscan Places* (London: Olive Press, 1994).

Pollnitz, Christopher, 'Cough-Prints and Other Intimacies: Considerations in Editing Lawrence's Later Verse', in *Editing D.H. Lawrence,* ed. Charles L. Ross and Dennis Jackson (Ann Arbor: University of Michigan Press, 1995).

Pollnitz, Christopher, *D.H. Lawrence and the Pensée* (Paris: Carrefour Alyscamps Press, n.d. [1996]).

Pollnitz, Christopher, 'Raptus Virginis: The Dark God in the Poetry of D.H. Lawrence', in *D.H. Lawrence: Centenary Essays,* ed. Mara Kalnins (Bristol: Bristol Classical Press, 1986).

Powell, Lawrence Clark, *The Manuscripts of D.H. Lawrence: A Descriptive Catalogue* (Los Angeles: Los Angeles Public Library, 1937).

Reeve, Neil H., *Reading Late Lawrence* (Basingstoke: Palgrave, 2003).

Roberts, Neil, *D.H. Lawrence: Travel and Cultural Difference* (Basingstoke: Palgrave, 2004).

Roberts, Warren and Poplawski, Paul, *A Bibliography of D.H. Lawrence*, third edn (Cambridge: Cambridge University Press, 2001).

Rowley, Stephen, 'The Quest for a Nucleate Trope in Lawrence's Poetry: Organic Becoming and Inorganic Collapse', *Etudes Lawrenciennes*, 30 (2004).

Sagar, Keith, *A D.H. Lawrence Handbook* (Manchester: Manchester University Press, 1982).

Sagar, Keith, *D.H. Lawrence: A Calendar of his Works, with a checklist of the manuscripts of D.H. Lawrence by Lindeth Vasey* (Manchester: Manchester University Press, 1979).

Sagar, Keith, *D.H. Lawrence: Poet* (Humanities-Ebooks L.L.P, 2007; Troubador, 2008).

Sagar, Keith, *The Art of D.H. Lawrence* (Cambridge: Cambridge University Press, 1966)

Sagar, Keith, 'The Genesis of "Bavarian Gentians" ', *The D.H. Lawrence Review*, 8 (Spring 1975), pp. 47–53.

Smailes, T.A., 'D.H. Lawrence: Seven Hitherto Unpublished Poems', *The D.H. Lawrence Review*, 3 (Spring 1970), pp. 42–6.

Squires, Keith, 'Introduction', *Lady Chatterley's Lover* (Cambridge: Cambridge University Press, 1993).

Tedlock, E.W., *The Frieda Lawrence Collection of D.H. Lawrence Manuscripts: A Descriptive Bibliography* (Albuquerque: University of New Mexico Press, 1948).

Viinikka, Anja, *From Persephone to Pan: D.H. Lawrence's Mythopoeic Vision of the Integrated Personality* (Turku, Finland: Turun Yliopisto Julkaisuja, 1988).

Welby, T.E., 'Lawrence's Etruria' (review), *Observer* (23 October 1932), p. 7.

Worthen, John, *D.H. Lawrence: The Early Years* 1885–1912 (Cambridge: Cambridge University Press, 1991).

Worthen, John, *D.H. Lawrence: The Life of an Outsider* (London: Allen Lane, 2005).

Works on Late Style and Intertextuality

Adorno, Theodor W., *Essays on Music*, ed. Richard Leppert, with new translations by Susan H. Gillespie (Berkeley, Los Angeles and London: University of California Press, 2002).

Anderson, William S., 'The Theory and Practice of Poetic Arrangement from Vergil to Ovid', in *Poems in Their Place: The Intertextuality and Order of Poetic Collections*, ed. Neil Fraistat (Chapel Hill and London: The University of North Carolina Press, 1986).

Bakhtin, Mikhail, *The Dialogic Imagination*, trans. Caryl Emerson and Michael Holquist (Austin: University of Texas Press, 1981).

Barthes, Roland, 'Pierre Loti: *Aziyad*', in *Le Degré zéro de l'écriture, suivi de nouveaux essais critiques* (Paris: Editions du Seuil, 1972).

Barthes, Roland, *S/Z*, trans. Richard Miller (Oxford: Blackwell, 1996).

Bayoumi, Moustafa and Rubin, Andrew (ed.), *The Edward Said Reader* (New York: Vintage, 2000).

Bloom, Harold, *The Anxiety of Influence* (New York: Oxford University Press, 1973).

Britton, Celia, 'Fiction, fact and madness: intertextual relations among Gide's female characters', in *Intertextuality: theories and practices*, ed. Judith Still and Michael Worton (Manchester: Manchester University Press, 1990).

Broch, Hermann, 'Introduction', in *On the Iliad*, Rachel Bespaloff, trans. Mary McCarthy (New York: Pantheon, 1947).

Fraistat, Neil (ed.), *Poems in Their Place: The Intertextuality and Order of Poetic Collections* (Chapel Hill and London: The University of North Carolina Press, 1986).

Frow, John, 'Intertextuality and ontology', in *Intertextuality: theories and practices*, ed. Judith Still and Michael Worton (Manchester: Manchester University Press, 1990).

Genette, Gérard, *Palimpsestes: la litterature au second degré* (Paris: Editions du Seuil, 1982).

Hand, Sean, 'Missing you: intertextuality, transference and the language of love', in *Intertextuality: theories and practices*, ed. Judith Still and Michael Worton (Manchester: Manchester University Press, 1990).

Harrison, Anthony H., *Victorian Poets and Romantic Poems: Intertextuality and Ideology* (Charlottesville: University Press of Virginia, 1990).

Holquist, Michael, *Dialogism: Bakhtin and his World* (London: Routledge, 1990).

Jefferson, Ann, 'Autobiography as Intertext: Barthes, Sarraute, Robbe-Grillet', in *Intertextuality: theories and practices,* ed. Judith Still and Michael Worton (Manchester: Manchester University Press, 1990).

Knight, Diana, 'Roland Barthes: an intertextual figure', in *Intertextuality: theories and practices*, ed. Judith Still and Michael Worton (Manchester: Manchester University Press, 1990).

Kristeva, Julia, 'Word, Dialogue and Novel', in *The Kristeva Reader*, ed. Toril Moi (Oxford: Blackwell, 1986).

Lipking, Lawrence, *The Life of the Poet: Beginning and Ending Poetic Careers* (Chicago: University of Chicago Press, 1981).

Lodge, David, *After Bakhtin* (London: Routledge, 1990).

Mann, Thomas, 'Freud and the Future', *Essays of Three Decades*, trans. H.T. Lowe-Porter (London: Secker and Warburg, 1947).

Miner, Earl, 'Some Issues of Study of Integrated Collections', in *Poems in Their Place: The Intertextuality and Order of Poetic Collections*, ed. Neil Fraistat (Chapel Hill and London: The University of North Carolina Press, 1986).

Orr, Mary, *Claude Simon: The Intertextual Dimension* (Glasgow: University of Glasgow French and German Publications, 1993).

Page, Tim (ed.), *The Glenn Gould Reader* (New York: Knopf, 1984).

Patterson, Annabel, 'Jonson, Marvell, and Miscellaneity?', in *Poems in Their Place: The Intertextuality and Order of Poetic Collections*, ed. Neil Fraistat (Chapel Hill and London: The University of North Carolina Press, 1986).

Riffaterre, Michael, 'Compulsory reader response: the intertextual drive', in *Intertextuality: theories and practices,* ed. Judith Still and Michael Worton (Manchester: Manchester University Press, 1990).

Robbins Landon, H.C., *1791: Mozart's Last Year* (London: Thames and Hudson, 1988).

Said, Edward, *On Late Style* (London: Bloomsbury, 2006).

Still, Judith, and Worton, Michael (ed), *Intertextuality: theories and practices* (Manchester: Manchester University Press, 1990).

Todorov, Tzvetan, *Mikhail Bakhtin* (Paris: Editions du Seuil, 1981).

Other Works

Blake, William, *Blake's Poetry and Designs*, ed. M.L. Johnson and J.E. Grant (New York and London: W.W. Norton and Co., 1979).

Broadwood, Lucy E. and Maitland, J.A. Fuller, *English County Songs* (London: The Leadenhall Press, 1898).

Burnet, John, *Early Greek Philosophy* (London and Edinburgh: Black, 1892).

Burnet, John, *Early Greek Philosophy* (London: Black, 1908).

Burnet, John, *Early Greek Philosophy* (London: Black, 1920).

Carter, Frederick, *The Dragon of Revelation* (London: Desmond Harmsworth Ltd, 1931).

Carter, Frederick, *The Dragon of the Alchemists* (London: Elkin Mathews,1926).

Dennis, George, *Cities and Cemeteries of Etruria*, vol. 1 (London: Dent, 1907).

Eliot, T.S., 'Four Quartets', in *T.S. Eliot: Collected Poems 1909–1962* (London: Faber, 1963).

Frazer, James, *The Golden Bough*, vol. iv (London: Macmillan, 1927).

Gill, Eric, *Art-Nonsense and Other Essays* (London: Cassell Walterson, 1929).

Inge, William Ralph, *The Philosophy of Plotinus*, vol. 1 (London, New York and Toronto: Longmans, 1929).

Jung, C.G., *Civilisation in Transition, the Collected Works*, vol. 10, trans. R.F.C. Hull (London: Routledge, 1964).

Keats, John, *The Complete Poems*, ed. John Barnard (London: Penguin, 1988).

Keats, John, *The Letters of John Keats: A Selected Edition*, ed. R. Gittings (Oxford: Oxford University Press, 1990.

Louis, Margot K., *Persephone Rises, 1860–1927: Mythography, Gender, and the Creation of a New Spirituality* (Aldershot: Ashgate, 2009).

Moffatt, James, *A New Translation of the Bible* (London: Hodder and Stoughton, 1926).

Murray, Gilbert, *Five Stages of Greek Religion* (Oxford: Oxford University Press, 1925).

Oman, John, *Book of Revelation* (Cambridge: Cambridge University Press, 1923).

Pearson, John, *Façades* (London: Macmillan, 1978).

Pryse, James M., *The Apocalypse Unsealed* (New York: J.M. Pryse, 1910).

Shakespeare, William, *The Complete Works* (Oxford: Oxford University Press, 1988). Shelley, Percy Bysshe, *Shelley: Selected Poems*, ed. Timothy Webb (London: Dent, 1991).

Shelley, Percy Bysshe, *Shelley's Prose*, ed. David Lee Clark (Albuquerque: University of New Mexico Press, 1966).

Tennyson, Alfred, *The Poems of Tennyson*, ed. Christopher Ricks (London: Longmans, 1969).

Thomas, Dylan, *The Poems*, ed. Daniel Jones (London: J.M. Dent, 1971).

Tylor, Edward B., *Primitive Culture*, vol. I (London: John Murray, 1903).

Whitman, Walt, *Leaves of Grass*, ed. Sculley Bradley and Harold W. Blodgett (New York and London: W.W. Norton & Co.,1973).

Whitman, Walt, 'Preface to *Leaves of Grass*, 1st Edition', in *Leaves of Grass*, ed. Sculley Bradley and Harold W. Blodgett (New York and London: W.W. Norton & Co., 1973).

Index

Note: Titles of poems, articles and essays (in inverted commas) or books (italicized) are by D.H. Lawrence, unless followed by an author name in parentheses. Titles beginning with articles are not inverted, following the scheme used in the 'Published Texts and Editions' section of the author's bibliography. Lawrence is referred to as 'L'.

Printed in Great Britain
by Amazon

44837676R00142